Essays on Russian Liberalism

ESSAYS ON
RUSSIAN LIBERALISM

Edited, with an Introduction
by Charles E. Timberlake

University of Missouri Press
1972

Copyright © 1972 by The Curators of the University of Missouri
University of Missouri Press, Columbia, Missouri 65201
Printed and bound in the United States of America
Library of Congress Catalog Number 70–185830
ISBN 0–8262–0120–2
All rights reserved
Pipes' essay reprinted by permission of the publishers
from Richard Pipes, *Struve: Liberal on the Left, 1870–1905.*
Cambridge, Mass.: Harvard University Press, Copyright,
1970, by Richard Pipes.

To Howard and Mabel

Preface

The essays contained in this volume were first presented to the Bi-State (Kansas-Missouri) Slavic Conference in Columbia, Missouri, in November, 1969. I thank the individual contributors for their participation in the conference and for the subsequent revision of their papers for inclusion in this volume.

I wish also to record my gratitude to a number of persons and offices, especially the Department of History, the Office of International Studies, the Graduate School, and the Dean of the College of Arts and Science at the University of Missouri—Columbia for their financial and other types of assistance to the conference. My colleagues on the Russian Studies Committee at the University of Missouri also contributed willingly their time and advice in arranging the conference.

To my wife I owe particular gratitude for her assistance at various stages in the preparation of the volume.

Transliteration from Cyrillic to Latin characters is according to the Library of Congress system with deviation only in cases involving German names (thus Hessen, not Gessen) and where a Russian name became well known in the West by a spelling different from the one produced by following the Library of Congress system. Thus, the book has Peter, rather than Petr, Struve, Paul, not Pavel, Miliukov, and A. Tyrkova-Williams, rather than A. Tyrkova-Vil'iams. Dates before February 18, 1918, are in Old Style, unless otherwise indicated, and in New Style thereafter.

C. E. T.
Columbia, Missouri
January, 1972

Contents

Contributors

Charles E. Timberlake is Assistant Professor of History at the University of Missouri—Columbia, where he has taught since 1967. Professor Timberlake obtained his B.A. degree from Berea College in Kentucky in 1957, his M.A. from Claremont Graduate School in California in 1962, and his Ph.D. from the University of Washington, Seattle, in 1968. Among his publications are "The Slavic Department of the Helsinki University Library," *Slavic Review*, 25:3(September, 1966), and "The Leningrad Collection of Zemstvo Publications," *Slavic Review*, 26:3(September, 1967). He is currently writing a political biography of I. I. Petrunkevich.

Kermit E. McKenzie, Professor of History at Emory University, where he has taught since 1960, received his B.A. degree from the University of Richmond, Virginia, in 1947. He earned his M.A. and certificate from the Russian Institute at Columbia University, 1949, as well as his Ph.D. in history in 1960. Professor McKenzie has published *Comintern and World Revolution, 1928–1943* (New York, 1964), translated into Italian as *Comintern e rivoluzione mondiale 1928/1943* (Florence, 1969), and he has contributed essays to Ernest Simmons, ed., *Continuity and Change in Russian and Soviet Thought* (Cambridge, Mass., 1955); John S. Curtiss, ed., *Essays in Russian and Soviet History* (New York, 1963); and George Simmonds, ed., *Soviet Leaders* (New York, 1967). He is currently working on a study of Fedor Rodichev.

Richard Pipes, Professor of History at Harvard University, and Director of the Russian Research Center there, earned his B.A. degree from Cornell University (1945), and his M.A. and Ph.D. degrees from Harvard (1947 and 1950). He has been on the Harvard faculty since 1950. Among his publications are *Formation of the Soviet Union* (Cambridge, Mass., 1954, 2nd rev. ed., 1964); *Social Democracy and the St. Petersburg Labor Movement, 1885–1897* (Cambridge, Mass., 1963); and *Peter Struve: Liberal on the Left, 1870–1905* (Cambridge, Mass., 1970). Professor Pipes is currently completing volume two of his study of Peter Struve.

David A. Davies is Associate Professor of History at the University of Waterloo, Ontario, Canada, where he has taught since 1964 and was Chairman of the Department of History from 1968 to 1970. He earned his B.A., M.A., and Ph.D. degrees in history from the University of Washington, Seattle, and studied for one year at the University of Leningrad. His dissertation was a study of Vasilii Maklakov. Professor Davies is currently engaged in research on the social history of the city of Moscow before the Bolshevik Revolution.

William R. Copeland, who obtained his B.A. from Georgetown University and his Ph.D. from Helsinki University in Finland, is Lecturer in Political History at Helsinki University, where he has taught since 1970. Professor Copeland's dissertation was on the role of Finnish politicians in the Russian Empire at the end of the nineteenth and the beginning of the twentieth centuries. His paper on Konni Zilliacus, presented to a conference in London in January of 1972, will appear in a volume on Finland to be published by Cambridge University Press. In addition to further work on the topic of his dissertation, Professor Copeland is conducting research on the migration of American Finns to Soviet Karelia in the 1920s and 1930s.

Judith E. Zimmerman, Associate Professor of History at the University of Pittsburgh at Greensburg, earned her B.A. degree from Swarthmore in 1960, and her M.A. and Ph.D. degrees from Columbia University in 1963 and 1967 respectively. Professor Zimmerman has translated N. Berdiaev, "Philosophical verity and intelligentsia truth," *Canadian Slavic Studies,* Summer, 1969, and with Marshall Shatz she has translated *Vekhi,* which was serialized from September, 1968, to December, 1971, in *Canadian Slavic Studies.* Her present commitments include working on the *Vekhi* group and serving as Assistant Editor of *Canadian Slavic Studies.*

William G. Rosenberg has taught at the University of Michigan since 1967 and is now Associate Professor of History there. He received his B.A. degree from Amherst College in 1960, his M.A. from Harvard in 1961, and a Ph.D. in history from there in 1967. Professor Rosenberg has published *A. I. Denikin and the Anti-Bolshevik Movement in South Russia* (Amherst, 1961) and articles on Russian liberalism in the *Journal of Modern History, Cahiers du Monde russe et sovietique, Soviet Studies,* and other journals. He is currently working on a history of the Constitutional-Democratic party from 1917 to 1921.

Theodore H. Von Laue, Professor of History at Clark University in Worcester, Mass., has taught at that institution since 1970. He received his B.A. degree in 1939 and his Ph.D. in 1944, both from Princeton. His publications include *Leopold Ranke* (Princeton, 1950), *Sergei Witte and the Industrialization of Russia* (New York, 1963), *Why Lenin? Why Stalin?* (Philadelphia, 1964), and *The Global City* (Philadelphia, 1969). Professor Von Laue is currently engaged in research on the process of modernization.

Essays on Russian Liberalism

INTRODUCTION: THE CONCEPT OF LIBERALISM IN RUSSIA

Charles E. Timberlake

I

Every person who attempts to discuss Russian liberalism in any detail soon becomes aware of the lack of precision in terminology. Shall he begin by explaining carefully the ideas the word *liberalism* represented during the first quarter of the nineteenth century in Western Europe (even if he can find a definition that applies to all its variations in Western Europe) and then search for some of those ideas in Russia? If he takes this approach, does he then call the Russians in whom he finds one or more of those ideas embodied *Russian liberals?* When he compares the Russian "liberal," identified by this method with a liberal in Western Europe in the nineteenth century, he often discovers gross dissimilarities and abandons the term *Russian liberal.* This, then, creates the problem of discussing liberalism in Russia without an identifiable group to which the liberal label can be affixed.

One of the two major works on Russian liberalism published to date is an example of the approach outlined above. Its title, *Geschichte des Liberalismus in Russland* [*History of Liberalism in Russia*],[1] reveals the emphasis of the work. It is an effort to find in Russia tenets of thought that characterized liberalism in the West. As the author, Victor Leontovitsch, explained, the book is a study in intellectual history, "a history of liberalism and not a history of the liberals." [2] As one might expect from this approach, Leontovitsch found elements of European liberalism in the thoughts of Russian emperors, empresses, and bureaucrats, as well as in members of the Constitutional-Democratic party (the group commonly regarded by historians as Russia's major liberal party). He

---

1. Victor Leontovitsch, *Geschichte des Liberalismus in Russland* (Frankfurt, 1957).
2. *Ibid.,* vii.

2 · **Essays on Russian Liberalism**

devoted more space individually to Catherine II, Alexander I, Alexander II, Mikhail Speranskii, Peter Stolypin, and Sergei Witte than to any member of the Constitutional-Democratic party, except for Kadet Vasilii Maklakov.

A second approach to the study of Russian liberalism is to start with a more functional definition. The researcher begins by seeking a Russian reformer who preferred to work peacefully through legal institutions in order to change the state structure and allow for more public participation, the same course West European liberals had taken. Such an approach assumes the existence of an identifiable behavioral pattern (or patterns) of liberals. Having found a suitable person, the researcher then analyzes his thoughts and actions in order to discover the nature of the Russian strain of liberalism. This cluster of ideas is then compared with West European liberalism or another previously identified type of liberalism to justify applying the term to the Russian group, or at least to establish a relative meaning of the term in its Russian context.

The second major work on Russian liberalism, George Fischer's *Russian Liberalism: From Gentry to Intelligentsia,*[3] is a product of the more functional approach. Having provided a very general definition of liberalism, Fischer distinguished between traditional West European liberalism and "have-not" liberalism, which is a minority movement in an underdeveloped society. Having decided that Russia's liberal movement fit into the have-not category, Fischer divided the have-not liberals in Russia into two types: those who pursued their goals "through the existing illiberal government" and those who sought its "overthrow or drastic transformation." Fischer focused on the latter group. Seeking to give relative meaning to liberalism as he defined it in Russia, Fischer said Russian liberals were more analogous to liberals in Spain and Greece in the 1820s or liberals in present-day Asia and Latin America than to liberals in Western Europe during the period of 1860 to 1905.[4] This approach virtually excluded the emperors, empresses, and bureaucrats who were the major characters in Leontovitsch's approach.

The problems of definition posed by Russian liberals and

---

3. George Fischer, *Russian Liberalism: From Gentry to Intelligentsia* (Cambridge, Mass., 1958).
4. *Ibid.,* viii–ix.

liberalism are not unique to present scholars. Russians were aware that the word *liberal* and its derivative, *liberalism,* which were born morphologically and semantically in Western Europe during the first two decades of the nineteenth century, described West European phenomena, but they had imported the words into Russia, nonetheless, by the 1820s. By the 1860s both words had become common in the political vocabulary of literate Russians, especially those of the capital cities. Twenty years later they were entering common usage in the provinces and appeared in a major Russian dictionary as early as 1881. In the 1860s, Russians began debating the relevance of the two words for Russian society. The modern scholar merely inherited this debate and the problem of applying the terms to persons and ideas in imperial Russian history. A short history of the usage of the word *liberal* and its derivatives in Russia and of the debate surrounding that usage can place the problem of definition in perspective.

Recent research reveals that Napoleon first used the term *liberal ideas* in a political sense in France in 1799, and that the *Liberales* in the Spanish Cortes of 1812 was probably the first group to designate itself as liberal. Shortly thereafter, the British Tories referred to the most progressive section of the Whig party as *British Liberals.* The *Oxford English Dictionary* included this usage in an entry for *liberal* in 1816. In France a political pamphlet published in 1817 included the word *liberal* in its title, and in 1819 the word *liberalism* appeared both in France and England.[5]

Although no systematic research has been done to trace the route by which these terms reached Russia, the Russians seem to have acquired them from the French. The Decembrist Pavel Pestel, citing the impact French writers had made upon him, referred to himself in his testimony of 1826 as imbued with "free-thinking and liberal ideas." [6] But from Pestel's

5. G. de Bertier de Sauvigny, "Liberalism, Nationalism, and Socialism: The Birth of Three Words," *The Review of Politics,* 32:2(April, 1970), 147–66.

6. Pestel's testimony is included in I. Ia. Shchipanov, ed., *Izbrannye sotsialno-politicheskie i filosofskie proizvedeniia dekabristov,* vol. 2 of 3 vols. (Moscow, 1951). See pp. 164 and 167, for instance, for usage of the terms *free-thinking (vol'-nodumnye)* and *liberal (liberal'nye) ideas.*

Pushkin also used the words *liberalism* and *liberal ideas. Slovar' iazyka Pushkina,* vol. 2 of 4 vols. (Moscow, 1957), 482.

testimony to the drafting of the Great Reforms in the 1850s, few things Russian were described as liberal.

The aftermath of the Crimean War and the drafting of the Great Reforms provided a new Russian context within which the word *liberal* had more meaning. In 1856 K. D. Kavelin, B. N. Chicherin, and N. A. Mel'gunov formed the first Russian group to refer to itself as advocates of Western-type liberalism.[7] They constructed a seven-point liberal political program to solve Russia's domestic problems. Alexander Herzen published the program in his emigré publication, *Voices from Russia,* in London in 1856. This group stated straightforwardly that the solution to Russia's problems was: "Liberalism! This is the slogan of every educated and sensible person in Russia. This is the banner which can unite around it people of all spheres, all classes, all tendencies. . . . In liberalism lies the whole future of Russia." The group's political program consisted of freedom of conscience, freedom of public opinion, freedom of the press, freedom of teaching, freedom from serfdom, and public, open conduct of government and administration of justice.[8]

After publishing the program, Herzen kept the word *liberal* before his readers in the periodical, *The Bell.* In letters from readers and in articles by himself and others he used various forms of the word. *Liberal* and its derivatives appeared especially frequently in 1859 and in early 1860,[9] but it was used less and less after the mid-1860s. By the beginning of 1866 qualifiers such as *gentry liberalism* and *bourgeois liberalism* replaced the terms *liberalism, liberal ideas,* and *our liberals,* which had characterized the period of 1856 to 1860.[10]

At the same time Herzen, Chicherin, and others made references to the positive role liberalism could play in Russia, liberals came under attack from both extremes of political opinion in Russia. Turgenev's character, Bazarov, exhibited the nihilists' scorn for the term when he said in *Fathers and*

---

7. V. Rozental', "Pervoe otkrytoe vystuplenie russkikh liberalov v 1855–1856 gg.," *Istoriia SSSR,* 2(1958), 113–30.

8. Quoted in Terence Emmons, *The Russian Landed Gentry and the Peasant Emancipation of 1861,* 46.

9. See, for example, *Kolokol* (April 15, December 15, 1859, March 15, 1860).

10. For use of the terms *bourgeois liberalism* and *gentry liberalism,* see *Kolokol* (December 1, 1865), 1711, and (April 15, 1866), 1782.

Children (first published in 1861), "Aristocracy, liberalism, progress, principles . . . if you think of it, what a lot of foreign . . . and useless words." [11] In the following year, a Russian student radical wrote a "political dictionary," in which he defined a liberal in Russia as: *"Liberal*——a man who loves liberty, generally a noble; for example, landlords, landed aristocrats. These men like looking at liberty from windows and doing nothing, and then go for a stroll and on to theaters and balls. This is what is called a Liberal." [12]

Dostoevsky also defined Russian liberals in a letter in 1868, in which he called them "obsolete and retrograde dregs. . . . The so-called 'educated society' of old is a motley collection of everything that has separated itself from Russia, that has not understood Russia and has become Frenchified—that is what a Russian liberal is, and that is why he is reactionary." [13]

These three quotations reveal several facts about the words *liberal* and *liberalism* in Russia. They show, first, that by the 1860s the words were widely used. Thus, the historian of Russia's intellectual and political development cannot ignore the words, even though he might deplore the way in which Russians used them.

More importantly, the quotations show that the words were used as pejoratives and that while the Russians who used the terms did not consider themselves liberals, they did not designate specific Russians as liberals. The liberal described in these quotations is merely a stereotype of a landlord with a taste for frivolous European culture, but lacking an understanding of the reality of contemporary Russia. Such descriptions leave the Russian liberals virtually anonymous and are, in fact, references to a social group rather than an explanation of a political philosophy.

The scholar who relies upon the Russians of the period to explain who the liberals were and what they believed learns little, and what he learns comes from nonliberal detractors,

---

11. Ivan Turgenev, *Fathers and Children* (New York, 1954), 55.

12. B. Kozmin, "K istorii 'Molodoi Rossii'," *Katorga i ssylka*, 6(1936), quoted in Franco Venturi, *Roots of Revolution* (New York, 1966), 299.

13. Fedor Dostoevsky, *Letters and Reminiscences* (New York, 1923), 39. Dostoevsky mentioned only Vissarion Belinsky by name.

because apparently no person or group after Chicherin adopted that label or articulated a set of political theories to which the person or group applied the liberal label. Early use of *liberal* and *liberalism* in France and England was also derogatory, but in those countries groups to which the liberal label was attached accepted it as an accurate description of their ideas. History is full of examples, in fact, where groups accepted titles given them by their detractors. The liberals in imperial Russia, however, are an exception. No group— not even the Constitutional-Democrats, as a party or individually—was willing to adopt the label, even though they held theories common among Western liberals. Several Kadets openly admitted that during their political activism in Russia they had always subscribed to the major beliefs of West European liberalism, but they made the admission only after they had emigrated to Western Europe after the Bolshevik Revolution. In this manner, the Kadets applied the word *liberal* to themselves retrospectively, just as historians have done and must do. Those who applied the label in the nineteenth century to the precursors of the Kadets were the nonliberal detractors and foreigners.

Clearly the label can be attached to individual Russians as early as the creation of the gentry committees in the late 1850s. Whether the scholar takes Leontovitsch's approach and identifies persons according to the content of their political philosophies or Fischer's approach and identifies a group of activists who sought reform through peaceful means, he identifies approximately the same group of people. The scholar's particular vantage point (whether he is studying intellectual, social, or institutional history) determines which Russian liberals he analyzes in detail and which he virtually ignores.

If the presence of liberals in Russia in the 1860s was so obvious that the nonliberal detractors of the time could identify them, why did Russian liberals at the time not accept the label? Two answers seem most likely. First, the word was foreign and therefore not comprehended by the ordinary Russian citizen. Even the words *constitutional* and *democratic* were so foreign to the Russian population in 1905 that the Kadet party chose as its official name "Party of Popular Freedom" and put *Constitutional-Democratic* in parentheses at the end of the party's name.

In addition to its foreign origin, the word *liberal* had acquired serious negative connotations by the end of the

1860s. Russian monarchists considered the liberals disguised radicals, and the revolutionaries considered them the product of a narrow class interest, as the terms *gentry liberals* and *bourgeois liberals* suggest. These connotations discouraged Russians from applying the liberal label to themselves, even those who consciously accepted the basic postulates of West European liberalism. Russian liberals preferred, instead, to designate themselves as society (*obshchestvo*) and their movement as the movement of society (*obshchestvennoe dvizhenie*). These purposely vague terms not only avoided the word *liberal,* but also suggested a movement that rested on a base much broader than merely the gentry or the bourgeoisie.

Despite the Russian liberals' refusal to claim the label, the word *liberal* remained in use by nonliberals in the 1870s. Near the end of that decade, populists spoke of possible alliances with the liberals, but they did not mention specific persons when they spoke of liberals. They certainly knew the names, however, of I. I. Petrunkevich and A. F. Lindfors, two liberals from the Chernigov provincial zemstvo who held a secret meeting with populists in Kiev in December, 1878.[14] The fact was that the objectives of the populists and liberals were so similar that the populists constantly felt the necessity to explain how they differed from the liberals. Had the differences been great, the frequent explanations would not have been necessary. The future member of the revolutionary society People's Will, Debogorii-Mokrievich, who participated for the revolutionaries in the meeting with Petrunkevich and Lindfors, reported that the terrorists agreed with the political objectives of the zemstvo men. They disagreed only with the contention that the imperial government would be more likely to grant a constitution if the terrorists suspended violence for a specified period of time.[15] Disagreement over terror as a means for achieving self-government was the major question that separated liberals and populists in the 1870s.

The writer Iuzov-Kablits in 1882 also contrasted populists and liberals in his book on the intellectual bases of populism.[16] V. A. Gol'tsev, in one of the rare defenses of Russian

14. See my essay in this volume for a discussion of the secret meeting in 1878.
15. Debogorii-Mokrievich, *Vospominaniia* (Paris, 1894), 300.
16. V. A. Gol'tsev, "Liberalizm i narodnichestvo," *Golos,* 320(1882).

liberals, published an attack upon the book. In an article entitled "Liberalism and Populism" Gol'tsev argued that the liberals shared the populists' objectives. "The liberal," Gol'tsev asserted, "might differ from the populist only in preference of means of achieving the desired independence." [17] The difference in means was, of course, the willingness of most populists to use violence. Gol'tsev, while he defended liberals, did not name any liberal, however, and he did not refer to himself as a liberal, although he clearly belonged to the group of zemstvo and professional men out of which the Kadet party was later formed. He was, for instance, the organizer of the first zemstvo congress in Moscow in April 1879.[18]

By 1881 the substantive *liberal* and five derivatives appeared in Vladimir Dal's *Defining Dictionary of the Living Great Russian Language*. Dal' defined a liberal as "a political free-thinker, one who thinks or acts freely; in general, one who desires great freedom for the people and self-government." In addition to the adjective *liberal'nyi* (defined merely as "that which related to the noun"), the dictionary included two abstractions: *liberal'nost'* (defined as "the property or characteristics of a liberal") and *liberal'stvo* (defined as "the abstract quality of being a liberal"), and it listed the verb *liberal'nichat'* (defined as "to exhibit the characteristics of a political free-thinker; to think freely") which meant, in short, to pretend to be a liberal. From this verb, the Russians formed the noun, *liberal'nichan'e,* which meant the pretense of being a liberal.[19] *Liberalism* did not appear in Dal's 1881 dictionary. Thus,

---

17. *Ibid.*
18. I. I. Petrunkevich, *Iz zapisok obshchestvennago deiatelia* (Berlin, 1934), 112, which is vol. 21 of *Arkhiv russkoi revoliutsii.*
19. See Vladimir Dal', *Tolkovyi slovar' zhivago Velikorusskago iazyka,* 2nd ed. (St. Petersburg, 1881), at the word *liberal.* In 1865, for instance, Herzen applied this term to Mikhail Katkov's newspaper, *Moscow News,* when the newspaper offered some statements in support of the peasantry. Herzen's typical description of the paper was that it was "an organ of neo-serfdom and the destruction of Poland." "Liberal'nichan'e *Moskovskikh Vedomostei,*" *Kolokol* (April 1, 1865), 1611. See *Slovar' sovremennogo russkogo literaturnogo iazyka,* vol. 6 of 17 vols. (Moscow-Leningrad, 1957), 207–10, which refers in several instances to Dal's dictionary, but supplies some additional examples.

a Russian who consulted this dictionary would have learned only that the liberal political program included more freedom for the people and self-government.

By the 1880s the words *liberalism* and *liberal party* had found their way into the provinces. The event that made them seem applicable was the formation of factions in the county and provincial zemstvo assemblies. As early as 1877 members of the Chernigov provincial zemstvo assembly used the words *left* and *right* to identify *parties* that had come into existence in that assembly.[20] In 1882 some members of the zemstvo assembly of Sudzhan County in Kursk Province began describing factions in their zemstvo as *liberal* and *conservative parties*.

The editor of the Sudzhan County zemstvo *Weekly* lamented in an editorial, "Our Zemstvo Parties," that, in the recent 1882 elections to the county zemstvo assembly, liberal and conservative parties had contested with each other. He considered the appearance of parties in the zemstvo a bad omen and blamed the Russian gentry for their existence, because the gentry imported the concept of parties from Western Europe and subsequently divided themselves into parties in their own gentry assemblies. In Western Europe, the writer explained, liberal and conservative political parties had some historical justification, but in Russia they had none.[21] Despite the formation in Russia of parties called liberal and conservative, the editorial contended, the Russian parties did not share common ideas and aspirations with their West European counterparts. The Russian conservatives did not wish to preserve the existing order created by the Great Reforms, yet preserving the *status quo* was the major objective of West European conservatives. In contrast, the Russian conservatives preferred a return to prereform conditions, although they would not, perhaps, reinstitute serfdom. The "so-called liberals," the writer asserted, "while extolling the existing renovated or newly established institutions, want their further, successive development. Thus, the opinions of our liberals come closer to the opinions of the Western conservatives, and why they are called liberals only God knows." [22]

---

20. See my essay on I. I. Petrunkevich.
21. "Nashi zemskiia partii," *Ezhenedel'nik Sudzhanskago zemstva,* 15(1882), 2.
22. *Ibid.*

The editorial made clear that in the term *liberal party,* the word *party* was as foreign to the Russian reader in the province as was the word *liberal.* In response to the editorial, a person calling himself "Minus" wrote a six-column article in which he defined the word *party* and explained the significance of the appearance of parties in Russia in 1882. Defining a party as "an aggregate of several persons, bound together by a conscious spiritual unity which is not contradictory to the unity of human society," the writer argued that: "The existence of parties in human societies is necessary and is summoned forth by the development of that society." [23] A society with petty factions rather than clearly formed interest groups, he said, exhibited signs of a lack of development, and such factions were a manifestation of a serious social inadequacy. "The moving of a person from one party to another, based upon the development of his social views, does not constitute an evil similar to betrayal or desertion, but is a necessary phenomenon in a developing society and a manifestation of that very development." The emergence of parties in the Sudzhan county zemstvo, as in other zemstvos, was, therefore, a sign that Russia was a healthy, developing society, rather than one beset by evils.[24]

Although members of zemstvo factions were the subjects of similar discussions in the 1880s, they almost always refrained from identifying themselves as liberals. When they did apply the label to themselves, they were addressing foreigners who, as the Russians knew, were accustomed to seeing the zemstvo activists and their allies among the liberal professions called liberals in the Western press.

Perhaps the first instance in which a zemstvo activist and future Kadet called himself a liberal occurred in the correspondence between I. I. Petrunkevich and the American journalist, George Kennan. Kennan, who had visited Petrunkevich in the early 1880s while conducting research on tsarist prisons, obtained a copy of an appeal to Minister of Interior M. T. Loris-Melikov by a group of Moscow lawyers, doctors, professors, and others who advocated a role in national legislation for zemstvo representatives. Kennan titled the document "The Last Appeal of the Russian Liberals," and he was translating it into English for

---

23. Minus, "K voprosu o nashikh partiiakh," *ibid.,* 18(1882), 2.

24. *Ibid.*

publication in an American journal in 1886 when he wrote to Petrunkevich for information about the origins of the appeal.[25]

For the purpose of responding to Kennan's query, Petrunkevich adopted the use of the term *liberal party* and called his group that met with the revolutionaries in Kiev in 1878 representatives of the liberal party. He explained, as Gol'tsev and Debogorii-Mokrievich had done, that the liberals and populists had many similarities: "Our parties: liberals, radicals, and *narod[n]ovoltsy* all have one common objective . . . ," he said, "the establishment in this country of a constitutional government in place of the absolute autocracy." He cautioned, however, that Russia still did not have "either the bases or sufficient numbers of adherents" to form genuine parties. Russia's "liberals, radicals, and revolutionaries are differentiated not by political objectives, but by temperament." [26] Prior to this letter, Petrunkevich had not called himself a liberal, and he did not do so afterwards.

The case of Paul Miliukov also illustrates the way Kadets refrained from calling themselves liberals at home, but adopted the label abroad. Miliukov rarely, if ever, referred to himself directly as a liberal in his Russian writings or speeches. But when he presented a series of lectures at the University of Chicago in 1903 and the Lowell Institute in Boston in 1904, he called the two major currents for reform in Russia "the liberal idea" and "the socialistic idea." Calling these the "moderate and the radical" opinions, respectively, he added (in less than perfect English) that the moderate opinion *"has always been called* in Russia by the party title 'liberals' of western Europe." The bearers of liberalism were, he said, "the representatives of Russian self-government, . . . men of liberal professions, and even . . . state officials; all of them for the most part belonging to the old Russian gentry." [27]

---

25. Kennan published the article with an introduction that is a translation of portions of Petrunkevich's letter in *The Century Magazine,* 35:1(1887), 55–63.
26. I. I. Petrunkevich to George Kennan, December 20, 1886/ January 1, 1887, Box 1, Folder 1885–1886, The George Kennan Papers, Manuscripts Department, Library of Congress.
27. Paul Miliukov, *Russia and Its Crisis,* 167. The emphasis supplied is my own. Miliukov said (p. 168) that in Russia the word *liberalism* was "worn out" from overuse.

Clearly, Miliukov considered himself in that group; yet
he chose to acknowledge the label only to an English-speaking
audience. Prior to these lectures, he had apparently used
the word *liberalism* only once to describe a Russian
phenomenon. In 1902 he had written that "populism arose
to replace slavophilism, and democratic liberalism of the
newest type replaced westernism [*zapadnichestvo*]." [28]

Fedor Rodichev also abstained from describing himself
as a liberal during his political activism. Yet, in 1923, as an
emigrant in Switzerland, he wrote for an English audience
a two-part article entitled "The Liberal Movement in Russia,
1855–1905," and he followed in 1929 with an article whose
title described his closest friend, Ivan Petrunkevich (whom
he had not previously called a liberal), as "The Veteran of
Russian Liberalism." [29] Peter Struve followed the same
pattern with an article in 1934 in which he described
Rodichev as a liberal. [30]

With the publication of Volume 34 of *Entsiklopedicheskii
slovar* (the *Encyclopedic Dictionary*) in 1896, the Russian
reader had at his disposal a more complete definition of
liberalism than Dal' had provided him. V. Vodovozov
wrote in the volume that "in state structure, liberalism
advocates constitutional order against absolutism; local
self-government against central; freedom of person against
police guardianship; equal rights for women; abolition of class
privilege; participation of the popular element in the
administration of justice; equality of distribution of the tax
burden; . . . and a direct income tax." [31]

28. Paul Miliukov, *Iz istorii russkoi intelligentsii*, 2nd ed. (St.
Petersburg, 1903), 267.
29. "The Liberal Movement in Russia (1855–1891)" and
"The Liberal Movement in Russia (1891–1905)" *The Slavonic
Review*, 2:4(June, 1923), and 2:5(December, 1923); "The
Veteran of Russian Liberalism: Ivan Petrunkevich," *ibid.* (1929).
See also Maklakov's *The First State Duma*, 1–2, where he defends
himself against Miliukov. The latter had claimed that Maklakov
opposed the ideas of liberalism, and Maklakov asserted that he
"did not reject these ideas. . . . Liberalism . . . had a good
chance for success in Russia since it fought for the country's
needs."
30. "My Contacts with Rodichev," *The Slavonic Review*,
12:35 (January, 1934). See p. 351 for an example.
31. V. Vodovozov, "Liberalizm," *Entsiklopedicheskii slovar'*,
vol. 34 of 86 vols. (St. Petersburg, 1896), 632–33.

The same author, defining a liberal party, wrote that "in the strict sense of the word, no liberal party exists in Russia," merely a "liberal tendency." The representatives of that tendency promoted the introduction of the Great Reforms and later "defended them against attacks of a conservative and reactionary character."[32] In the supplement to the encyclopedia in 1906, Vodovozov revised his article on the liberal party to include contemporary events. The liberal tendency he had referred to earlier in Russia, he said, had always been "painted in the hue of democraticism." No clear boundary between Russian liberalism and socialism existed, he said. Using almost the exact words Petrunkevich used in his letter to Kennan in 1886, Vodovozov said that "the difference lies more in the area of temperament than in the area of world view." He defined liberals as "those who act exclusively through legal means, refraining from revolutionary methods of struggle." Laissez-faire liberalism had always been weak in Russia, he said, and never constituted "a specific tendency." Of the parties in existence in Russia before 1906, "the Constitutional-Democratic party was, from the beginning, the only one which can be called liberal," although the Party of Democratic Reform, founded only at the end of January, 1906, also appeared to him to be liberal.[33]

With the formation of the Kadet party, Russia had a cohesive group to which Russians and foreigners alike could point when they discussed the embodiment of liberal ideas in Russia. Men who had been the bearers of merely "liberal tendencies," and who often had no contact with each other or merely met once per year in zemstvo assemblies, now formed a party similar to political parties in Europe and America. Direct references to Kadets replaced earlier references to ill-defined groups.

II

The present collection of essays on Russian liberalism has several objectives. The first and most obvious is to make available the findings of substantial research on topics in the area of Russian liberalism. The book is an outgrowth of a conference on Russian liberalism that met simultaneously with

32. "Liberal'naia partiia," *ibid.*, 637.
33. "Liberal'naia partiia," *ibid.*, 3/d (St. Petersburg, 1906), 75–76.

the Eighth Annual Bi-State Slavic Conference in Columbia, Missouri, in the autumn of 1969. The aim of the conference was to bring together every Western scholar who had completed but not yet published research on various aspects of Russian liberalism. The collection reflects, within these limits, the status of research completed by 1969 and familiarizes the general reader with the approaches of those who have begun research on the topic within the past decade.

The volume does not attempt to deal systematically with the whole area of Russian liberalism or to offer final conclusions about the movement. It lacks, for instance, an essay on Paul Miliukov, an analysis of the Kadet agrarian policy and its origins, and a work of synthesis emphasizing the Russian sources of Russian liberal thought and action that would balance Professor Von Laue's article stressing the European sources of Russian liberalism. The organizer of the conference sought essays on each of these three topics, but was unable to locate persons who had progressed far enough with their research to publish their findings on the topics.

The second objective of the volume is to analyze the origin and evolution of Russian liberalism. By presenting analyses of the major figures in the Russian liberal movement (in chronological order of their participation), the volume notes the similarities and differences among the liberals studied, and it reveals the issues which those persons, prior to 1905, considered important for Russia's future. The influence Herzen had upon the generation of Rodichev and Petrunke-vich, for instance, is significant. Both Petrunkevich and Rodichev were members of the Russian gentry, and both chose to live in rural areas to work through institutions created by the Great Reforms in order to shape the newly emancipated peasant into a citizen capable of participation in self-government. The later generation of Maklakov, Struve, and Miliukov differed from the Petrunkevich-Rodichev generation in that the three members of the later generation were urban dwellers engaged in liberal professions. None had worked in the zemstvos, and only one (Maklakov) was a member of the Russian gentry.

After presenting sketches of these four important liberals, the volume analyzes the policies the Kadets pursued in national politics when the creation of the Duma in 1905 presented them with that possibility. The areas of concern for zemstvo liberals, and the policies they pursued through the zemstovs, provided background for several members of the Kadet party after 1905. The program that the party drafted in 1905–1906 was not a purely abstract one drafted at the moment; rather, it was the result of many years of concern and consolidated several objectives that Kadets had been pursuing through the zemstvos for several decades.

The third objective of the volume is to shed further light on the question of the role of Western Europe as the model after which Russian liberals sought to shape Russia's future. Clearly, the Russian liberals wanted Russia to develop an economy and culture equal to those of the countries of Western Europe. They were conscious of a contact between Russia and Europe and the enormous impact of European ideas upon Russia since the reign of Peter I, and they considered the Russian educated class (of which they were a part) a product of the forces set in motion by Peter I's reforms.

Russia's economic and cultural backwardness was most evident in the Russian peasantry's low level of production and education, however. This fact constituted the major problem for the liberals, because the peasantry had to be the primary basis for constitutional self-government that the liberals sought. The liberals' goal was, therefore, to remove the economic and educational differences between the citizens of West European countries and the illiterate, impoverished Russian peasantry. In this sense the liberals were Westernizers, as Maklakov said; in this sense they constituted the minority movement in an underdeveloped society, as Fischer observed.

The liberals' assumptions about the unpreparedness of the Russian peasantry to participate in self-government led them to expect no immediate spectacular successes. They set about a long-range plan to use the institutions created by the Great Reforms to complete the emancipation of the peasantry, a process begun but not completed by emancipation legislation. They sought, especially through the zemstvos, to improve the peasant's material conditions and to prepare him through education to play a new role in a society undergoing rapid transformation after the Great Reforms. They assumed that an educated peasant would inevitably choose self-government over autocracy. For this reason, the liberals considered the construction of schools a political act.

Because of their assessment of the peasantry's condition, the liberals regarded any forceful overthrow of the government as useless. For that reason, terror was also counterproductive. The liberals felt the best guarantee for the preservation of self-government to be an educated citizenry that would strongly defend that form of government. Until such a citizenry emerged, the people would neither defend nor utilize the opportunities self-government afforded. To create such citizens, the institutions established by the Great Reforms were better instruments than the instrument of terror. The tsarist government could stand, therefore, until the citizenry was prepared for a parliament. In the meantime, the liberals wanted the tsarist government to grant freedoms of press, speech, assembly, and the inviolability of person, all of which would facilitate the liberals' task of educating the peasantry.

By 1917 the liberals still opposed violence. During the Duma monarchy, as the essays by Professors Zimmerman and Rosenberg show, the Kadets sought to be the agency expressing the demands of the peasantry and society to the government, but the Kadets sought at the same time to steer the peasants' frustrations through nonviolent opposition. As long as events in Russia kept open the hostility between the population and the government, the Kadets, attempting to retain the favor of both, could be the real representative of neither and were bound to arouse the suspicions of both. This was the problem a minority faced when it attempted to lead and restrain the majority at the same time, the problem of a liberalism that had no firm social base, or that was "intellectual rather than bourgeois," as Miliukov characterized Russian liberalism.[34]

Given that such conditions faced Russian liberals, what were the prospects for a peaceful, liberal alternative to autocracy in Russia before 1917? Professor Von Laue answers that the prospects were so remote that the question is irrelevant. To arrive at this conclusion is to choose the first approach outlined above in this essay: the approach that defines liberalism in its Western context and looks for those tenets in Russia, the approach of Leontovitsch carried to its logical conclusion. This collection of essays provides evidence that the Russian liberals knew not only the ideas of West European liberals, but they also knew the unique conditions

---

34. Miliukov, *Russia and Its Crisis,* 169.

that prevailed in Russia, and they had drafted specific, practical solutions for many of those problems. Professor Davies's essay on Maklakov is devoted specifically to illustrating that the Russian liberals were aware that the West was not always an applicable model for Russians to follow.

The approach the liberals took to reform required more time than events allowed, but they were convinced they could achieve parliamentary government without violent revolution. They cannot have been irrelevant to Russian history, of course, for they were a very important part of it from the middle of the nineteenth century to the Bolshevik Revolution. If the Russian liberals thought a nonviolent alternative to autocracy possible, certainly the student of Russian liberalism must study that possibility. This volume of essays is a further effort in that direction.

IVAN IL'ICH PETRUNKEVICH:
RUSSIAN LIBERALISM IN MICROCOSM

Charles E. Timberlake

The history of Ivan Il'ich Petrunkevich's political life is an inner history of the Russian liberal movement from the period of the Great Reforms to the emigration of Russia's liberals after the Bolshevik Revolution. His activities in the zemstvo institutions of Chernigov Province from 1868 to 1879 and in Tver Province from 1891 to 1905 constituted an important part of the zemstvo movement. From 1905 onward he also began to play an important role in national politics, especially in 1906 when he was chosen chairman of the "parliamentary fraction" of the Kadet party in the First Duma. After the dissolution of the First Duma in 1906 he served until 1915 as chairman of the central committee of the Kadet party. In 1915 he retired to the Crimea, but the Russian Civil War in that area compelled him to seek safety abroad. He died in emigration in Czechoslovakia in 1928 and was buried in Prague.

By 1867 when Ivan Il'ich Petrunkevich, at age twenty-two, left Saint Petersburg University to enter public life, he had already decided upon the objectives he wished to pursue. His youth had coincided with the period of the Great Reforms in Russia, and his political ideas were heavily influenced by the debate in society that accompanied the drafting of those reforms. Born in Chernigov Province in 1844, he was ten years of age when the Crimean War began; he was sixteen when the serfs were emancipated, and during his nineteenth year (while a student at Saint Petersburg University), university autonomy was restored. During his twentieth year, the zemstvo and judicial institutions were created, and the following year, precensorship of the press was abolished. In addition, revolutionary societies sprang up in the early 1860s, and in 1866 D. V. Karakozov, a member of one of the revolutionary societies, made an attempt upon the life of Emperor Alexander II. The intense and ubiquitous debates

over the best form of social and political organization for
the future of Russia stimulated Petrunkevich's interest in these
questions. Through his concern for these issues he formed
the bases of the political philosophy that guided his actions
during the remainder of his life.

Petrunkevich was a student in the "special course" in the
cadet corps (*kadetskii korpus*) in Kiev during the period when
the Emancipation Statute was being drafted. One of his
teachers, M. A. Domontovich, received considerable
information about the internal operations of the Editorial
Committee from a relative who was a member of the committee. Domontovich, Petrunkevich said, "let me in on all the
details of this question, arousing in me an interest and a
more or less clear understanding of this [serfdom], the greatest
of evils through which Russia had passed." [1]

Domontovich also introduced Petrunkevich to the works
of Alexander Herzen. In London, Herzen followed closely
the work of the Tver gentry committee (to draft suggestions
for Emancipation) and published extracts from its report
in 1860. He also published the Tver gentry assembly's
address to the Tsar in 1862 calling for the convocation of a
national assembly and an end to the gentry's exemption
from taxation. In 1865 he published the Moscow gentry
assembly's appeal to the Tsar to "crown the edifice" with a
national assembly. Petrunkevich said that he "read and
reread" *Poliarnaia zvezda* and *Kolokol*. Having experienced
serfdom first-hand, Petrunkevich considered himself
"sufficiently prepared soil" for Herzen's articles, and he
soon found himself "under the strong influence of Herzen." [2]
Near the end of his life Petrunkevich still credited Herzen
with ideas which "remained dear to me all my life. Further,
they determined my direction in political and social questions.
Since that time, more than sixty years have passed, but to
this day I consider Herzen my guide who taught me not only
to follow him but to discern in him that which constitutes
the immutable principles of human life from those which are

1. I. I. Petrunkevich, *Iz zapisok obshchestvennago deiatelia:
vospominaniia*, 15, which is vol. 21 of the 22 vol. *Arkhiv russkoi
revoliutsii*. (These, the memoirs of Petrunkevich, will be cited
hereinafter as *Iz zapisok*.)
2. *Kolokol* (April 1, 1858, January 15, 1860, March 22, 1862,
March 1, 1865); *Iz zapisok*, 15.

hypothetical in character and are relevant to time, place and circumstance." [3]

Like Herzen, Petrunkevich was critical of the Great Reforms. He referred to "their obvious insincerity, their fear of granting more than what was absolutely necessary and inevitable, their illegality and inconsequentiality." [4] Yet, his first experience with a zemstvo assembly made a very favorable impression on him. In 1865 when the Chernigov provincial zemstvo assembly convened for the first time, Petrunkevich, a twenty-one-year-old law student, was visiting his parents during a recess at the university.

This "local parliament," as the zemstvo was called, presented Petrunkevich with his first opportunity to be in a large public assembly, which included not only the delegates, but also had regular citizens in attendance. "There was not the slightest resemblance between the old gentry assembly and the zemstvo assembly." Petrunkevich said. "Everything was new to me, and everything was different. . . . My imagination went far beyond the limits of this hall and of this moment and painted for me a picture of the future which seemed to me so close." [5] He was particularly interested in the five peasant delegates who, in his words, "took refuge" at the end of the "chamber" (at a large green table around which the delegates sat). Petrunkevich approached these "authentic representatives of the popular mass" during recess, volunteered them his advice, and proofread the written statements they intended to present.[6]

Between the 1865 Chernigov zemstvo session and his graduation from Saint Petersburg University in 1867, Petrunkevich had met with a small group of friends in Chernigov Province to establish a program that they would pursue through the county and provincial zemstvo institutions in Chernigov Province. Despite his reservations about the Great Reforms, he chose to settle in the small village of Pliski, Borzna County, Chernigov Province, where he was born. There, he planned to "dedicate myself to public affairs, for which a broad field . . . had been opened by the Great Reforms—peasant, zemstvo, and legal . . . I knew, while

3. *Iz zapisok,* 15.
4. *Ibid.,* 41.
5. *Ibid.,* 13–14.
6. *Ibid.,* 16.

settling in the village among the common people, in the midst of whom I was born and raised and whose difficult life I had seen and felt with all my heart, that I should devote my life to the interests of the people, to their material, spiritual, civic, and general human needs." [7]

The members of his group were all "the type of people who later received the name 'people of the 60s.' " They believed that the Great Reforms had provided the public with:

> a foothold and some ground for socially useful work which within itself would inevitably extend the limits fixed by the government and prepare the country for the very broadest self-government. . . . We were few, but that did not bother us, for our program exceeded the limits of the county and our plans embraced all of Russia. We did not doubt that soon we would find supporters not only in other counties of our province but also in other provinces.

The fundamental point of the program of this group was "to convert the zemstvo institutions into a school of self-government and by this means prepare the country for a constitutional state order." [8]

The group assumed that the basis of self-government should be democracy, but the group was aware of the low level of understanding and preparation of the peasantry for constitutional government. Given the low educational, economic, and social levels of the peasantry, the group did not expect immediate or spectacular results at the national level. Any change of government through "forcible upheaval" would be "going beyond the objective," for such an upheaval could be successful only "when the popular mass raised itself to the understanding that it was possible to be not the object, but the subject of state government." [9]

What was the program the group felt would transform "the popular mass"? The program can be reduced to three major areas of concern: (1) free, public education at the primary level for the peasantry; (2) improvement of the material conditions of the peasantry; and (3) justice for the peasantry based upon the principle of equality of all persons and classes before the law.

Inadequacy of space prevents a detailed examination of

7. *Ibid.*, 19–20.
8. *Ibid.*, 41.
9. *Ibid.*, 41–42.

Petrunkevich's efforts in each of these three areas. Certain incidents illustrate well, however, the manner in which he hoped to use the zemstvos, the degree to which he achieved his objectives through them, the way in which his efforts contributed to the formation of factions in the Chernigov assembly, and the process by which his program in the zemstvos was complemented after the 1890s by extrazemstvo political activities.

Free public, elementary education for the peasantry Petrunkevich considered the most important of the many goals of the zemstvos. In 1867 he built a school on his property, hired a teacher from his own funds, and successfully offered the school to the Borzna zemstvo in 1868. He hoped that the zemstvo would administer the school and by that act assume a role as promoter of public education in the county.[10] During his first session in Borzna County's zemstvo assembly in September, 1868, he presented a forceful argument for the zemstvo's involving itself in directing education, an argument that resulted in the creation of a special committee to investigate the role the Borzna zemstvo could play in education.[11]

The following year the committee presented a recommendation that the assembly vote 1,000 rubles for maintaining schools. Petrunkevich, considering this an inadequate sum, argued that the question of public education was "the question of the zemstvos' future" and taunted the gentry members (who held a majority in the assembly) that they were still living off the labor of the peasantry. "We have in existence postal and transport roads which the peasants hardly ever travel," he said:

> However, they do not find unjust the collection of a tax from themselves for repairing these roads! We have zemstvo post offices, the blessings of which, as is known, the agricultural working population does not take advantage of, but it also pays this tax without a murmur. Why does the gentry class, enjoying the blessings created at the expense of the zemstvo and which other classes do not take advantage of, not consider itself obligated to accept expenditures on public education, even if it does not consider this a blessing for itself? Such a uniform distribution

10. *Ibid.*, 30–31; *Zhurnaly zasedanii Borzenskago uezdnago zemskago sobraniia, 1868* (Chernigov, 1868), 27.
11. Borzna, *Zhurnaly,* 1868, 65–67.

of expenditures in one instance and such class insulation in the other are extreme inconsistencies.[12]

After this speech, the Borzna assembly voted 6,585 rather than 1,000 rubles, sufficient to maintain fifteen schools in the county.[13]

Having been successful in the county zemstvo assembly, Petrunkevich argued the same case in the 1869 session of the Chernigov provincial zemstvo assembly, to which he was one of Borzna County's delegates. The specific issue being debated was the proposal to create a special, permanent school fund through taxation on land to support education in the province. This issue brought clearly into the open two different interpretations by the delegates of the powers granted to the provincial zemstvos in the Zemstvo Statute of 1864, and the difference in interpretation revealed the conflicting aspirations of two groups in the zemstvo assembly of Chernigov Province. The conflict was similar in many respects to the argument that raged in the United States during the first decades of the Constitution between the strict constructionists and loose constructionists over the powers of Congress.

The loose constructionists in the zemstvos wished to use such elastic clauses in the Zemstvo Statute of 1864 as "care for the local economic needs and wants" to expand the scope of zemstvo activities to the greatest possible degree. A person who wished to replace autocracy with self-government would, obviously, wish the zemstvos to steal out from under the autocracy as much control over rural life as possible. Petrunkevich was the foremost exponent of expanding the powers of the zemstvo institutions in Chernigov Province.

The strict constructionists argued that the Zemstvo Statute of 1864 delegated specific powers to the zemstvos. Unless a right was clearly granted in the statute, the zemstvos had no right to take such action. To prevent the provincial zemstvo from expanding its powers to the greatest degree possible, the strict constructionists also used the tactic of referring matters to the county zemstvo assemblies for resolution.

Strict constructionists opposed creation of a special fund by the provincial zemstvo assembly for maintaining schools.

---

12. *Zhurnaly zasedanii Borzenskago uezdnago zemskago sobraniia, Sentiabr' 1869 goda* (Kiev, 1870), 17–19.
13. *Ibid.*

They argued that their county zemstvo assemblies had not granted them power to levy such taxes and that maintenance of public schools was a matter for the county zemstvos to decide for themselves; the provincial zemstvo should not attempt to decide this question for the counties. Delegate Rachinskii, the most articulate spokesman for the strict constructionists, stated that faction's position succinctly when he said: "It is fitting for us to centralize some kind of expenditure only when such a centralization is called for by necessity emanating from the very existence of the matter. For instance, we decided to found a provincial teachers' seminary because it is obvious that to parcel out such an institution would be inconceivable." [14]

Petrunkevich objected strenuously to this assertion and argued for centralization. The budgets for the county zemstvos were vastly different, he said. Borzna's budget was over 50,000 rubles while Grodno County's budget was only 29,000. This difference stemmed not from a difference in needs, but from "the extreme inequality of means" to satisfy those needs. Petrunkevich stated categorically that he could not:

> see any kind of injustice in the wealthy's coming to the aid of the poor in our common concern of public education. It is impossible to expect otherwise. Only by a concentration of the expenditures for the province on the construction of schools can we achieve a distribution which is just and which corresponds to the needs of the population. By sending the question to the county assemblies for discussion, we would postpone the solution of the problem for an indefinite time. [15]

On this occasion, however, the majority of the delegates agreed with Rachinskii's argument and submitted the question to the county assemblies. The question was not referred again to the provincial assembly during Petrunkevich's membership. [16] This incident reveals the manner in which the zemstvo imposed a limitation upon its own activities. Scholars traditionally blame the Saint Petersburg government

---

14. *Zhurnaly ocherednago Chernigovskago gubernskago zemskago sobraniia 1869 goda*, 113. *Zhurnaly* of the 1869 session are appended to *Zemskii sbornik Chernigovskoi gubernii*, 1 (1870). The *sbornik* is hereinafter cited as *ZSChG*.

15. *Ibid.*, 113–14.

16. *Ibid.*, 115.

for limiting the activities of the zemstvos, and, after the mid-1870s, such was increasingly the case. But the zemstvos clearly had a larger area allowed them by the Tsar's government than the majority of the deputies chose to use.

Despite Petrunkevich's failure to win a majority vote for a permanent school fund in the provincial zemstvo assembly, he returned the following year (1870) to Borzna, where he won a vote of approval from the county assembly for precisely the same scheme for education in Borzna County. The permanent fund allowed the county zemstvo to maintain sixty schools—one for each village in the county.[17] Clearly, in the field of education, the zemstvo was providing Petrunkevich with the type of lever he felt he needed to "transform the popular mass"—the first step, he felt, in bringing about eventual self-government. He was not completely satisfied with the decisions of the provincial assembly, but he had his way on virtually every proposal he submitted to the Borzna county zemstvo assembly.

Petrunkevich's efforts to improve the economic conditions of the peasantry took several forms. Before he was elected, the Borzna county zemstvo assembly had already voted to convert the "natural obligations" of the peasantry (road maintenance, carting, and quartering obligations) into a money obligation that would be paid by the zemstvo with funds it obtained from a tax levied on all classes. In the 1869 session, Petrunkevich proposed that the Borzna assembly add to the list of obligations it assumed from the peasantry an annual expenditure of 3,874 rubles to pay for the military recruitment obligation of the peasantry. Such a sum would provide sufficient funds for the four recruits per thousand required by the Saint Petersburg government. The assembly did not accept this proposal, however, and the peasantry bore the expense until 1874 when military reform altered the situation.[18]

In the regular session of the 1875 Chernigov provincial zemstvo assembly, Petrunkevich proposed another approach to the economic problem of the peasantry of Chernigov Province. Noting that the famine of 1870–1871 in Surazh and Mglin counties had created a large rural proletariat, he proposed that the zemstvo petition the government to create a

17. *Zhurnaly zasedanii Borzenskago uezdnago zemskago sobraniia 1870 goda* (Chernigov, 1871), 14–16.

18. Borzna, *Zhurnaly*, 1869, 41–42, 47–48.

special committee to determine the location of fertile lands in other parts of Russia. With this information available, the zemstvos would assist the peasants who had lost their land (through failure to meet arrears and through sales in hopes of migrating) in making the arrangements necessary for migration to areas where land was available. This request would also be accompanied by a recommendation that the government ease the restrictions on migration. Largely because of the accompanying request, the marshal of the nobility, ex officio chairman of the assembly, refused to allow further debate on this question, and Petrunkevich and his group marched out of the assembly hall. The Senate (Russia's Supreme Court) later upheld Petrunkevich's right to discuss the question, however.[19]

The first step necessary for further improvement of the peasants' economic condition was, Petrunkevich felt, reform of the tax structure. This meant a reduction of the obligations forced upon the peasant by the Saint Petersburg government and an equitable assessment of taxes by the zemstvos.

The extraordinary session of the Chernigov provincial zemstvo assembly in 1871 provided Petrunkevich with a rare opportunity to address himself directly to the central government on behalf of tax reforms beneficial to the peasantry. The assembly was convened to offer its comments on proposed revisions of the tax structure, which had been drafted by a special committee created within the ministry of finance. Petrunkevich proposed and defended a sweeping reform in place of the special committee's scheme. The major points of his program were: a tax-free minimum income for each citizen to be determined by the local zemstvos upon the basis of what constituted the income "absolutely essential to sustain life" in the zemstvo's geographic area; collection of the tax by the zemstvos; allocation of state funds by the zemstvos; and cooperation between government officials and zemstvo members in any final legislation affecting tax reform.[20]

---

19. *Zhurnaly ocherednago Chernigovskago gubernskago zemskago sobraniia 1875 g.*, 282–335; Petrunkevich, *Iz zapisok*, 86. See also S. F. Rusova, "K sorokaletiiu chernigovskago zemstva, 1865–1905 gg.," *Russkaia mysl'*, 12(1904), 110.

20. *Zhurnaly chrezvychainago Chernigovskago gubernskago zemskago sobraniia 1871 goda*, 9–12. Appended to *ZSChG*, 6(1871).

Of particular interest is the manner in which Petrunkevich discussed obligations imposed upon the peasantry by the Emancipation statutes. He proposed that, in determining the income of the peasantry for tax purposes, *obrok* and redemption payments first be deducted from the peasant's income so that the peasant would pay taxes merely on the adjusted income. In support of this arrangement, Petrunkevich presented the following argument to the assembly:

> It is impossible to look at the redemption payments as the result of a private, voluntary transaction by the peasants with their former owners. Serfdom, introduced by the state, was abolished by the state. During the abolition, the relationship of the peasants to the land acquired by them was determined by legislative process; the redemption payments, as a result of this, have the complete character of a tax laid by the state on a given type of property.[21]

The Chernigov zemstvo assembly, although not one of the most assertive assemblies in Russia, adopted most of Petrunkevich's points. It voted that any tax should be levied on all classes (instead of merely on the peasants, as the special committee proposed), and that the tax should be on net income with the redemption payments and *obrok* payments excluded from the income of peasant taxpayers. Furthermore, the assembly expressed its "hope that during the solution of the question of the reform of the system of direct taxes the Government, as on the occasion of the former great reforms of the present Tsar's reign, will not exclude from participation in the final discussion of the matter persons familiar with the needs and economic conditions of all the localities of the Empire." [22] One can hardly fail to be reminded here of the Tver gentry's 1862 address calling upon the government to tax all classes and to convene an assembly of representatives from all Russia to consider "the questions raised but in no way solved" by the Emancipation.[23]

Although this was, apparently, the only occasion Petrunkevich had from 1868–1879 to address himself directly to the central government on taxation, he devoted constant efforts to an equal assessment of zemstvo taxes, based on

---

21. *Ibid.,* 4–5.
22. *Ibid.,* 6–7.
23. The address is included in Vladimir L. Burtsev, *Za sto let (1800–1896)* (London, 1897), 61.

income, or income potential, by the zemstvos of Borzna
County and Chernigov Province. The first step necessary for
taxation based on income was to determine the income of
persons in the province. To accomplish that task Petrunkevich
proposed and the assembly adopted the creation of a
statistical bureau by the provincial zemstvo assembly in 1875.
By 1877 three counties had been surveyed, and two others
were being completed.

In the 1877 session, however, several delegates had become
impatient with the amount of time required for the work.
After a debate that lasted more than three days, the assembly
voted to discontinue the statistical work. During the debate
Petrunkevich had been the most ardent defender of
continuing.[24] Unable to establish a revised taxation policy
for the whole province, he set to work to create a revised
system for Borzna County, one of the three for which the
work had been completed. In 1878 the Borzna assembly
adopted his scheme,[25] but the governor of the province
"objected" to the change and submitted the question to the
Chernigov provincial zemstvo assembly session for 1878
(which met in January, 1879). There Petrunkevich, after a
few uncomplimentary words for the governor's critical
abilities, defended his revised tax system; the provincial
zemstvo assembly consequently sustained Petrunkevich's
system and the Borzna county zemstvo assembly's ratification
of it. The governor's objections had been based upon the
"unfair" burden the new scheme placed on gentry and state
lands in Borzna County.[26]

During the debate on the question of the statistical survey,
in the 1877 Chernigov provincial zemstvo assembly, the words
right and *left* were used to describe factions in the zemstvo
assembly. One delegate argued that the reason the whole
assembly did not favor the work was that the project had
been initiated by the left faction of the assembly, and the work

---

24. *Zhurnaly chernigovskago ocherednago gubernskago zemskago sobraniia, 1877,* 303–4. Appended to *ZSChG,* 1(1878).
Petrunkevich pledged his support of the work, even though he as
a representative of a "wealthier county" would suffer more
financially than several delegates who were opposing the work.

25. *Iz zapisok,* 87–88.

26. *Zhurnaly chernigovskago gubernskago zemskago sobraniia
ocherednoi sessii 1878 goda, sostoiavsheisia v Ianvare 1879 goda,*
7–8. Appended to *ZSChG,* 1–4 (1879).

had been done in those counties represented by the left faction of deputies in the provincial assembly. Had the statisticians begun their work in the counties represented by the right, the speaker said, the delegates from those areas would have been able to see the value of the work more clearly. Petrunkevich objected to this interpretation of the reasons for failure, trying to prevent the statistical work from becoming a partisan issue, but he used the right and left labels himself during his rebuttal.[27]

This was the first open acknowledgment recorded in the minutes of the Chernigov provincial zemstvo sessions of the existence of factions. The division was obvious to any reader of the minutes, however, by the presence of the two interpretations of the Zemstvo Statute of 1864. The *strict* and *loose* constructionist descriptions imposed by me can be replaced after 1877 by right and left, respectively. The division within the assembly certainly must have been perceived by the delegates much earlier than 1877, exemplified by the fact that delegate Shrag used the word "parties" (*partii*) during the debate to describe the factions within the assembly.[28] The 1877 debate on the statistical bureau is a significant event for the scholar who wishes to study the process of faction formation and group identity in the zemstvos.

By 1878 Petrunkevich had accomplished a great deal that he felt was crucial for the transformation of Russian society —the "popular mass"—from the bottom upward. Although he suffered several reverses, he also achieved many successes. A man who wished to use the zemstvos as an instrument of change need not be completely disillusioned, especially if he felt education to be the most vital area for his efforts.

Coupled with his work in the zemstvo assemblies, Petrunkevich was also active as a justice of the peace from 1869 to 1879. The total of his efforts in both areas was, he felt, highly significant. Although he had an enormous case load and little compensation, Petrunkevich was quite willing to take on the tasks performed by a justice of the peace. It provided him with an opportunity to use his training in law, and he used that training in a way he felt directly applicable

27. Chernigov, *Zhurnaly,* 1877, 302–3.
28. *Ibid.,* 305.

toward preparing the population for eventual participation in self-government. The justices of the peace, he said,

> formed an inseparable part of self-government, its special organ fulfilling not only a legal but also an educational function, not confining itself to the formal, inflexible prescriptions and forms. On the justices of the peace lay the practical task, in living examples and instances, to expose the whole sense of legal principle and to show the population that law is the realization in human society and within the limitations of human capabilities of those moral truths which have been accepted by Christian culture, civility, and civilization of the whole world.[29]

In the winter of 1878–1879 Petrunkevich began seeking out persons in other zemstvos in order to create a common front powerful enough to obtain reforms from Alexander II. He contacted members of several zemstvo assemblies, a group of Ukrainian nationalists, and even members of revolutionary societies in Kiev, with the objective of dissuading the revolutionaries from the use of terror long enough to allow the zemstvos to use their regular sessions during the winter to direct appeals to the Tsar for reform.[30]

Petrunkevich failed to obtain the broad response he would have preferred from the zemstvos, but he did directly influence at least three zemstvos to make such appeals. The most crushing defeat for him personally he suffered in his own zemstvo in Chernigov Province. A majority of delegates in the assembly favored adopting the famous "Chernigov address," which he and a committee representing both factions drafted, but the marshal of the nobility refused to allow discussion or even a reading of the address to the assembly. The marshal had obtained a copy in advance and had, apparently, been instructed by the local authorities to prohibit discussion of it. During the incident, the right defected and sided with the marshal. Petrunkevich and his group left the hall, and the session was closed for lack of a quorum.[31]

Despite this failure, Petrunkevich did not blame the zemstvo itself. He placed the blame upon the bureaucracy

---

29. *Iz zapisok,* 63–64.
30. See Charles Timberlake, "The Birth of Zemstvo Liberalism in Russia: Ivan Il'ich Petrunkevich in Chernigov" (Ph.D. diss., University of Washington, 1968), chap. 3, for an analysis of these secret negotiations.
31. Chernigov, *Zhurnaly,* 1878, 482–83.

that was represented in this case by the marshal of the nobility. His only criticism of the zemstvos for their failure to act in 1878–1879 (and this was extended to the city dumas also) was that the deputies therein had failed as yet to realize the vital position they occupied in society and the possibilities for action before them. The best solution for the zemstvos' ills, he wrote in 1879, was for a reconstitution of their membership.[32] The demands he included in a pamphlet of 1879, *The Most Immediate Tasks of the Zemstvo,* were the same as those he had been making in the assemblies since 1868. The major change the experiences of 1878–1879 produced in Petrunkevich's program was the addition of a national effort to accomplish at the national level those changes for which he had been working at the county and provincial levels.

He divided the tasks of the zemstvos into two categories. The first included freedoms of press, speech, assembly, and was, in fact, a restatement of the demands presented in the Chernigov address, which failed to be confirmed by the Chernigov assembly.[33] These reforms were for the zemstvos to demand immediately. The second category was the demand for a "constituent assembly." According to the research of V. Ia. Bogucharskii, this was the first statement drafted in Russia demanding a constituent assembly,[34] and Petrunkevich listed it as a long-range objective of the zemstvos.

The call for a constituent assembly reflects Petrunkevich's disillusionment with the central government. Before 1878–1879 he had believed that the zemstvos could obtain reforms, but the government refused to listen. His emphasis shifted from the traditional appeal to the Tsar to "crown the edifice," to an appeal for the zemstvos and other institutions representing the people to crown the edifice themselves. Despite some disappointment, which his pamphlet reflected, with the zemstvos, his disillusionment was more with the Saint Petersburg government.

Early in 1879 Petrunkevich was exiled for seven years for

32. "Blizhaishiia zadachi zemstva," *Iz zapisok,* 456. (This pamphlet was first published anonymously in 1879. In 1914 it was published under its author's name and included as an appendix to Petrunkevich's memoirs published in 1934.)

33. *Ibid.*

34. V. Ia. Bogucharskii, *Iz istorii politicheskoi bor'by v 70-kh i 80-kh gg. XIX veka* (Moscow, 1912), 414–15.

being a "troublemaker" in the Chernigov zemstvo assembly.[35] Nonetheless, the Borzna gentry curia elected him one of its delegates to the Borzna county zemstvo in 1880, and the Borzna zemstvo assembly then elected him one of its delegates to the provincial zemstvo assembly. The governor of the province objected to both elections, and the Chernigov provincial zemstvo assembly took up the matter in its regular session for 1880, which met in January, 1881. The assembly voted 56 to 4 to confirm Petrunkevich's right to hold the title "provincial delegate," and 57 to 3 to petition the government to grant him "the possibility to fulfill his obligations as a provincial and county delegate." Although the zemstvo did not receive a favorable decision from the government on this petition, the provincial zemstvo continued to list Petrunkevich as a member of the assembly and merely marked him absent until the end of his period of exile.[36]

Petrunkevich's exile ended in 1886, which was also the year for the regular elections to the zemstvo institutions of Chernigov Province. He was elected once again to the county and provincial assemblies, and he returned to Chernigov from Tver Province, where he had lived during the last years of exile. Before he had an opportunity to participate in zemstvo work, the governor of Chernigov Province, acting upon instructions from his superior—Governor-General Drentel'n —to "find a legal basis" for preventing Petrunkevich from participating in zemstvo work, summoned Petrunkevich to his office. He presented Petrunkevich with the choice between retaining the title of zemstvo delegate without attending sessions or being exiled from Chernigov Province. Petrunkevich refused the former and received the latter. In fact, in early autumn he was exiled from all of Little Russia.[37] He returned to Tver Province, where his brother was a physician

---

35. V. Khizhniakov, *Vospominaniia zemskago deiatelia* (Petrograd, 1916), 157–58.

36. *Zhurnaly chernigovskago gubernskago zemskago sobraniia ocherednoi sessii 1880 goda, sostoiavsheisia v Ianvare 1881 goda,* 516, 109, 126–29. Appended to *ZSChG*, 1–4(1881).

37. I. I. Petrunkevich to George Kennan, December 20, 1886/ January 1, 1887, Box 1, Folder 1885–1886, George Kennan Papers, Manuscripts Department, Library of Congress. The introduction Kennan published to his "Last Appeal of the Russian Liberals," *The Century Magazine*, 35:1(1887), 55–63, is a virtual translation of portions of the long letter.

and member of the Tver provincial zemstvo, and became an active member of the Tver zemstvo from 1891–1905.

Exile increased Petrunkevich's bitterness toward the bureaucracy, but he did not become disillusioned with his approach to political and social reforms; he remained convinced of the inevitability of representative government in Russia. The proper bases for such government had not been built by the end of the 1880s, but, he believed, much work had been done by persons like himself using the institutions created during the Great Reforms. Without the zemstvos and the justices of the peace, he wrote in 1886, "all life . . . [would] move backward to serfdom." [38] He felt his work through these institutions would merely hasten the inevitable.

Petrunkevich's bitterness toward the central government did not change his repudiation of terror. He referred in 1886 to those persons engaged in terror as "passionate and young, more relying on their strength than paying attention to our pitiful history, less sensitive to all the cold of our social 'tundra'." Their terror was, however, merely a reflection of terror perpetrated by the government. He was opposed to both forms of terror, but he knew the government did not understand the difference between himself and the terrorists. Not only was the government unable to distinguish one group from the other, he wrote, but it also "instinctively senses an internal connection uniting all opposition parties, and is indiscriminately ruthless toward them all." [39]

Petrunkevich's sensitivity to Russia's "pitiful history" and the "cold of our social 'tundra' " in 1886 reveals that the popular mass had still not been transformed to the degree he felt necessary to guarantee the success of self-government. For this reason, he approached zemstvo work in Tver Province in 1891 even more diligently than he had in Chernigov from 1868 to 1879. Through the zemstvo institutions of Tver Province he pursued the same objectives he had previously in Chernigov. By 1891, however, the major force retarding his work in the zemstvo assembly was no longer the right faction he had faced in Chernigov. It was, rather, the Saint Petersburg government and its provincial bureaucracy. To deal with the central government, he supplemented his work in the zemstvo

38. *Ibid.*
39. *Ibid.*

assemblies by forming secret societies for constitutional agitation outside the assemblies.

The move to Tver Province opened in Petrunkevich's life a chapter that ended only with his departure to Saint Petersburg to participate in the First Duma in 1906. Even before he was elected to the zemstvo assemblies of Novotorzhok County and Tver Province, he became involved in the work of those zemstvos. The provincial zemstvo board in Tver had set up a statistical bureau, as Chernigov had done earlier, to collect data on the counties of Tver Province. The data had been collected on Novotorzhok County in 1884, but had not been analyzed before Petrunkevich undertook that task and completed it in 1889. In that year the provincial zemstvo published his work as volume two of its series, *Sbornik statisticheskikh svedenii po Tverskoi gubernii* (*Collection of Statistical Data on Tver Province*). By 1891 he had performed the same task for Bezhetsk County, the publication of which constituted volume six of the series; he also prepared volume twelve of the series for Ostashkov County. It appeared in two parts in 1895 and 1896. One portion of the volume he prepared twice, for a fire in the publishing house burned the original manuscript.[40]

Shortly after his election in 1891 to the Novotorzhok and Tver zemstvo assemblies, Petrunkevich became one of the most active and influential deputies in both assemblies, and he remained such until his last year in the assemblies in the winter of 1905–1906. In 1892 he became active in the committee on provisions (*Prodovol'stvennaia kommissiia*) and undertook a detailed study of conditions in Tver Province during the famine of 1891. His long report is cited as one of the most detailed studies available on the effects of the famine in central European Russia.[41] The assembly adopted resolutions he submitted in the name of the committee to help

40. See vypusk no. 2, 1895, foreword, for this explanation. This complete series is available in Helsinki University Library and has recently been made available on microfiche by the Inter Documentation Centre.

41. Petrunkevich's report, "Doklad chlena prodovol'stvennoi kommissii I. I. Petrunkevicha po obezpecheniiu narodnago. prodovol'stviia," was forty-three pages in length in the *Protokoly zasedanii Tverskogo ocherednago gubernskago zemskago sobraniia 8–19 Dekabria 1892 goda*. It was later published by the Tver zemstvo as a separate item.

alleviate the plight of the peasantry. One such resolution approved by the assembly committed the zemstvo to retaining "permanently under its control" the right to consider the question of the food supply of the population. He also sought to raise taxes and to establish a county-wide and province-wide system for educational planning.[42]

Petrunkevich's interests in Novotorzhok and Tver were extensions of the interests he had pursued in Borzna and Chernigov zemstvos. He devoted much time, thought, and energy to free public education and to attempts to improve the material conditions of the peasantry. He became chairman of both the important standing committees of Novotorzhok zemstvo before 1900 (the editorial and auditing committees) and of the budget committees. His son Mikhail was elected marshal of the Novotorzhok nobility and became the chairman ex officio of the Novotorzhok zemstvo assembly, thereby removing a possible source of resistance to Petrunkevich's schemes for the county.[43]

Petrunkevich expanded his activities beyond the zemstvo during his residence in Tver. Since his experiences of 1878–1879 in Chernigov, he had supplemented his efforts in the zemstvos by pursuing his objectives through extrazemstvo groups as well. His desire for reform and for a zemstvo press, outlined in the 1878 Chernigov address and the brochure of 1879, remained intact. Seeing that it was impossible to obtain a press for the zemstvo, and wishing to utilize the growing public sentiment for reform, he began to work through small circles of friends in the 1890s to plan the best possible means for disseminating constitutionalist ideas in Russia.

Out of such meetings came the decision to establish a newspaper abroad and have it smuggled into Russia as Herzen had done earlier with *Kolokol*.[44] By 1900 Peter Struve had

---

42. See *Protokoly* for Novotorzhok, 1893 and 1898, 6–8.

43. He was also on all the major committees for the Tver provincial zemstvo assembly. See *Materialy dlia istorii Tverskogo Gubernskago Zemstva 1886–1908 gg.*, vol. 6 of 10 vols. (Tver, 1909), 17, for the judicial committee's membership list, 93–97 for the editorial committee's membership list, and 110–11 for membership lists for the auditing committee.

44. Petrunkevich began writing of Struve's visits to the Petrunkevich household in Tver in a letter dated August 7/20, 1900. After a four-day visit had ended, Petrunkevich referred to Struve as "an extraordinarily intelligent and nice person." Letter from Ivan to Alexander I. Petrunkevich, Box I, Petrunkevich Col-

chosen Tver as his place of residence during exile, and he and Petrunkevich had become close friends. Paul Miliukov also began to participate in these circles, and in such a manner the group jointly prepared the first number of *Osvobozhdenie,* which Struve escaped abroad to edit.[45] Petrunkevich's long-standing desire for a press that would disseminate ideas which he felt were the key to Russia's future happiness became a reality at last.

The same group that had founded the publication transformed itself into the nucleus of a secret, conspiratorial society in 1903. Petrunkevich was one of the leading participants in the series of meetings held in Switzerland in 1903, the result of which was agreement to form the Union of Liberation. The founding congress in January, 1904, elected Petrunkevich chairman, and he also was a member of the Union of Zemstvo Constitutionalists, which had been formed by the same group late in 1903, although the membership of the two groups did not overlap entirely.[46]

At what seemed the height of his role in the "liberation movement," Petrunkevich was exiled from Tver Province on January 29, 1904. This exile saddened him deeply, for his work was just beginning to have the broad and profound influence he had hoped for all his life. In a letter to his son on February 12/25, 1904, he informed him of the exile and observed plaintively that: "Life does not stand in one place.

lection, Yale University. In a letter from Same to Same, December 17/30, 1900, Petrunkevich spoke still more favorably of Struve, "the young writer," and expressed the hope that he would be in the village of Mashuk again next summer.

45. A. A. Kizevetter described one of these small gatherings after Struve's move to Tver. At the date of the meeting (which is not given specifically by Kizevetter), Struve had already emigrated, and Struve and Petrunkevich had written the program for *Osvobozhdenie.* "I . . . found there a very small group. There were the two Petrunkevich brothers, [V. I.] Vernadskii, and [P. I.] Novgorodtsev [V. Ia.] Bogucharskii, and [D. I.] Shakhovskoi. Petrunkevich read the program and the lead article by Miliukov. This and other topics were approved by all present. . . . We then discussed a plan to create throughout Moscow a series of such small, secret meetings . . ." to distribute the new journal. *Na rubezhe dvukh stoletii: vospominaniia 1881–1914* (Prague, 1929), 336–37.

46. See George Fischer, *Russian Liberalism: From Gentry to Intelligentsia,* 135–49 for a discussion of Petrunkevich's role in the formation of the Union of Liberation.

It follows its course, and I can no longer dream that I will adapt again to its movement, for each individual existence is assigned its limit, and I have already come close to it." [47]

But Petrunkevich's indomitable spirit would not surrender. "While there is strength left in me," he said, returning to his old fighting stance, "I cannot await my end with the fatalism of a Tatar; rather, I will try to direct [my energy] . . . toward other work." He was contemplating more active participation than previously in the writing of an encyclopedia of self-government, which he and a small circle of his acquaintances in Moscow had decided to begin before his exile.[48]

Although Petrunkevich feared that he had been cast aside by fate, he stood, in fact, on the eve of his finest hour. He remained in exile until October, 1904, but used the occasion to write an article on the war for the periodical, *Pravo*, which provoked a long chain of letters to the editor of *Moskovskiia vedomosti* denouncing him.[49] He also went on a tour of Western Europe and was in Paris when he learned that as one of the government's concessions, Minister of the Interior Sviatopolk-Mirskii had rescinded the order exiling him from Tver Province and from Saint Petersburg.[50]

Petrunkevich returned from Paris on the eve of the zemstvo congress held November 6–9 in Saint Petersburg. He played the role of initiator of a set of resolutions that was adopted by the majority of the congress and then presented by a delegation to a representative of the Tsar.[51]

After this congress, Petrunkevich returned to Novotorzhok County in Tver and participated in the zemstvo assembly session for 1904 (which met January 11–15, 1905). The

47. I. I. Petrunkevich to A. I. Petrunkevich, February 12/25, 1904, Box I, Petrunkevich Collection.

48. *Ibid.*

49. Petrunkevich entitled his article, "Voina i nashi zadachi," *Pravo*, 41 (October 10, 1904), 1951–1955. The public response to the article began in the November 2/15 number of *Moskovskiia vedomosti* with "Otkrytoe pis'mo g. Petrunkevichu" by "Dvorianin Pavlov" and ran through the month of November. All denounced him for speaking in the name of "the Russian people." Petrunkevich's views, the writers claimed, were not the same as those of the Russian people.

50. I. I. Petrunkevich to A. I. Petrunkevich, February 12/25, 1904. Petrunkevich Collection.

51. See Fischer, *Russian Liberalism,* chap. 5, for an analysis of the work of this congress.

session began only two days after the "Bloody Sunday" incident in Saint Petersburg, and the assembly was concerned with the violence during and after that event. Petrunkevich spoke in favor of a resolution introduced by deputy E. V. de Roberti that the Novotorzhok zemstvo send aid to those of "the Russian people" suffering as a result of the conflict with "the Russian military." Petrunkevich expressed feelings of regret and sorrow over the "blood spilled in the streets of St. Petersburg," but noted that what was worse than the event itself was that: "These feelings are aggravated by the thought that the possibility of such events in the future will not be removed and that the country might experience still more terrible shocks, for they have their roots in those disorders of our life which were condemned from the height of the throne in the ukase of December 12 of the past year." [52]

The ukase of December 12, 1904, had stated the government's "plans for the improvement of the system of government" in response to the many resolutions and appeals sent from the institutions of society, such as the eleven-point program for reform drafted by the zemstvo congress in November, 1904, in which Petrunkevich had participated.

Petrunkevich said he was "deeply convinced that the reforms promised by this ukase can bring to the country peace and tranquility if their implementation is entrusted to representatives of the people and that this is the only path which will lead the country to peaceful and beneficial labor for the welfare of the motherland." He ended the speech by introducing a resolution that the Novotorzhok zemstvo inform the government of its convictions that an assembly of representatives of the people should be called to implement the promised reforms. The assembly approved the resolution.[53] The original draft by Sviatopolk-Mirskii had, in fact, called for broadening the membership of the State Council through election of representatives from the zemstvos and other social institutions, but this clause was deleted by the Tsar upon the advice of Witte.[54]

During the spring of 1905 Petrunkevich stated the demand

---

52. *Protokoly novotorzhskago uezdnago zemskago sobraniia: Ocherednoi sessii 1904 goda s prilozheniiami k nim* (Torzhok, 1905), 9.

53. *Ibid.*

54. Michael T. Florinsky, *Russia: A History and an Interpretation,* vol. 2 of 2 vols. (New York, 1960), 1171n7.

for an elected assembly more openly and more categorically in a speech to the extraordinary session of the Novotorzhok zemstvo assembly that was convened to discuss the ukase of February 18, 1905. The resolutions of the zemstvo congresses of November 6–9, 1904, and of April 22–28, 1905, were read to this assembly and were included in the minutes. Petrunkevich expressed "the joy of the occasion" on which zemstvo and city governments "for the first time in their existence" could discuss "questions of national importance." The assembly, he proposed, should "demand the convening of a people's assembly on the basis of universal, equal, direct and secret" ballot to deal with the problems raised by the ukase of February 18, 1905.[55]

During 1905 Petrunkevich initiated steps to combine his many circles and groups into an open political party to participate in elections to the First State Duma. He attended the founding congress of the Constitutional-Democratic (Kadet) party in October and was also present at its second and third congresses in 1906. He was chairman of the third congress during formulation of its program on the land question.[56]

During the elections to the First State Duma Petrunkevich was elected a deputy from Tver Province. When the Kadet party obtained the largest number of seats in the First Duma, he was elected by the Kadet deputies as chairman of the party's "parliamentary fraction," a position that made him floor leader—or majority leader in Western vocabulary. He was responsible for coordinating the work of the many committees created to draft the party's program for various questions. When these committees reported back to a general session of the fraction, he was chairman of the session. This position imposed upon him an extremely fast pace for a man of sixty-three during the First State Duma. On occasion he presided over sessions at working breakfasts, went from breakfast to the morning Duma session, presided over a working lunch, returned for the afternoon Duma session, presided over a working dinner, attended an occasional Duma

---

55. *Protokol chrezvychainago novotorzhskago zemskago sobraniia ekstrennoi sessii 1905 goda* (Torzhok, 1905), 2–3.

56. See *Protokoly III obshcheimperskago delegatskago s"ezda partii narodnoi svobody (konstitutsionno-demokraticheskoi)* (St. Petersburg, 1906), 97–160, which contain the debate on the agrarian question and Petrunkevich's remarks on that problem.

session which met in the evening, then presided over another committee meeting after the Duma recessed for the day. Frequently these ran into the early hours of the morning.[57]

By a prearranged parliamentary tactic of the Kadet party, Petrunkevich became the first elected delegate to address the Duma, the first national representative body ever convened in Russia—an event that gave him enormous pride. He used the occasion, while government ministers and various other high bureaucrats listened, to demand amnesty for all political prisoners in Russia.[58]

The government refused to grant amnesty or to accept the majority of the Duma's resolutions, however. The Kadets on their part voted no confidence in the government and refused to compromise. When the government ended the deadlock in July, 1906, by dissolving the Duma, Petrunkevich notified all the Kadets to meet at a hotel in Vyborg, Finland, to discuss the action the party could take against the government. Despite his knowledge of the consequences for himself and others, he insisted that a manifesto to the Russian people be drafted and signed by all Kadet deputies in the First State Duma. Having achieved so much in at last obtaining a national representative institution, he and many others chose to sacrifice their political rights in order to prevent further violence and to defend an ideal that the government, it seemed, was attempting to destroy.[59]

Deprived of his political rights and forced to spend three months in jail, as were all the signers of the Vyborg Manifesto, Petrunkevich could not seek election to the Second State Duma. The Kadet party had lost many of its popular orators

57. See "Parlamentskaia fraktsiia partii narodnoi svobody," which was a weekly section carried in *Vestnik partii narodnoi svobody* shortly before and during the First State Duma, for Petrunkevich's activities outside the daily sessions of the State Duma.

58. This speech made an enormous impression on the public and was printed verbatim in several newspapers and periodicals of the day. It is printed in the stenographic notes of the First State Duma.

59. See M. M. Vinaver's pamphlet "Istoriia Vyborgskago vozzvaniia," published by the central committees of the Kadet party in 1917 in Petrograd, for an attempt to evaluate the willingness of the participants to engage in "self-sacrifice." Cf. P. N. Miliukov, "M. M. Vinaver, kak politik" in *M. M. Vinaver i russkaia obshchestvennost' nachala XX veka* (Paris, 1937), 25–26.

and capable delegates from further participation in the State Duma. In Saint Petersburg, Petrunkevich published the newspaper, *Rech'*, which Paul Miliukov edited and which they made into an instrument for the party (although it was not officially its organ) from 1908–1917.[60] In 1909 he became chairman of the central committee of the Kadet party, a position he retained until 1915 when he resigned the chairmanship and retired to his villa on the Crimean peninsula. At that time he was elected honorary chairman of the party for life.

Even in retirement, the major events of Russia followed Petrunkevich. In the Crimea he found himself amid World War I, the Bolshevik Revolution, and the Civil War. After the German withdrawal, he became involved in the government created in the Crimea. In 1920 he left the Crimea, fearful for his life, and came to America where he lived for approximately one year with his son in New Haven, Connecticut.[61] In 1921 he returned to Europe to be nearer events in Russia. He had also come into conflict with Miliukov over decisions by the Kadet party in its emigration in Paris, and in 1921 resigned his position as honorary chairman. He was convinced that soon the Bolsheviks would be overthrown and that he would return to Russia.[62]

Petrunkevich never returned to Russia, however. Death came peacefully to him in Prague on June 14, 1928, the year Stalin began the first five-year plan in Russia. It seems unlikely he could have died so peacefully in Russia. The tragedy of his life and the tragedy of Russia were intertwined. The connection was stated by V. A. Rosenberg at Petrunkevich's graveside in Prague: "The remains of Ivan Il'ich Petrunkevich should not lie here, but in Moscow in a Russian Pantheon." [63]

60. See Thomas Riha, *"Riech':* A Portrait of a Russian Newspaper," *Slavic Review,* 22(December, 1963), 663–82.
61. See D. S. Pasmanik, *Revoliutsionnye gody v Krymu* (Paris, 1926), for some comment on Petrunkevich's role in the Crimea. "Pis'mo I. I. Petrunkevicha o russkoi intelligentsii" is an appendix to this book. See also I. I. Petrunkevich, "The Bolsheviks in the Crimea," *Yale Review,* 10:1(October, 1920), 57–71.
62. I. I. Petrunkevich, "The Russian Problem," *Yale Daily News* (October 19, 1920). Cf. letter from Anastasia Sergeevna Petrunkevich to Sof'ia Panina, May 2, 1921, Panina Collection, Columbia University Archive on Russian and East European History and Culture, Folder 4.
63. "Pokhorony I. I. Petrunkevicha," *Rul'* (June [20?], 1928).

THE POLITICAL FAITH
OF FEDOR RODICHEV

Kermit E. McKenzie

In a speech before the deputies of the Third Duma on
November 17, 1907, the Kadet "Knight of Liberty," Fedor
Izmailovich Rodichev, while making a passionate plea for
governmental commitment to justice and the rule of law,
uttered the startling phrase "Stolypin necktie" to characterize
negatively the policies and methods of the Tsar's chief
minister. This euphemism for the hangman's noose provoked
an instantaneous and bitter reaction. The clamor of outraged
deputies cut short Rodichev's words, and only with difficulty
was he kept safe from bodily assault.

Stolypin, who was present with his fellow ministers, turned
pale and strode from the chamber. Unable to restore order,
the chairman of the Duma left his post, thereby enforcing by
Duma rules an hour's recess. Shaken by the unanticipated
impact of his hastily conceived expression, Rodichev made
his way to the ministers' quarters and there explained to
Stolypin that no personal insult had been intended.
Stolypin brusquely replied, "I forgive you," turned his back,
and walked away. On reconvening, the majority of the
deputies were of no mind to let the incident pass and
punished Rodichev for his "insult" by voting, with only 96
(out of approximately 400) opposed, to exclude him from the
next fifteen sessions, the most severe penalty possible under
the circumstances.[1]

---

1. Rodichev's account of this incident is in his letter to A. R.
Lednicki, written October–December, 1932, a copy of which is
in the Rodichev Collection at the Archive of Russian and East
European History and Culture at Columbia University, hereinafter cited as Rodichev Collection. For the full text of his speech,
see Gosudarstvennaia Duma, Tretii sozyv, *Stenograficheskie
otchety*, Part I (St. Petersburg, 1908), columns 390–97. The
Third Duma had 442 members and was predominantly conservative. Rodichev's daughter sought to clarify the circumstances on
two occasions: "F. I. Rodichev i P. A. Stolypin (pis'mo v
redaktsiiu)," *Novyi zhurnal*, 34(1953), 294–96, and "Pis'mo v

Fedor Rodichev was not only one of the principals in this brief but dramatic confrontation of 1907, but he was also one of the outstanding veterans of the Russian liberal movement. His long career of public service, which ultimately extended over four decades, and the distinguished reputation he gained through his zemstvo activity in the liberal movement and in all four dumas, all suggest a remarkable figure in the social and political life of the Russian Empire. Like other high-minded representatives of the privileged upper stratum of Russian society, Rodichev aspired and worked toward a free society of equals in rights and opportunities. Born into the *dvorianstvo,* or gentry class, he championed the abolition of all class privileges; a member of the *obshchestvo,* or educated society, he devoted himself to aiding the cause of universal education; a Great Russian, and accordingly privileged, he fought consistently against national discrimination in any form. His weapons were not violence or terror, but legal activity and peaceful persuasion. Rodichev was generous, sensitive, and humane, and espoused his ideals in a warm and honest manner.

A brief sketch of Rodichev's life suggests by itself the richness of his activity in public service as well as the strength of his commitment to the cause of liberty in Russia.[2] He was born in Saint Petersburg on February 9, 1854. His family, descended on both sides from the aristocracy of pre-Muscovite Novgorod, possessed estates in Ves'egonsk County in Tver Province, and was registered in the sixth part of the nobles' genealogical book.[3] Rodichev grew up, then, in that province which Sir Bernard Pares judged to have the

redaktsiiu," *Novyi zhurnal,* 38(1954), 302–4. See also A. Tyrkova-Williams, *Na putiakh k svobode* (New York, 1952), 370–73, and Paul Miliukov, *Political Memoirs, 1905–1917* (Ann Arbor, 1967), 169–70.

2. This portrait is based largely upon the memoirs Rodichev wrote as an emigré after the Russian Civil War. Although the memoirs were never completed, several selections were published before and after Rodichev's death, and much unpublished material is contained in the collection assembled by his daughter, Alexandra Fedorovna, and now deposited in the Rodichev Collection.
I have prepared for publication an edition of the most important memoir materials in the collection.
3. "Biografiia F. I. Rodicheva," manuscript in the Rodichev Collection, 1. This was evidently written by Rodichev's daughter.

"finest tradition of liberalism in Russia," [4] and which George Fischer called the "birthplace of constitutionalism" in the Russian Empire.[5]

Rodichev's childhood and youth coincided with the era of the Great Reforms under Alexander II. As he writes in his memoirs, "My first memories begin with the year 1861. All my life has been spent under the sign of liberation." [6] In 1870, Rodichev entered the University of Saint Petersburg, where he first completed studies in natural science and then turned to law, passing his examinations in 1876.[7] That same year, along with many other idealistic young Russians, he volunteered for service under Gen. M. G. Cherniaev in Serbia's war against the Ottoman Empire, believing, as he put it, that "the cause of Slavic freedom is the cause of Russian freedom." [8]

During Rodichev's absence, the zemstvo of his native county in Tver Province unanimously elected him an honorary justice of the peace.[9] Two years later he became county marshal of the nobility, a position that he held for the next thirteen years. From 1878 to 1895 he was a deputy both to the Ves'egonsk county zemstvo assembly and to the Tver

4. Bernard Pares, "Fedor Rodichev," *Slavonic and East European Review,* 12 (July, 1933), 199.

5. George Fischer, *Russian Liberalism, From Gentry to Intelligentsia,* 28. For information on the liberal tradition in Tver Province, see the excellent study by Terence Emmons, *The Russian Landed Gentry and the Peasant Emancipation of 1861,* especially chaps. 4 and 8. Also available is the unpublished dissertation by the Soviet scholar, M. A. Rozum, "Tverskie liberaly v reformakh 60-kh gg. 19-ogo veka," Lenin Pedagogical Institute, Moscow, 1940, which the author kindly permitted me to inspect when I was in Kalinin in 1964. See also his "Podgotovka krest'ianskoi reformy v Tverskom komitete," *Uchenye zapiski Kalininskogo pedagogicheskogo instituta,* 10:1(Kalinin, 1945).

6. "Detstvo," *Poslednie novosti* (Paris, August 20, 1933), typescript in Rodichev Collection.

7. "Universitet," typescript in Rodichev Collection, 2.

8. "Serbiia 1876," typescript in Rodichev Collection, 1.

9. Rodichev was elected an honorary (*pochetnyi*) justice of the peace rather than a full or regular (*uchastkovyi*) one because of one negative vote; as he was under twenty-five years of age, unanimity was required by law for election. *Protokoly ocherednago Ves'egonskago uezdnago zemskago sobraniia za 1876 god* (Tver, 1877), 3. In 1878 he was elected *uchastkovyi.* Ves'egonsk, *Protokoly,* 1878 (Tver, 1879), 18. From 1885 to 1891 he served as chairman of the congress of justices of the peace.

provincial zemstvo assembly, in which at various times his father and his older brother Dmitrii also served.[10] In 1879 Rodichev displayed his reforming zeal as the prime mover behind the well-known address of the Tver zemstvo, which appealed to Alexander II to grant the Russian people "those blessings of lawful freedom and free institutions" that had recently been bestowed upon Bulgaria following her liberation by Russian arms.[11] In 1891 Rodichev was honored with the highest elective post in local government—that of chairman of the zemstvo board (*uprava*) of Tver Province. This election, however, opposed by the governor,[12] was not confirmed by the minister of the interior and Rodichev was replaced by the appointed B. V. Stürmer, who years later in 1916 was to become chairman of the Imperial Council of Ministers.[13]

Upon the accession of Nicholas II in 1894, Rodichev became the main author of that most famous of all addresses of the Tver zemstvo, which in moderate and respectful language requested the new Tsar to listen to the voice of his people and not simply to his bureaucrats. The address, expressing faith in the possibility of peaceful progress and indicating the primary condition for such progress, reads in part:

We look forward, Sire, to its being possible and rightful for public institutions to express their views on matters concerning them, so that an expression of the requirements

---

10. On the history of the Tver zemstvo there is the old study by B. B. Veselovskii, *Istoricheskii ocherk deiatel'nosti zemskikh uchrezdenii Tverskoi gubernii (1864–1913 gg.)* (Tver, 1914). The organization is topical, but the final chapter gives an over-all sketch of the political highlights in the history of the Tver zemstvo.

11. F. Rodichev, "The Liberal Movement in Russia (1855–1891)," *Slavonic and East European Review,* 2 (June, 1923), 7.

12. In his report for 1891 the governor of Tver Province, P. Akhlestyshev, expressed hope for an end to the "dictatorship of the liberal party" in the Tver zemstvo by the nonconfirmation of the election of the "clearly compromised and politically unreliable" Rodichev. Central State Historical Archive, hereinafter cited as TsGIAL, *fond biblioteka,* 1886, *opis'* 1, *delo* 98, 35.

13. On Stürmer's appointment in 1891 and his personal ambitions at that time, see the interesting comments of I. I. Petrunkevich, *Iz zapisok obshchestvennago deiatelia: vospominaniia,* 268–72, and V. I. Gurko, *Features and Figures of the Past* (Stanford, 1939), 185–87.

and thought of representatives of the Russian people, and
not only of the administration, may reach the heights of
the throne. We expect, Sire, that in your reign Russia will
move forward along the path of peace and truth with a full
development of living forces of the public. We believe that
in intercourse with representatives of all classes of the
Russian people, equally devoted to the Throne and Fatherland, the power of Your Majesty will find a new source of
strength and a pledge of success in the fulfilment of Your
Imperial Majesty's generous intentions.[14]

This petition met with a sharp rebuff from the young
emperor, whose phrase "senseless dreams" became
notorious throughout Russia and shattered hopes for a change
in governmental policies and attitudes.[15] As punishment,
Rodichev was deprived of his political rights for the next
decade. Turning to a rather unrewarding practice of law in
Saint Petersburg, he was subsequently banished from that
city in 1901 for signing a collective letter to the ministers of
interior and justice on behalf of certain student demonstrators.
In 1904, Minister of the Interior Sviatopolk-Mirskii restored
Rodichev's political rights, and Rodichev took part in the
several congresses of zemstvo delegates and of Zemstvo-
Constitutionalists during 1904–1905. In the fall of 1905, he
was one of the organizers of the Constitutional-Democratic
party, and was named to its central committee in 1906.[16]

Rodichev was one of the very few public figures during the
semiconstitutional period after 1905 who was a member of
all four dumas. Before the dissolution of the First Duma, he

14. Quoted in Peter Struve, "My Contacts with Rodichev,"
Slavonic and East European Review, 12(January, 1934), 350.
For the record of the sessions of the Tver zemstvo assembly on
December 8 and 10, 1894, at which the address was first adopted
enthusiastically and only later critically debated, see *Materialy dlia
istorii Tverskago gubernskago zemstva,* vol. 6 of 10 vols. (Tver,
1909), 128–35.

15. Rodichev's reaction is in his "Pervaia rech' Imperatora
Nikolaia II," typescript in the Rodichev Collection, which was
published anonymously as *Pervaia tsarskaia rech'* (Geneva,
1895), and his "Adres Tverskogo Zemstva," *Sovremennye
zapiski,* 52(1935).

16. Rodichev was one of nine new members added to the Central Committee at the Second Kadet Party Congress in January,
1906. For the members elected at the First and Second Congresses, see Thomas Riha, *A Russian European: Paul Miliukov in
Russian Politics,* 93, 106.

had gone to England to take part in the Inter-Parliamentary Congress; he was, therefore, not a signer of the hapless Vyborg Manifesto and did not suffer the penalty of disfranchisement that befell so many of the Kadet leaders. In all four dumas Rodichev came forward as one of the principal spokesmen for the Kadets, exercising his natural gift for public speaking and gaining a reputation as one of the ablest Duma orators. Bernard Pares judged him to be "one of the two most eloquent orators ever produced by the Duma"—the other being the Kadet leader V. A. Maklakov.[17] Peter Struve called Rodichev "one of the three great speakers of modern Russia"—the others being Maklakov and Stolypin.[18] Maklakov in his memoirs generously cited Rodichev as "the best Duma orator,"[19] while Lenin, always a harsh critic of liberals, castigated Rodichev as one of the Kadet "windbags" (*krasnobai*).[20]

Rodichev's speeches were always delivered without notes, and his style was often dramatic—too much so in the opinion of Maurice Baring—[21] and Miliukov complained that Rodichev's "fiery temperament often led him beyond the limits demanded by fractional discipline and the political conditions of the moment."[22] Pares recalls that "Rodichev depended on the inspiration of the moment, and if it came, one had the feeling of a rocket rising higher and higher, and ultimately breaking in a shower of sparks."[23] Voicing the opinion of many, that Rodichev was an orator "by the grace of God," Struve judged that had Rodichev had the "vast general and literary-rhetorical culture as Jaurès possessed, he would have become a really colossal phenomenon in Russian spiritual culture."[24]

With the establishment of the Provisional Government in

17. Pares, "Fedor Rodichev," 199.

18. Struve, "My Contacts with Rodichev," 363.

19. V. A. Maklakov, *Vtoraia gosudarstvennaia duma* (*vospominaniia sovremennika*), 101.

20. V. I. Lenin, *Sochineniia,* 3rd ed., vol. 9 of 30 vols. (Moscow, 1935), 381.

21. Maurice Baring, *A Year in Russia* (New York, 1907), 199.

22. P. N. Miliukov, *Vospominaniia (1859–1917)*, vol. 2 of 2 vols., 17.

23. Pares also remarked: "When I have sat with him in the tea-room after one of his speeches, he perspired like a race-horse." Pares, *My Russian Memoirs* (London, 1931), 134.

24. Struve, "My Contacts with Rodichev," 363.

February, 1917, Rodichev became for a brief time its representative to Finland and later served on the Extraordinary Investigating Commission. Like many Kadets, he became a supporter of Gen. Lavr Kornilov and, in the election campaign for the Constituent Assembly, his name was fourth on the Kadet ticket in Petrograd, coming after Miliukov, M. M. Vinaver, and N. N. Kutler; only these four Kadets were elected from the capital.[25] After the dispersal of the Constituent Assembly in February of 1918, Rodichev went into hiding in Petrograd and Moscow. When Mikhail Uritskii, head of the Petrograd Cheka, was murdered, Rodichev was arrested but not recognized, and was released. He then went south to the Crimea and the Don region and later went abroad as a member of Denikin's delegation to Yugoslavia, never to return to Russia. He lived for many years in Switzerland, traditional haven for Russian political exiles, with his wife and daughter. On February 28, 1933, Rodichev died in Lausanne, having just passed his seventy-ninth birthday.[26]

This brief account of Rodichev's career emphasizes that he was above all a public figure and a political activist, who held numerous public and party offices by virtue of election rather than appointment. Unlike Miliukov and Struve, he was not a scholar. After returning from Serbia in 1876 he decided to enter public life, although he had sufficiently impressed the esteemed historian of law, A. D. Gradovskii of the University of Saint Petersburg, for the latter to urge him to pursue an academic career in legal history.[27] While not a writer in the sense of being a systematic producer of lengthy studies, he frequently contributed short pieces to various newspapers and journals. Unlike Maklakov, he was not a truly professional jurist; law served him not as an end in itself but as a means toward realizing more effectively his vocation in politics.

Without question, the supreme goal for Rodichev was the

---

25. James Bunyan and H. H. Fisher, eds., *The Bolshevik Revolution, 1917–1918: Documents and Materials* (Stanford, 1934), 345–47.

26. For other summaries of Rodichev's career, see P. P. Gronskii, "F. I. Rodichev," *Le Monde Slave* (January, 1934), 115–22, and Sergei Shtern, "75-letie F. I. Rodicheva," *Segodnia*, 53(1929). The latter is in the Rodichev Collection.

27. F. I. Rodichev, "Obshchina i lichnost', *"Poslednie novosti* (September 19, 1931).

ideal of achieving human liberty—the love of which became profoundly rooted in his spirit. Liberty meant many things for Rodichev, but the content of his writings and speeches as well as his practical work in public life richly testifies that the following were foremost for Rodichev: freedom of speech, especially the right of the people to express their views directly to the sovereign without bureaucratic interference; increasing and equalizing the rights of the Russian peasantry with those of the rest of the population; abolition of arbitrariness and brutality as techniques of rule; release of human, and therefore national, energy; and, most important, realization of the principle of human dignity and worth. These goals were consistently pursued over a long career, first at the provincial level and later on the national stage.

Rodichev's involvement with his goals was highly emotional, at times romantic, and permeating his thought and activity was a high sense of decency, magnanimity, and fair play. Pares had frequently characterized Rodichev, whom he knew well, as "generous," and "the most generous of men." [28] Rodichev was easily hurt when he felt that he had not been treated fairly, as when he was punished by Nicholas II for the Tver address of 1894 and by the Third Duma for the Stolypin necktie speech. His faith—as much a liberalism of the heart as of the mind—left him a vulnerable man.

The figure of Alexander Herzen stands as the supreme inspiration in Rodichev's life. It is important to appreciate that Rodichev revered Herzen not as the founder of Russian populist socialism, or *narodnichestvo,* but as the great teacher and personification of the ideal of human liberty.

Rodichev's "discovery" of Herzen occurred during a European tour in 1872, when in Berlin he came upon a collection of Herzen's writings. "I could not tear myself away from this book," Rodichev writes. "For me it was the revelation of a free spirit." [29] Later that year, in Geneva, he was to acquire an edition of Herzen's autobiography, *My Past and Thoughts.* "Thus I became acquainted with this amiable man and all my life loved him."

> Herzen represented for me the living tradition from the first heralds of free thought, from Novikov and Radishchev, from the Decembrists, to the men of the sixties. He was

28. Pares, *My Russian Memoirs,* 89, 107, 174, 211.
29. F. I. Rodichev, "Vstrechi s Ogarevym," *Poslednie novosti* (May 5, 1934).

the vital link between Russian liberation and the European movement. But above and beyond all else, the value of Herzen is in the freedom of his spirit—he bent his knee before no dogma whatsoever.[30]

Herzen had died in 1870, but his lifelong friend and companion in exile, Nikolai Ogarev, was living in Geneva during Rodichev's visit to that city. The young university student felt a strong compulsion to talk with this intimate disciple of Herzen and requested in writing a meeting. From the interview the admiring Rodichev came to know much about this personal link to Herzen. At a second meeting and in subsequent correspondence Rodichev informed the older man of events in Russia.[31] These letters reveal an exaggerated estimation of the strength of popular unrest in the 1870s, but also a perception of the lack of confidence by the masses and their sympathizers in the upper classes. In one letter Rodichev wrote: "It is often said that the people will always be loyal, that they will never rise up against the Tsar, to whom they are grateful and whom they love. This is untrue. Without any exaggeration . . . I say that love for the Tsar you will not find in a single Russian *muzhik*." [32] In another letter he expressed concern lest the revolution catch the upper-class liberals unprepared and isolated. "It seems to me," he wrote,

> that all is not so peaceful with us in Russia as those at the top think and that not far off is the time when the Russian Tsar with all his family and loyal gentry will go into retirement. Our task is to look forward to and prepare for this time and, mainly, to try to make the people not look upon us as foreigners or as unwelcome guests at their festivity.[33]

Rodichev's identification of himself with Herzen and Ogarev remained strong throughout his life. On the hundredth anniversary of Ogarev's birth, Rodichev published an appreciation of the poet in *Russkie vedomosti,* in which love of liberty was once more the theme.[34] At the Seventh

---

30. *Ibid.*
31. Copies of three letters are preserved in the Rodichev Collection.
32. Letter dated March 10/22, probably written in 1874.
33. This letter bears no date.
34. Typescript of "Pamiati Ogareva" in the Rodichev Collection, published in *Russkie vedomosti* (November 24, 1913).

Congress of the Kadet party in March, 1917, Rodichev reminded the gathering that March 25 was the anniversary of Herzen's birth and should not pass unnoticed. Asserting that "Russia has not yet paid her debt to Herzen," he concluded with stormy applause from his listeners: "As long as Russian is spoken and as long as the human heart beats with love for liberty, the glorious name of Herzen will not be forgotten." [35]

Writing the introduction for the first complete edition of Herzen's *My Past and Thoughts,* which was published in 1921 in Berlin,[36] Rodichev singled out freedom and reason as the "two basic principles for Herzen, the two guiding stars," and sought to encourage his fellow expatriates by reminding them that Herzen "had believed in the future of Russia when there was no justification for hope." [37] Later, in his years of exile in Lausanne, considerable comfort was afforded by the friendship between Rodichev's family and Herzen's daughters, Natalia and Ol'ga.[38]

Returning in 1872 to Petersburg University from Switzerland and his meetings with Ogarev, Rodichev wrote that he "began to preach Herzen to my comrades on the right and on the left." [39] But he found his hero rejected in favor of highly conservative or militantly revolutionary doctrines. The socialism of Russian populism was especially attractive. As he comments, "In Russian political currents of that time socialism was the ABC of political understanding. . . ," [40] but, he adds, "I never shared this view." Characteristically, the explanation for his minority position was based on the belief that individual liberty would be endangered by the establishment of a socialist society. For him, socialist theories of his day served as thin veils for a future serfdom in the form of a "socialist enslavement of the personality,"

---

35. *Rech'* (March 28, 1917). A Kiev delegate, Professor Kosinski, was so moved that he called for, with general applause, the return of Herzen's remains (which were in Nice) to "free Russia."

36. A. I. Herzen, *Byloe i dumy,* first complete ed., vol. 1 of 5 vols. (Berlin, 1921), 9–23.

37. *Ibid.,* 9.

38. "Biografiia F. I. Rodicheva," handwritten manuscript in the Rodichev Collection, reverse of p. 3.

39. Typescript of "Khotel ia proverit' svoe proshloe," in the Rodichev Collection, 6.

40. "Vstrechi s Ogarevym," *Poslednie novosti* (May 5, 1934).

and he quotes with obvious approval the words of Proudhon: "Je suis pur des infamies socialistes." [41]

The enthusiastic reception of Herzen by the young Rodichev in 1872 was not, however, the first awakening of a social consciousness in the future liberal leader. There were earlier influences, going back even to his childhood. One of these was his governess, Maria Evgrafovna Pavlovskaia, who was later to marry the great populist thinker, N. K. Mikhailovskii. Rodichev relates how she "instilled in me democratic ideas about the equality of people, and I very willingly made these notions my own." [42] He admits that as a child under rather strict supervision he had a confused understanding of the emancipation of the serfs in 1861. He recalls that he "envied the liberty of the peasant boys, and dreamed of equality with them in rights and freedom." [43]

In his adolescence Rodichev was much impressed by events in France during the last years of the Second Empire and the Franco-Prussian War. Speeches of liberal opposition leaders like Jules Favre, Jules Simon, and Léon Gambetta stimulated his thought and interested him in the study of French history. What Rodichev self-revealingly termed the "romanticism of liberation" attracted him to the French Revolution. "I adopted the Declaration of the Rights of Man," he wrote, "at first as a discovery and then as an ideal." [44] In a long letter written a few months before Rodichev's death to his close friend, Polish lawyer and statesman A. R. Lednicki, he traced the highlights of his career and named Herzen and the French Revolution as the chief mentors in shaping his public philosophy. "My political consciousness," he wrote, "was formed under the impact of my reading of Herzen and the history of the French Revolution. The Declaration of the Rights of Man became and remained for me axiom and ideal." [45]

It is of interest to note that a reading of Ernest Hamel's biography of Robespierre, whose doctrinaire spirit must have appeared quite uncongenial to Rodichev, led him to conclude

41. *Ibid.*
42. "Detstvo," *Poslednie novosti* (March 20, 1933).
43. *Ibid.*
44. "Vstrechi s Ogarevym," *Poslednie novosti* (May 5, 1934).
45. Typescript of letter to A. R. Lednicki, written October–December, 1932, in the Rodichev Collection, 2.

that the French Jacobin could never become one of his heroes.[46] Rodichev continued to combine study of French revolutionary history with constant observance of contemporary events in France. The Franco-Prussian War deepened his admiration for the French liberals and left him with an intense dislike for Bismarck, in whom Rodichev saw a "cynicism" and "militarism" that had a persistent and baleful influence on the next several decades of European history.[47]

During Rodichev's long period of provincial activity from 1876 to 1895, members of two gentry families in Tver helped shape and bolster his commitment to public service. The Korsakov family, including the brothers Ivan and Pavel Assigkritovich, who for several terms were deputies in the Tver zemstvo, lived in Rodichev's native county of Ves'egonsk. Pavel headed the progressive faction in the Ves'egonsk zemstvo known as "Young Ves'egoniia." In 1874 he not only had entered the county and provincial zemstvos but also had been elected to the zemstvo board of his own county.[48] It was Pavel who persuaded Rodichev to choose zemstvo service as a career. "He exerted a decisive influence on my life," Rodichev wrote; "he attracted me to zemstvo activity when after finishing the university I hesitated about what to do." [49]

In Novotorzhok County lived the Bakunin family and the younger brothers of the famous anarchist Mikhail Bakunin. Of these, Pavel and Alexander played a leading role in Tver zemstvo work for decades. Together with the physician M. I. Petrunkevich they made Novotorzhok County another center of progressive zemstvo activity in Tver Province, even before the famous veteran of Russian liberalism, I. I. Petrunkevich, settled in Novotorzhok in 1890. Of the Bakunins, Pavel, a philosopher, seems to have had the greatest influence on Rodichev, who planned but did not live

46. "Vstrechi s Ogarevym," *Poslednie novosti* (May 5, 1934).
47. *Ibid.*
48. On Korsakov, see I. K. Gudz', *Zemskie deiateli Tverskoi gubernii*, vol. 1, *P. A. Korsakov* (Tver, 1909). The "Young Ves'-egoniia" group also included P. E. Gronskii, father of P. P. Gronskii, member of the Fourth Duma and coauthor of *The War and the Russian Government* (New Haven, 1929). The group was especially active in developing primary education, fire insurance, and savings and loan societies.
49. "O semeistve Bakuninikh i Tverskom zemstve," *Poslednie novosti* (April 22, 1932).

to carry out the writing of an extensive study of the Bakunin family.[50]

Armed with the ideal of liberty and strengthened by the warm support of kindred spirits, Rodichev now launched upon that practical service which brought him face to face with the peasant question. For almost two decades after 1876 he worked continuously with the north Russian peasantry of Tver as a justice of the peace and as a zemstvo deputy. Rather soon his thinking respecting the peasant commune, or *mir,* underwent a change. At first he approached his work "with the conviction, then widespread among young people, of the great significance of the commune"; and he recalls that, while in Serbia, he had confidently told an Italian journalist that: "We will not have a labor problem . . . the *mir* protects us from social upheavals. The *mir* serves as a guarantee of the rights of each to the land. We need only liberty—the rest will follow." [51]

Experience with the peasantry and closer observation of communal realities, however, soon changed his views. "Life taught otherwise," Rodichev writes, and by 1881 he had become firmly convinced that the power of the commune should be broken, that individual property in land should become the rule, and that the peasantry should fully possess all rights enjoyed by the other classes. He registered his new position in 1881 in a memorandum submitted to the abortive Kakhanov committee on reorganization of local government. The memorandum describes the peasantry's status as "State serfdom," in which the peasant is subjected to the *mir* and to the bureaucracy, and asserts that "this special status of the peasants is nowadays no longer justified either by reasons of State necessity, or still less from the point of view of justice and humanity." [52] Rodichev's conclusion is a call for the further emancipation of the peasant and the abolition of restrictions "which place him in the peculiar position of a man who lives not for himself and not as he likes, but for the Treasury and in a way advantageous to the latter." [53] In much

---

50. *Ibid*. See also "Biografiia F. I. Rodicheva" in the Rodichev Collection, p. 4 and reverse.

51. "Obshchina i lichnost'," *Poslednie novosti* (September 19, 1931).

52. Quoted in Struve, "My Contacts with Rodichev," 362.

53. *Ibid.*

of this, as Struve has noted, Rodichev anticipated the later Stolypin agrarian reform.[54]

The *mir*, then, was a retarding factor upon the growth of a consciousness of human worth and a sense of personality that Rodichev ardently wished to arouse in the north Russian peasantry of Tver, and he set about to achieve these aims by putting his greatest efforts as a zemstvo deputy into the work of expanding the meager system of public education.[55] He was violently opposed to the establishment in 1889 of the office of land captain (*zemskii nachal'nik*), which he interpreted as a reactionary measure critically endangering the desired growth of freedom and self-esteem among the peasants. It was in keeping with his whole philosophy that Rodichev should protest by resigning his long-held position as county marshal of the nobility. As Ves'egonsk marshal of the nobility he would have had to preside over meetings of the county land captains, an institution with which he did not care to identify himself.[56]

Consistent with Rodichev's concern for political liberty in Russia and justice for the peasantry was his position with respect to the nationality question. Here he stood firmly for equality of rights and an end to any form of discrimination. On different occasions he defended the use of the Ukrainian language, came out during World War I against persecution of the German subjects of the Empire, and after the Revolution wrote a pamphlet refuting the equation of Jews with Bolsheviks.[57]

Most frequently, however, Rodichev served, as did Herzen, as a generous champion of the Poles, going further in support of their aims than Miliukov deemed suitable.[58] One of his most intimate friends was the Polish national leader, A. R. Lednicki, who became a member of the

54. *Ibid.*, 367.
55. On Rodichev's efforts to promote education, see his "Zemstvo i narodnoe obrazovanie," *Poslednie novosti,* (June 21, August 20, September 24, 1932).
56. "Avtobiografiia F. I. Rodicheva," typescript in the Rodichev Collection, 1. This was written in 1932 to support a petition for a pension from the Czechoslovak government.
57. See in particular his *Bol'sheviki i Evrei* (Lausanne, n.d.), copy in the Rodichev Collection.
58. Miliukov, *Vospominaniia,* 2:76.

Central Committee of the Kadet party and was the persistent
organizer of Russian-Polish fraternity among liberal circles
in Petersburg. Rodichev's letter, written shortly before his
death, to Lednicki reveals the strength of their friendship,[59]
as does testimony by Lednicki's son, Waclaw Lednicki,[60]
and by Maklakov, who worked in Lednicki's law office as
pomoshchik, or lawyer-in-training.[61] Maklakov maintained that Rodichev's fight against national discrimination
was grounded on his patriotism, which led Rodichev to
seek reforms that would remove nationalist discontent among
the non-Russians and therewith preserve the Empire from
disintegration. To quote Maklakov, Rodichev "believed
that a great Russian Empire could be maintained and could
flourish only when it had correctly solved the *national*
question." [62] Such was Rodichev's reputation as a champion
of the Poles that, when Lednicki at the Seventh Congress
of the Kadet party in 1917 stood to acknowledge the
recently granted independence of Poland, spontaneous cries
arose from the audience that Rodichev should make reply
on behalf of the party.[63]

These broad issues—liberty, the peasant question, and
the problem of nationalities—were central concerns for
Rodichev during his career. The question was, how might
one best encourage a suspicious and bureaucratized autocracy
to ameliorate Russian conditions in these particular areas?
Refusing to be a revolutionary or to resort to violence,
Rodichev clearly hoped that the path of gradual, loyal, and
constructive activity at the local level would be a feasible
means of narrowing the gulf between *vlast'* ("the regime")
and *obshchestvo* ("educated Russian society"), of winning
greater confidence from the Tsar and his bureaucrats, and
of ultimately extending the principle of elected representative
bodies to the highest echelons of the state.

Rodichev undoubtedly held in mind even in his early
years of public service the ideal and goal of a constitutional
monarchy, with equal justice and freedom under law for

59. See note 1.
60. V. Lednitskii [Lednicki], "Vokrug V. A. Maklakova,"
Novyi zhurnal, 56(1959), 241, 249.
61. V. Maklakov, "F. I. Rodichev i A. R. Lednitskii [Led-
nicki]," *Novyi zhurnal,* 16(1947), 240–51.
62. *Ibid.,* 241.
63. *Rech'* (March 28, 1917).

all. That such a goal was as yet remote was clearly indicated
by Alexander III's rejection of the Loris-Melikov project,
the dissolution of the Kakhanov committee, and the triumph
of reactionary bureaucrats in legislation affecting local
government from 1889–1902. Thus the liberals' first step
was to encourage not constitutionalism, but an enlightened
or liberal absolutism. The central role of the monarch was
recognized, for the monarch had the power to open new
lines of communication with his subjects, to curb bureaucratic
abuses, and to check arbitrary punishments. The Tver
address of 1894, in which Rodichev played the leading
part, made no bold demand for a constitution. The choice
before the new emperor, as Victor Leontovitsch has noted,
was not between constitutionalism and absolutism, but
between liberal absolutism and antiliberal absolutism.[64]
Rodichev, dismayed and disappointed years afterward, asked
in 1923: "What kind of mind and heart must a man have
had, to be affronted by that address, and to reply to it in
the way that Nicholas II replied?" [65] Even after the 1905
Revolution, Rodichev believed, Nicholas "could never
reconcile himself to the thought that he was no longer an
unlimited monarch, that he too was bound honourably to
observe the Fundamental Laws." [66] The proper course for
Nicholas should have been a return to the spirit of his
grandfather's reign and a sincere compliance with the
implications of the October Manifesto. For Rodichev, the
"road to salvation" ran from February 19, 1861 to
October 17, 1905. "The monarchy of Nicholas did not wish
to follow this road, and it has perished." [67]

The period opened by the October Manifesto placed
Rodichev squarely upon the national political stage, and
a fresh opportunity for a new and more constructive era
in Russian political history presented itself. Looking back
in 1934 upon this period, the historian Peter Struve offered

---

64. Victor Leontovitsch, *Geschichte des Liberalismus in Russland* (Frankfurt-am-Main, 1957), 261. He cites Maklakov's similar interpretation in the latter's *Vlast' i obshchestvennost' na zakate staroi Rossii* (Paris, 1936), 134–35.

65. F. Rodichev, "The Liberal Movement in Russia (1891–1905)," *Slavonic and East European Review*, 2(December, 1923), 250.

66. *Ibid.*, 262.

67. *Ibid.*

the following provocative judgment: "The tragedy of Russian Liberalism and at the same time the tragedy of the Russian State idea consisted in this: that instead of being political allies, Rodichev the Liberal and Stolypin the Conservative proved to be political adversaries and even enemies." [68] Struve argued that the two men, political emotions and prejudices aside, need not have been opponents and, in fact, were actually not far apart in their aspirations, especially with regard to the peasantry. Stating his case in broad terms, Struve contended that after 1905 "the real danger to freedom and to a regime of legality in Russia came no longer from the Right, but from the Left," that is, from that political current which Struve called "revolutionary maximalism." [69]

The late Michael Karpovich dealt with the same problem in respect to the differing viewpoints represented within the Kadet party by Miliukov and Maklakov.[70] Miliukov, like Rodichev, saw the main enemy on the right—the Tsar's government; Maklakov feared the left and desired cooperation with Stolypin. No political alliance between government and Kadets was forthcoming, however, and opposition between them continued; final victory went to neither, but rather to the Bolshevik variant of revolutionary maximalism.

It is altogether natural, after the victory of a totalitarian movement has led to the dismal extermination of its rivals, that an explanation be sought for the lack of timely and appropriate cooperation among the nontotalitarian elements, whether radical, liberal, conservative, or even moderately authoritarian. Why, indeed, was there not collaboration between Rodichev and Stolypin, between Russian liberalism and the chiefs of the imperial bureaucracy? One might go further and speculate whether such collaboration, had it developed, could have been sufficient to ward off the forces of revolutionary maximalism, given those numerous problems of awesome magnitude that history had set for the Russian Empire during its last years.

The prospects for cooperation in 1906 were certainly dim. The long heritage of mutual suspicion and hostility, the

---

68. Struve, "My Contacts with Rodichev," 367.
69. *Ibid.,* 365–66.
70. Michael Karpovich, "Two Types of Russian Liberalism: Maklakov and Miliukov," in Ernest J. Simmons, ed., *Continuity and Change in Russian and Soviet Thought,* 129–43.

differing political philosophies, the excessive optimism of
the Kadets, the inflexibility of the bureaucracy, and the
political prejudices of Nicholas II—all these determined
that the new era opened by the October Manifesto would be
a difficult one. The scales were weighted against, rather
than for, cooperation between liberals and government.

To Rodichev, the experience of the preceding years of
Nicholas' reign could not have appeared encouraging.
Everything that Rodichev despised—injustice, arbitrariness,
oppression—had been practiced in abundance by the Tsar's
government and caused the most serious doubt concerning
the good faith behind governmental overtures for a coalition
ministry. It was apparently too much to ask of Rodichev and
the Kadets that they should have compromised themselves
in the eyes of the Russian public by joining hands with
that bureaucracy against which they had long been leading
the opposition.

In Rodichev's case, several factors militated against
compromise. The Tsar's government had subjected him to
a good deal of personal punishment: he had been victimized in
1891, rebuffed and denied public office in 1895, banished
from the capital in 1901, and placed for many years
under police surveillance. Furthermore, his strong emotional
commitment to his political ideals would have made any
significant compromise with the Tsar's government profoundly uncongenial, if not repulsive. Certainly, after
Stolypin's arbitrary revision of the Duma electoral law, the
chances for collaboration became virtually nil. Any personal
relationship between Rodichev and Stolypin was under
considerable strain after the necktie speech of 1907.

Struve argued that there should not only have been a
policy of mutual concessions but that the concessions on
the part of the liberals should have been, "both in substance
and in spirit, much more drastic and resolute than on the
part of the historical power [the Tsar]." [71] One might venture
to suggest, on the contrary, that the burden of proof was
more to be placed on the Tsar's government than on the
liberals. The government had to convince the liberals and
the country as a whole of its desire to fulfill the spirit of
the October Manifesto, of its willingness to attempt a new
policy, of its rejection of the old practice of placing obstacles

---

71. Struve, "My Contacts with Rodichev," 366.

in the path of healthy public activity. This it largely failed
to accomplish, or, as Rodichev believed, did not even
seriously try to effect. Of course, neither the liberals nor the
government should be faulted for failing to perceive that in
little more than a decade there would occur the triumph of
one party and the beginnings of a totalitarian system.
Although many voices predicted future revolution, the
options were still open, at least until the First World War.
More time was needed and only after the war created a new
emergency situation may it be argued that a victory for the
forces of revolutionary maximalism was probable or
inevitable.[72]

Rodichev and his fellow liberals were not, of course,
without their own faults and weaknesses; they were probably
too idealistic and too doctrinaire. Rodichev's weakness as
well as his strength lay in his refusal to compromise with
arbitrary power. One can agree with Struve in his judgment
that Rodichev "was not in the least a 'Real-Politiker.'"[73]
Rodichev's liberalism was deeply principled, and his spirit
was not that of a bargainer or compromiser. Whatever
inflexibility this political faith imposed upon his tactics,
that faith did not prevent him from being a good servant
of his fellow countrymen in Tver province and, on the
national stage, a bold articulator of commendable and needed
values.

Rodichev clearly saw himself in the great tradition of
the struggle for political and social liberation in Russia, a
tradition that for him went back to Radishchev and Novikov
and had as its most outstanding figure Alexander Herzen.
His favorite word, recurring frequently in his speeches and
writings, was *osvobozhdenie* ("liberation"). In 1905, when
his fellow liberals were discussing a name for their new
party, Rodichev voiced objection to "such un-Russian words

---

72. It is clear that I do not find convincing the arguments put
forward by adherents of the "pessimist" school on the prospects
for liberal constitutionalism in Russia. Again, more time was
necessary. Had not World War I intervened, the matter of mutual
distrust might well have been resolved and a more stable social
and economic milieu might have developed. See especially the
thoughtful article by Arthur Mendel, "On Interpreting the Fate of
Imperial Russia," in T. G. Stavrou, ed., *Russia Under the Last
Tsar* (Minneapolis, 1969), 13–41.

73. Struve, "My Contacts with Rodichev," 365.

as 'constitutional-democratic party.' I would suggest putting
into the name of the party the word *'osvobozhdenie,'* the
mention of which, for me at least, makes the heart beat
powerfully." [74]

74. *Osvobozhdenie* (October 5/18, 1905).

PETER B. STRUVE:
THE SOURCES OF HIS
LIBERAL RUSSIAN NATIONALISM

Richard Pipes

It should be stated at the outset that very little is known of Struve's childhood and youth. He left no memoirs and, except for occasional reminiscences which he scattered in obituaries of friends and public figures, kept his memories to himself. His earliest available writings date from 1892, when he had already completed two years at the university and was about to begin work on what became his first book.[1] There is little mention of his early years in memoirs of others, and the little there is was written after a lapse of half a century by old men. Such dearth of information on a man's formative years would be a handicap to any biographer, but it is particularly frustrating in the case of Struve because he was an extraordinarily precocious youth who made himself a name in Saint Petersburg intellectual circles while still a gymnasium student, and became a national celebrity at twenty-four.

The earliest description of him, written in 1944 by V. A. Obolensky, a fellow student from Saint Petersburg, depicts him as a pallid and sickly young man of nineteen: "He was a slender, tall youth, with a sunken chest. His hair was closely cropped, fair, with a reddish tint. Despite his rather regular features he seemed unattractive because of his unusually pale face, full of freckles, and his moist mouth subscribers and avid readers of the leading Pan-Slav organs,

---

1. Sergei Vodov says that Struve published his first article in the newspaper *Russkie vedomosti* on January 31, 1890: "P. B. Struve," *Studencheskie gody*, 1/18 (Prague, 1925), 34. There is indeed in this issue a brief item on German school reform signed with the initial "S," but neither in content nor in style does it bear any resemblance to Struve's authenticated writings. According to I. F. Masanov, *Slovar' psevdonimov*, vol. 3 of 4 vols. (Moscow, 1958), 47, the letter "S" was a cipher used by Struve's oldest brother, Vasily.

2. V. A. Obolensky, untitled reminiscences of Struve written in 1944, manuscript in the B. I. Nikolaevsky Archive, Hoover Institution, Stanford, Calif.

his unappealing mouth and let his hair reach to the shoulders
to hide his equally unattractive thick and protruding ears.
His whole appearance as a young man had something utterly
helpless about it, and Vera Zasulich, on meeting him in
1896 in Geneva, at once dubbed him *telënok* ("the calf");
this name stuck as his Social Democratic code word.

In this limp frame there burned a moral and intellectual
fire of such constancy and intensity that all who met Struve
soon forgot his external appearance. Struve was an intellectual
of a type that has become nearly extinct and that in another
century will probably be as difficult to imagine as a
medieval ascetic, a Renaissance humanist, or a Prussian
Junker are today. From the moment of earliest awareness
until his death, Struve's life centered on an inner dialogue.
He was forever debating with himself. Everything that
went on around him, even when it concerned his own
person, was to him utterly insignificant unless it related in
some way to that which occupied his mind. He had no
particular interest in other people except as they either
taught him or were willing to learn from him. Although
capable of forming warm friendships, he selected his friends
from among those who shared his way of thinking and
were in tune with his outlook. Obolensky aptly said that
just as there are many "egocentrists of feeling" Struve was
a "singular egocentric of thought." He never attended to his
private interests unless they grew desperate; indeed, the
very notion that he might exert himself to live better seemed
to him somehow indecent. In 1938, when he was living in
Belgrade in destitution, a friend suggested that he do something to improve his situation. Struve replied indignantly:

> It follows from my entire "nature" that I never impose
> myself on anyone and never seek anything for myself as a
> public figure and only in extreme need for myself as a
> private person, and never "arrange" anything. For that
> reason in my day I have done only that which I could not
> help doing, "inspired by some demon" (in the Greek sense
> of the word). . . . This is my "nature," and I could not
> act otherwise.

If his life needed "arranging," he added, that was for his
friends to worry about, not for him.[3] These were not the

3. Letter to N. A. Tsurikov, dated March 31, 1938, manuscript
in possession of Gleb Struve, Berkeley, Calif.

idle boasts of a man struck by misfortune and attempting to justify himself, but a firm principle of conduct to which he adhered even when life was good to him and when it would have taken little effort on his part to feather a comfortable nest.

For Struve, to think meant to speculate not *in vacuo* but from a position of knowledge. From his earliest years he thirsted for it. So important was learning to him that in the snatches of recollections that he left behind he talks of nothing else; where others measure the stages of their life by what once happened to them, he measures it by what he learned. Even as a schoolboy he displayed an extraordinary range of intellectual interests and read widely on sociology, politics, literature, philology, economics, philosophy, and history. Before reaching his teens, he mastered the classics of Russian prose, including Tolstoy, Turgenev, and Dostoevsky,[4] as well as the standard sociological literature, encompassing most of Darwin and all of Spencer.[5] He followed regularly the "fat" journals, and while still in grade school devoured political periodicals and pamphlets. Many years later he recalled the vivid impression made on him by Ivan Aksakov's protest against the Treaty of Berlin and Dostoevsky's Pushkin speech, events that occurred when he was eight and ten, respectively.[6] He was so impatient to learn that he plowed through his elder brother's university notes [7] and attended disputes of doctoral dissertations on

4. *Rossiia i Slavianstvo,* 83(June 29, 1930), and *Vozrozhdenie,* 362(May 30, 1926).

5. "Pamiati V. A. Gerda," *Vozrozhdenie,* 450(August 26, 1926).

6. Struve, "Aksakovy i Aksakov," *Russkaia mysl',* 6–8(1923), 350, and *Rossiia i Slavianstvo,* 117(February 21, 1931). "This discovery and disclosure of Pushkin by the prophetic utterances of Dostoevsky represents for me, who was then still a child, the first strong, purely spiritual, purely cultural experience, upheaval, and revelation." "Dukh i slovo Pushkina," in E. V. Anichkov, ed., *Belgradskii Pushkinskii Sbornik* (Belgrade, 1937), 270. Struve also recalled the powerful impression made on him when he was eleven (1881) by Vladimir Soloviev's funeral oration for Dostoevsky, although in this case he says that he was more moved than enlightened. "Iz vospominanii o Vladimire Solov'eve," *Rossiia i Slavianstvo,* 95(September 20, 1930).

7. "Iz vospominanii o S.-Peterburgskom universitete," *Rossiia i Slavianstvo,* 65(February 22, 1930).

historical and philological subjects, and funerals of writers and scholars of note.[8]

All this happened before Struve had graduated from school. By his graduation he had acquired an astonishing store of information on a wide variety of subjects; and what he learned he retained, for he had a photographic memory that never let go of any information imprinted on it.

> His memory, which he retained to old age, astonished all who knew him. Everything he had read, seen, or heard he remembered for the rest of his life. He remembered even the most useless trivia, which were sealed in his memory as it were automatically, without any exertion on his part, even without an effort of attention and so contrary to his characteristic absentmindedness. He could repeat in detail a conversation which he had with you twenty years ago, tell you where it took place and under what circumstances. If his memory retained trivia that were utterly indifferent and uninteresting to him, it must be apparent how firmly it retained all that which he took in with interest. . . . He was a remarkable bibliographer. He knew where, by whom, and when this or that book had been published. And as concerns great and even not so great men of all nations and times, writers, scholars, musicians, artists, crowned heads and statesmen, he not only knew accurately their names, but he could often furnish the precise dates of their birth and death. Peter Berngardovich carried in his head, as it were, a whole library, which in the course of his long life filled with new volumes.[9]

These remarks, applied to the mature Struve, also hold for the very young man. A. Meiendorf, who entered school in Stuttgart shortly after the twelve-year-old Struve had departed with his parents for Russia, recalled being told wonders about the Struve boy who, perched on a table, recited poems by heart.[10]

In Struve's youth, passion for knowledge in general and for knowledge that had no social and political "relevance" in particular was not only out of fashion but decidedly frowned

---

8. "Russko-slavianskie pominki," *Rossiia i Slavianstvo,* 223 (August, 1933). In June, 1889 Struve witnessed the obsequies of Orest Miller. *Slovo* (May 10/23, 1909).

9. V. A. Obolensky's unpublished memoirs of Struve.

10. A. Meiendorf, "P. B. Struve," unpublished manuscript in the possession of Gleb Struve, Berkeley, Calif.

upon. Young Russians, raised in the spirit of an anarchism that worshiped action, regarded pure learning as incompatible with service to the people. As they saw it, one had to choose between study and revolution. Active revolutionaries, by the very nature of their vocation, had little time to read and were poorly informed on any subject outside of radical polemics. But even their sympathizers who stayed in school and cheered the revolutionaries from the sidelines—that is, the vast majority—confined their reading to standard "progressive" monthlies, sociological treatises, and pamphlets. In belles lettres their tastes were confined to novels that portrayed "realistically" or "naturalistically" (in other words, unfavorably) Russia's condition. Even such literature, however, was regarded as inferior to literary criticism, which in the 1860s had developed in Russia into a powerful instrument of political propaganda. Poetry and the fine arts were altogether ignored unless, like Nekrasov's verse or the paintings of the "Ambulants," they dealt with social themes. Of academic subjects, the intelligentsia between 1860 and 1890 favored only the natural sciences, especially chemistry and biology, which were useful in fighting the idealism and religion of the older generation.

Struve, sufficiently a child of his time to share the passion for sociology and respect for natural science, was constitutionally incapable of putting fences around his curiosity or of judging that which intellect or taste had created by the standard of "relevance." He regarded the ignorance and militant anti-intellectualism of the Russian intelligentsia of the 1880s with profound contempt as a symptom of cultural deficiency.

He was never, therefore, not even in his teens, a true Russian intelligent. His unstinted admiration for every great achievement of the human spirit, whatever its political orientation or utility, perplexed those who knew him, especially his friends among radical youth. N. K. Krupskaia, Lenin's plodding wife, recalled with amazement the sight of Struve, tired from work on some Marxist publication, withdrawing to relax with a volume of poetry by Fet.[11] Her

---

11. N. K. Krupskaia, "Iz vospominanii," in *O Lenine,* vol. 1 of 2 vols. (Leningrad, 1925), 19. Struve discovered Fet in 1888, when in the library of a friend he chanced on a volume of Fet's poetry called *Vechernye ogni.* He read it with enormous

Volodia, in this respect a far more representative Russian intelligent of the period, could never have done anything like that, for he had little use for any poetry, and certainly none for that written by a reactionary like Fet. The radicals, in the midst of whom Struve spent much of his life until the age of thirty, instinctively (and rightly) interpreted his insistence on separating knowledge and art from politics as symptomatic of an imperfect commitment to the "cause." For that reason they never fully trusted him, and he reciprocated by treating them with a certain measure of disdain. Struve's quarrel with the Russian intelligentsia, which was to break into the open after 1905 and form one of the stormiest chapters in his biography, may be said, therefore, to derive from a fundamental trait of his character, one of which he gave evidence from his earliest years.

Nationalism constituted the lowest substratum of Struve's mind. Before he was anything else—a liberal, a Social Democrat, or what he himself called a liberal conservative— he was a monarchist, a Slavophile, and a Pan-Slavist. Nationalism is one of the several continua in his intellectual biography, a constant of which most of his other political and social views were merely variables. A great, vital, cultured Russian nation was for him, from the earliest moments of political awareness, the principal objective of public activity.

He absorbed this nationalism at home. His parents were subscribers and avid readers of the leading Pan-Slav organs, Ivan Aksakov's *Rus'* and Dostoevsky's *Diary of a Writer,* as well as of the "semilegal, oppositional conservative" (as he calls them) pamphlets of A. I. Koshelev and R. A. Fadeev.[12] The intellectual hero of the Struve household was Ivan Aksakov, to whom the Struves wrote letters expressing gratitude and admiration for his courageous critique of the government's domestic and foreign policies. In the summer of 1882, when on their return from Stuttgart to Saint Petersburg, they stopped in Moscow at the Slav Bazaar, the city's leading hotel, and Aksakov came to thank them personally for their expressions of support.[13] Struve's

---

excitement, even though aware of Fet's reactionary political opinions. "O Fete—'prozevala'-li Rossiia Feta?" *Rossiia i Slavianstvo,* 214(February 11, 1933).

12. Struve "Vremena," *Vozrozhdenie,* 264(February 21, 1926).

13. "Aksakovy i Aksakov," 350–51.

mother also entered into a correspondence with Dostoevsky, from whom she sought spiritual guidance.[14] From these clues it is not difficult to reconstruct the political atmosphere of the home in which Struve grew up: loyalty to the crown, hatred for nihilism and terror, admiration for the Great Reforms, unbounded faith in Russia's future as a great nation, and support of imperial expansion in the Balkans. Peter Struve's father had belonged to the ideology of the upper echelons of the enlightened imperial bureaucracy. Until the age of fifteen, Struve tells us, he shared these ideas. "I had patriotic, nationalistic impulses, tinged with dynastic and at the same time Slavophile sympathies, verging on hatred of the revolutionary movement. Ivan Aksakov and Dostoevsky, as the author of *Diary of a Writer,* were my principal heroes in the realm of ideas." [15]

The nationalism to which these statements refer was a very special phenomenon connected with the reforms of Alexander II. The purpose of the Great Reforms was to bring Russian society into closer participation in shaping the life of the country and to transform it from a body of passive subjects into one of active citizens. By introducing them in the 1860s the monarchy for the first time departed from the ancient tradition of bureaucratic authoritarianism and estate privilege and sought to bring to life a Russian nation. The mood of the country during these years resembled that of Prussia half a century earlier, in the age of the reforms of Stein and Hardenberg. Those who had been active during that decade or had grown up in its shadow never quite rid themselves of that optimistic liberal nationalism characteristic of societies in transition from traditional to modern politics, from static bureaucratism to dynamic democratism. As the reign of Alexander II drew to a close, the monarchy, responding to revolutionary violence, gradually abandoned its earlier course and returned to a policy of reliance on bureaucracy and police. But the liberal nationalism that it had stimulated in the 1860s remained very much alive in society during the following decade, when the precocious Struve began to interest himself in politics. His mind was

---

14. *Rossiia i Slavianstvo,* 117(February 21, 1931). "Aksakovy i Aksakov," 350.
15. Struve, "My Contacts and Conflicts with Lenin," *Slavonic Review,* 12:36(April, 1934), 575.

molded by the Great Reforms and he always held fast to
the belief that national greatness was attainable only through
popular involvement, which had inspired this experiment.

The thinker from whom Struve had absorbed this brand
of nationalism, and who of all the figures in the history of
Russian thought exerted on him the profoundest influence,
was Ivan Aksakov. Struve's admiration for him was born
early and never flagged. At twelve, Struve recalled, "his
first love in the realm of ideas were the Slavophiles in general
and [Aksakov] in particular." [16] As a child, carried away
by Aksakov's powerful editorials, he wrote in secret from
his family an article for *Rus'*.[17] Forty years later, on the
occasion of Aksakov's centennial, Struve described him as
the "foremost among Russia's publicists," ranking him higher
than both Herzen and Katkov, who, as he put it, "had
played themselves out performing for their own generation." [18]
Aksakov indeed provides the key to the innermost recesses
of Struve's political thought. His unique conservative-liberal-
nationalist ideology explains a great deal that is otherwise
puzzling in Struve.

Aksakov's politics cannot readily be fitted into the
familiar categories of Western political thought. He was
the leading spokesman of Slavophilism in its final phase,
after it had abandoned the cultural idealism of its early years
and turned into a political movement with strong xenophobic
overtones. As he grew older, Aksakov became increasingly
paranoid, inciting his readers against Poles, Germans, and
Jews, all of whom he blamed for Russia's misfortunes,
and whipping up public frenzy for imperialist ventures.
Viewed from this side, he may be characterized as a
reactionary nationalist and one of the ideological forerunners
of twentieth-century fascism.

But Aksakov's nationalism had to it another side, a strong
liberal strain not commonly associated with someone of his
xenophobic disposition. Like all the Slavophiles, he drew
a clear line separating the state (*vlast'*) from the land
(*zemlia*), or people (*narod*). To the state he conceded full
political authority, unrestrained by either constitution or
parliament, with the customary Slavophile qualification that

16. *Slavonic Review,* 2:6(1924), 515.
17. "Aksakovy i Aksakov," 350.
18. *Ibid.,* 349.

it respect the civil liberties of the people. In interpreting the state-land relationship, however, he went beyond the usual vague generalizations of his fellow Slavophiles. Unlike them, he did not idealize the common people of Russia. He did not think that the *narod* carried in its soul the secret of some higher truth lost to the educated; nor did he think that it was capable—as then constituted—of giving Russia a true national culture. Illiterate, and therefore of necessity culturally passive, the Russian people were to him only potentially a nation. To become one in reality, the *narod* had to raise itself to the higher level of *obshchestvo,* a term Aksakov understood in the sense of "society," and occasionally referred to by that English word.[19] "Society" was what the people created at a more advanced stage of Russia's historic evolution. It was "that environment in which a given people carries out its conscious intellectual activity, an environment which is created by the entire spiritual might of the people engaged in working out its national consciousness." [20]

The achievement of this level of consciousness was not possible without civil liberty. A passive people could create an active "society" only when permitted to educate itself, to engage in open discussion, and to gain experience in local self-government. True to his conviction, Aksakov fought relentlessly to improve and extend Russia's elementary and secondary schools, to safeguard the power of the zemstva and of the reformed courts, and to assure for the country freedom of speech. He detested the bureaucratic police regime of Nicholas I, which he had known in his youth. In the 1880s, when reactionaries were urging Alexander III to liquidate what was left of the reforms of his father and revert to the authoritarian regime of Nicholas I, Aksakov's was one of the loudest voices warning against the disastrous consequences of such a course. He thought it essential that the government draw its strength from the support of an enlightened citizenry and not from police repression. For his blunt critique of the government's foreign and domestic policies he was constantly harassed by the authorities, and he had more publications shot from under

19. Aksakov's remarkable essays on "society" from the early 1860s can be found in vol. 2 of his *Sochineniia,* 7 vols. (Moscow, 1886).
20. *Ibid.,* 33.

him than any contemporary liberal or radical publicist.

Aksakov's nationalism was as hostile to the radical intelligentsia as to the bureaucracy and police. To him, the intelligentsia was not an acceptable alternative to the Westernized elite that had run the country since Peter the Great, for it too had arrogated to itself the right to speak for the people. Its desire to reorganize the country in a preordained manner was as contrary to Russia's true interests as were the efforts of the bureaucrats to prevent Russia from developing at all. The people alone, speaking and acting freely, could work out the organization's national destiny. No one had the right to prevent it from so doing, and no one could act on its behalf.

Struve early adopted Aksakov's national ideal, which envisaged the creation of a Russian nation through the exercise of freedom of speech, education, and local self-government. Like Aksakov, he never treated the nation as something already given, something that, in order to flourish, merely required insulation from foreign influences, as did the run-of-the-mill Russian nationalists. From his earliest years he regarded Russian nationhood as lying still in the future: to him it was a task, not an inanimate object. That which Aksakov called by the English word "society" Struve described by the German word *Kultur* (culture). It was one of the basic terms in his vocabulary, meaning the conscious creation of an environment assuring the individual's and society's unrestrained search for identity. When in 1894 Struve spoke of the United States as enjoying the highest level of culture in the world,[21] he used the word in this Aksakovian sense; and so it appeared often in his subsequent writings.

Until the age of fifteen Struve adhered to this kind of nationalism, partly conservative, partly liberal. He expected the monarchy to continue along the lines chartered by the Great Reforms, to raise the level of culture and help the country create a nation, and he detested the revolutionaries for hindering this work. If the monarchy had indeed remained faithful to the reformism of the 1860s, Struve probably would never have changed his political views, for in his heart he was very much a German with an instinctive respect

---

21. *Kriticheskie zametki k voprosu ob ekonomicheskom razvitii Rossii*, 1(St. Petersburg, 1894), 91–92.

for the state as a creative force. But the government, as is
known, chose otherwise. In 1881, after brief hesitation, it
decided to abandon further attempts at bringing society into
partnership and to rely henceforth on repressive administration by the bureaucratic-police apparatus. The story of
Russian politics during the quarter of a century that followed
the assassination of Alexander II was one of relentless
constriction of that relatively limited sphere of public
activity granted society by the Great Reforms.

Aksakov saw all that happening, but was too old to
change. He expected to the end of his life to work for
Russian "society" within the framework of monarchical
absolutism. He rejected constitution and parliament,
convinced that they would serve only to divert the attention
of the Russian people from more urgent cultural tasks and
to perpetuate the domination of the country by the
Westernized elite. He was therefore content to confine his
demands to civil liberty.

As long as Aksakov was alive, Struve seems to have
thought in a similar manner. Then, in the winter of 1885–
1886, came an intellectual crisis, the first of several to come;
his faith in the monarchy was shaken. He became aware of
a fatal disparity that had developed between the government
and the country. The autocracy that since Peter the Great
had led a reluctant country toward culture had, after 1881,
lost its capacity to lead; worse than that, it had become a
burden that prevented the country from developing further
on its own. An ossified bureaucratic police establishment
could not direct a people whose leading spokesmen had
created a world literature and art, and whose educated
classes were engaged in an endless and impassioned discussion
of fundamental religious, political, and social questions. The
country had outgrown its government and could not survive
any longer without political liberty. As Struve recalled
half a century later, his love of political liberty was "born
of the enormous wealth of Russian spiritual and cultural
life, which obviously [had] ceased to fit the traditional legal
and political framework of autocracy or absolutism, even if
enlightened." [22]

This conviction must have come to him as a sudden
illumination, for he says his conversion to liberalism occurred

---

22. "My Contacts and Conflicts with Lenin," 584.

"with something like an elemental force." [23] Under what circumstances this happened can only be surmised, but there are strong indications that the crisis was connected with the last brush Aksakov had with censorship just before his death in January, 1886.

In November, 1885, Aksakov published in *Rus'* a particularly audacious attack on the government's policies in Bulgaria and blamed Russian diplomats for the deterioration in Russia's position in the Balkans. For this editorial he was formally reprimanded by the minister of the interior, who sent him a note accusing him of interpreting events "in a tone incompatible with true patriotism." As required by law, Aksakov published the reprimand without comment in the next issue of *Rus'*; but in the following issue he took it as the text for a scathing indictment of the whole bureaucratic conception of patriotism prevalent in the Russian government:

> We take the liberty of saying that the law itself does not empower the Main Publishing Administration to use such a formula of accusation, that it does not authorize the police, even its uppermost ranks, to cast doubts on anyone's "patriotism." We say "the police" because the Ministry of the Interior, in whose charge Russian literature has been since being removed, in 1863, from the competence of the Ministry of Education, is in the main a ministry of state police and can only administer literature from the police point of view. . . .
> Indeed, what is "true" and "untrue" patriotism? What are reliable symptoms of one and the other? What are the criteria for evaluating or even distinguishing them? From our point of view, for example, for a publicist true patriotism is to tell the government the truth, courageously and to the best of his understanding, no matter how hard and unpalatable; and for the government it is to listen to the truth, even when it is hard and unpalatable. In the opinion of many from the so-called higher spheres, the most genuine patriotism consists in cowering silence. . . .
> Is the government itself always acting in the spirit of faultless patriotism? . . . After all, the Russian enthusiasts of the Treaty of Berlin considered themselves also "true patriots," while "untrue patriots," like the editor of *Rus'*, see in their actions only patriotic thoughtlessness and cowardice. And can one, for instance, call unpatriotic that

23. *Ibid.*, 576.

sense of alarm which sent a shudder through all Russia
when it learned the terms of this treaty, an alarm which the
writer of these lines expressed in a public speech for
which the government meted out to him the well-known
punishment? . . . If this were so, then one would have
sometimes to charge all of Russian society and the whole of
the Russian people with lack of "true patriotism," and
to bestow a monopoly of genuineness exclusively on official
circles! . . .

The point is that in Russia the very word "patriotism"
still has a very imprecise meaning. Translated, it means
"love of fatherland." However, because of the special
circumstances attending the development of our public
life since the time of Peter the Great, there have emerged
in Russia, especially among its higher social strata, not a
few "patriots" who manage to separate the idea of the
"fatherland" from that of Russian nationality, and who
are ready to sacrifice their lives on the field of battle to
protect the fatherland's frontiers and honor, while at the
same time being estranged from their Russian nationality
and from Russian history and its legacy, of which they
want to know nothing and, of course, know nothing! In
other words, loving the vessel they scorn its content! Loving the "fatherland" they ignore and even feel contempt
for that which contains the inner meaning and cause of its
spiritual, moral, and political place in the world, and
which, consequently, defines its very destiny and mission.
It is understandable that such empty or one-sided patriotism
often enters into unconscious contradiction with Russian
national life, with the true national interests of Russia, caus-
ing between the one and the other at times a vast unbridge-
able chasm of tragic misunderstandings.[24]

This editorial made an overwhelming impression on
Struve. "Men of our generation read and reread it literally
with trembling and exultation," he wrote, "as a condemnation,
unexampled in its courage, of bureaucratic stupidity, and
an equally courageous defense of free speech." [25] "In our
family everybody read with enthusiasm Aksakov's passionate
and forceful answer to the censorship department, and in
my case it acted as the warm or even hot breeze in which
my own love of freedom finally matured." [26]

---

24. *Rus'* 23(December 6, 1885), 1–2.
25. "Aksakovy i Aksakov," 352.
26. "My Contacts and Conflicts with Lenin," 575.

For Struve, the essential point of Aksakov's reply lay in the final sentence of the excerpt: the implication that the imperial government and its ideologues had ceased to represent the "true national interests of Russia." Aksakov himself did not draw from his charge the obvious political conclusions. True to his Slavophile heritage, he treated the government as simply misguided. He was content to play the role of critic on the assumption that, by telling the government what the nation felt, he would bring it to its senses. Struve, however, pushed Aksakov's premise further: if it was true that the autocratic government no longer served Russia's national interests, then it had lost its usefulness and had to go.

The impulse of Struve's liberalism thus came from nationalism and remained rooted in it. Struve never gave up the hope that the government would come to realize the country's absolute need for freedom, and would of its own accord, for the sake of the future of Russia, transfer power to the people. Its stubborn refusal to do what he considered both right and unavoidable incensed him and drove him steadily leftward, from hatred of revolutionaries to admiration and even verbal support. But he was always willing to make peace with the monarchy, and would at all times have preferred to have it grant political liberty on its own accord than to have liberty wrested from it. To understand Struve's political evolution it is essential to keep this fact in mind. His opposition to absolutism was the fruit of the disappointment of a man who had grown up on the ideals of the Great Reforms, who throughout his youth saw them betrayed, and who had as his fondest hope seeing them reactivated.

Between 1885 and 1888 Struve drew his liberal inspiration mainly from two sources. One was the monthly *Messenger of Europe* (*Vestnik Evropy*). Around 1885 he met and made friends with K. K. Arseniev, the leading writer for the *Messenger*. Struve greatly admired the column "Domestic Survey" (*Vnutrennee obozrenie*), in which Arseniev month after month flayed the bureaucracy and championed the cause of law and freedom.[27] In his apartment on the Moika, Arseniev held a literary salon to which he invited young men to lecture to his guests—luminaries of the Saint Petersburg intelligentsia—among them many contributors

27. *Ibid.*, 575–76.

to the *Messenger*. Struve began to frequent this salon while still a gymnasium student and continued to do so after enrolling at the university. There he became acquainted with the philosopher Vladimir Soloviev, the literary historian Alexander Pypin, the trial lawyer A. F. Koni, and many others.[28] There too he made his literary debut. At Arseniev's invitation he read two papers, one on Shakespeare's *Tempest,* the other on the poetry of Nadson. The Shakespearean lecture was so brilliant that it dazzled even Arseniev and his sophisticated audience.[29] Arseniev took Struve under his wing and by his patronage helped him to enter unusually early in life the circle of Saint Petersburg literati.[30]

The other source of Struve's liberal inspiration was the novels of Saltykov-Shchedrin, his favorite reading in school.[31] The picture that Saltykov-Shchedrin painted of contemporary Russia, like Gogol's somber to the point of grotesqueness,

28. Struve left scattered recollections of Arseniev's salon in the following newspaper articles: "Pamiati A. F. Koni," *Rossiia,* 12(November 12, 1927); *Rossiia i Slavianstvo,* 38(August 17, 1929), 39(August 24, 1929), and 214(February 11, 1933). Among those who frequented it he listed, in addition, the literary historians V. D. Spasovich and S. A. Andreevsky and his university friends B. V. Nikolsky, N. D. Vodovozov, and N. P. Pavlov-Silvansky.

29. I. V. Hessen, *V dvukh vekakh* (Berlin, 1937), 252. On Struve's Nadson lecture, see his own remarks in *Rossiia i Slavianstvo,* 214(February 11, 1933).

30. On November 15, 1907, on the occasion of Arseniev's literary jubilee, Struve sent him the following letter: "In your person I would like to hail a remarkable Westerner-humanist, a man who firmly upheld the standard of true liberalism during the most difficult years in Russia's existence. I would like to tell you how much I owe to you in my political development both as an individual and as a representative of that Russian youth which in the 1880's and 1890's learned so much from the *Messenger of Europe.*" Manuscript, Pushkin House, Leningrad, Arkhiv Arsen'eva, *Fond* 359, Item No. 467. The same archival deposit has another letter from Struve to Arseniev, dated December 3, 1894, expressing admiration for the masterly survey—which was printed in the *Messenger*—of the reign of the recently deceased Alexander III. See *Vestnik Evropy,* December, 1894, 840–53. In one of those casual asides so exasperating to his biographer, Struve said that while a student he had contributed regular listings of current books to "a periodical." *Mech,* 42/75(October 27, 1935). This periodical was almost certainly the *Messenger of Europe.*

31. "My Contacts and Conflicts with Lenin," 576.

increased Struve's loathing for absolutist Russia and sharpened his resolve to see it radically changed.

As he entered the last year of gymnasium (1888–1889) he was a nationalist and a liberal, but as yet lacked a political program. Struve knew what he wanted but not how to get it; his politics were still less of an ideology than an attitude. It is in this mood that he began to read Marx and between 1888 and 1892 became a Social Democrat.

V. A. MAKLAKOV AND THE
WESTERNIZER TRADITION IN RUSSIA

David A. Davies

With Russian liberalism intimately connected to the
whole process of Russia's Westernization, Russians who
aspired to the development of liberal institutions were
consequently compelled to come to grips with the essential
elements of European liberalism. They were also confronted
with the necessity of discerning how European liberalism
could best be fostered in a land that did not include much
of Europe's institutional heritage. In some respects the
variations among Russia's liberals were reducible to the old
problem of Russia and Europe: that is, how they viewed
European liberalism and how they saw Russia in relation
to it.

Vasilii Alekseevich Maklakov, a prominent Moscow lawyer,
Duma member, and Kadet, classified Europe and Russia
in different categories than did most of the other leaders
of his party. At the root of his liberalism lay a different
understanding of what the essence of European liberalism
was, and, among Russian liberals, a somewhat different
perception of what Russia was. As a result, he was able to
contribute some fresh and important insights to the problems
connected with Russian liberalism.[1]

---

1. Maklakov is familiar to most students of Russian liberalism
as a liberal who differed in some important respects from the
dominant thinking in the Kadet party. This reputation derives
less from his pre-1917 career than from his post-1917 writings,
which included a retrospective analysis of Russian liberalism and
established him as the chief liberal critic of his party's tactics.
These writings include four books: *Vlast' i obshchestvennost' na
zakate staroi Rossii* (Paris, 1936); *Pervaia gosudarstvennaia duma*
(Paris, 1939); *Vtoraia gosudarstvennaia duma: vospominaniia
sovremennika* (Paris, n.d.); and *Iz vospominannii* (New York,
1954), as well as numerous articles, many of which were published
in *Sovremennye zapiski* between 1929 and 1936.

Two recent historians of Russian liberalism have found

Maklakov's attitude toward Europe fell within the Westernizer tradition. He thought of himself as a European and looked to the West as the main source of example for Russia's future. He also could appreciate that Russia's past was not a blank sheet of paper, and that her "peculiarities" were not merely anachronisms but viable traditions that hindered the immediate full application of Western social theories to Russian reality. Aware of the immense differences that still existed between many aspects of Russia and those of Western Europe, he believed that revolutionary upheaval, far from bringing Russia closer to Europe, could instead eradicate those European features that had begun to emerge in Russian life. Maklakov was not the first one to face this Westernizer dilemma, but his insights into it have particular relevance in understanding the problems accompanying true Westernization in the last years of the tsarist regime.

In its purist form, the Westernizer tradition in Russia was simply a commitment to the path of West European development. It did not imply so much a love of the West as it did a rejection of Russia's pre-Petrine past as a possible source for a unique Russian development outside of a European framework. It also carried a possible radical bias, since it regarded so much of Russia's past as a blank sheet and consequently ignored possible impediments to full Westernization. By Maklakov's time, however, the whole Westernizer concept had taken on greater complexity. The West was increasingly seen not as one entity, but as many different components simultaneously conservative, liberal,

---

Maklakov's writings to be so persuasive that their interpretations of the failure of Russian liberalism are based almost exclusively on them. See Victor Leontovitsch, *Geschichte des Liberalismus in Russland* (Frankfurt, 1957), and Jacob Walkin, *The Rise of Democracy in Pre-revolutionary Russia* (New York, 1962). Other historians who do not accept his arguments, nonetheless have felt compelled to deal with them. See Mare Raeff, "Some Reflections on Russian Liberalism," *Russian Review,* 18(1959), 218–30, and Thomas Riha, *A Russian European: Paul Miliukov in Russian Politics,* 334–35. Maklakov has been portrayed as a liberal of a different type in a penetrating article by Michael Karpovich "Two Types of Russian Liberalism: Maklakov and Miliukov" in Ernest J. Simmons, ed., *Continuity and Change in Russian and Soviet Thought,* 129–43. The present essay is concerned less with Maklakov's polemics than with some of the fundamentals of his thought.

and radical. Bismarck was undeniably European, for example, but so was Marx.

This variety of composition meant that Westernizer attitudes in Russia could follow diverse paths. Russian Marxists, for example, could be consistent Westernizers even while simultaneously showing the deepest hostility to what they conceived to be the basic reality of the West—capitalism. They were, instead, committed to a belief in the European future as revealed in the writings of Marx and Engels, the seeds of which they thought had already appeared. In a broader sense, all Russians who shared a positivist outlook were also committed not so much to the European present, but to the promise of progress in the European future which, they believed, would be Russia's future as well.

The dominant leaders of Russia's Constitutional-Democratic party were Westernizers in this sense. Most of them had strong intellectual roots in European positivism, believed in the universality of European institutions, and shared the assumption, common to much of European thinking in the nineteenth century, that these institutions were progressing inexorably toward parliamentary democracy. As the name of their party implied, these Kadets particularly identified with the contemporary neo-Liberal elements in England and France—the Lib-Labs and the French Radicals. They shared with these groups a belief that liberalism should be wedded to democracy and the democratic state used positively as an instrument for realizing the liberal ideal. They were critical of many aspects of Europe that impeded the full flowering of this ideal, but they believed these aspects to be vestiges of a European past that would have no place in the European future.[2]

Maklakov did not share this positivist background. Born in 1869, he was a whole generation removed from the older leaders of his party, most of whom had reached maturity before the assassination of Alexander II. Their formative years preceded the disillusionment of the 1880s, which helped emancipate Maklakov's generation from much of the

---

2. See, for example, Paul Miliukov's speech at the founding congress of the Constitutional-Democratic party in 1905, in which he said: "Our party closest of all approaches those intellectual Western groups who are known under the name of social reformers." K-D Partiia, *S"ezd 12–18 oktiabria, 1905* (St. Petersburg, 1905), 7.

intelligentsia heritage. In his memoirs, Maklakov recalls that "some kind of precipice already divided us"[3] from the previous generation and some of its assumptions.[4] "The enthusiasm of the [eighteen] sixties seemed naïve to us," he later wrote.

> We were carried away neither by "materialism" nor "atheism" nor "positivism." All this we outgrew and did not understand how [people such as] Pisarev could have been a ruler of men's minds. But we did not have opposing faiths. We looked on everything with the eyes of skeptics.[5]

Maklakov's liberalism was, therefore, conditioned very early by a skepticism that shunned neat formulas and the all-encompassing explanations of reality associated with the intelligentsia heritage. If the period of his youth corresponded with a time when the Russian intelligentsia was more passive, it also corresponded with the beginning of a major change in European thinking away from the prevailing rationalism and materialism of the nineteenth century toward that more complex and less systematic view of the world that forms the intellectual background to the thought of our own century. Whether it be labeled the "revolt against positivism," or against "formalism," or "a change in the public spirit of Europe," most historians recognize that the trend away from the optimism of the nineteenth-century thought had its roots in the 1880s.[6]

Maklakov's particular evolution must be seen as occurring within the early undefined stages of this important shift in European thinking. His liberalism took form in contact with

---

3. Maklakov, *Vlast' i obshchestvennost'*, 80.
4. This generation gap was later dramatized by the controversy within the liberal intelligentsia in 1909 when contributors, born mostly in the 1870s, published a book of articles criticizing the intelligentsia tradition. M. Gershenzon, ed., *Vekhi: sbornik statei o russkoi intelligentsii* (Moscow, 1909). This evoked a sharp counterattack by the older generation of liberals in I. I. Petrunkevich and P. Miliukov, eds., *Intelligentsiia v Rossii: sbornik statei* (St. Petersburg, 1910).
5. Maklakov, *Vlast' i obshchestvennost'*, 83.
6. These phrases derive from the following studies in intellectual history: H. Stuart Hughes, *Consciousness and Society* (London, 1959); Morton White, *Social Thought in America: The Revolt Against Formalism* (Boston, 1959); Bennedetto Croce, *History of Europe in the Nineteenth Century* (London, 1931).

critical-minded Russian liberals, such as Paul Vinogradov, his mentor at Moscow University, whose views, while wholly sympathetic to the ultimate ideals of European liberalism, were characterized by a willingness to re-examine the root assumptions of liberal democracy in the face of mounting doubts about its inevitability. In the introduction to his highly praised book *Villainage in England,* published while Maklakov was his student, he wrote that the

> liberal creed has been, on the whole, an eminently idealist one, assuming the easy perfectability of human nature, the sound common sense of the many, the regulating influence of consciousness of instinct, the immense value of high political aspirations for the regeneration of mankind. In every single attempt at realizing its high-flying hopes the brutal side of human nature has made itself felt very effectually, and has become all the more conspicuous just by reason of the ironical contrast between aims and means.[7]

Aware of, in his own words, "a growing distrust among scholars for preconceived theories . . . ," Vinogradov sought to base his genuine liberal aspirations for Russia on foundations other than the idea of progress. Rather than viewing liberal ideals as some sort of inevitable historical trend, he worked to advance the currents of Russian life that contributed to these hopes, not forgetting the existence of other realities less favorable, or the persistence of what he called "unconscious tradition" which, as he showed in all his studies, would always play a role in human development.

Vinogradov's views strikingly foreshadow the assumptions that became the foundations of Maklakov's particular brand of liberalism. Maklakov's attitude toward Europe did not include the future-mindedness of many of his liberal contemporaries. He did not identify primarily with Europe's anticipated future; rather, he responded to the European present. He admired European civilization for its existing accomplishments and past history, which he appreciated as producing a milieu conducive to liberalism.

By 1905, Maklakov was thoroughly familiar with much of Europe, especially France, which he had visited extensively first in 1889, again in 1890, and then virtually every year after 1896. He spoke French fluently and gradually gained

7. Paul Vinogradoff, *Villainage in England* (London, 1892), 30.

close contact with French society, acquiring with these experiences an admiration for French life and an attraction to its special characteristics.

That Maklakov closely identified with France is clear from his later account of his first visit to Paris in 1889, as a college youth of twenty. This visit coincided with the centennial of the French Revolution, and he was overwhelmed by the exhibitions that commemorated it, as well as by the general vitality of French society. He was duly impressed, for example, by the newly completed Eiffel Tower and saw in it not only Western technical achievement, but also the triumph of modern organization where complexity had been ordered into the shaping of a single magnificent whole. In his own mind he compared the tower to the Egyptian pyramids, but noted that it "was built not as the pyramids were built, not by a despotism of pharaohs with slave labor, but by a Republic under a regime of freedom." [8] What most impressed Maklakov was not so much the technical excellence manifested in the building of the Eiffel Tower, but rather the kind of society that had produced it.

In other ways too, he was amazed at the open, organized activity apparent to him in French public life. During his visit he witnessed the election in which General Boulanger seemed to challenge the institutions of the young Third Republic and was impressed by the way French society supported those institutions and the existing state. In fostering spontaneous initiative in public life, the French Regime had apparently contributed to its own stability and strength. "It was useful," he later wrote,

> to see in Europe that the pressure of state power on a person was not at all an attribute of a strong state, that the right of the state could be combined with the rights of the "individual.". . . it was instructive to observe with my own eyes that in France people valued not only their own freedom, but also the system of their state. [9]

While in France in 1889, the young Maklakov established close ties with the leaders of student associations in Paris. He noted the wide latitude of organized activity in which students could legally engage and admired the spontaneity and initiative that French students possessed in confronting

8. Maklakov, *Iz vospominanii*, 92.
9. *Ibid.*, 92–93.

many of the practical problems of student life. He left France at the end of the summer in a mood of euphoria, completely convinced of the advantages that societal initiative gave to French citizens, and hopeful that he could foster among his fellow students at Moscow University a possibility of similar organization and initiative. He left Paris not only bewitched, but also committed to the form of society and institutions reflected by that city.

These observations reveal that what Maklakov most admired in France was its institutional pluralism, which allowed French society autonomy in its activities in a way that did not undermine order and stability in the state. What attracted Maklakov was "the way Frenchmen related to their regime." [10] He perceived that in France the relationship between state and society was not antithetical, but reciprocal, the state providing a stable framework of law and fostering societal development in a way beneficial to both France and her citizens. By doing this the political institutions in France seemed to reconcile not only state and society, but also order and freedom, authority and spontaneity. This was in striking contrast to relationships in his native Russia where a gulf of suspicion and hostility separated state and society.

Maklakov thus regarded the French example with much sympathy and in many ways it became the touchstone for those aspects of European liberalism he particularly wished to see develop in Russia. With this in mind it is not too much to suggest that, for Maklakov, European liberalism consisted of an institutional pluralism in which both the state and elements of society outside the state—both as groups and individuals—have substantive rights, and in which the inevitable conflicts between them are settled by recourse to law.

Undoubtedly his ideas in 1889 were not this concretely formulated and the account in his memoirs in part represents the later thinking of the mature Maklakov; yet his activities and early ideas upon his return to Russia in 1889 clearly suggest a close connection with his later thinking. The young Maklakov thought in categories conducive to awareness of social pluralism in Europe, and his activities in Moscow represented an attempt to be a part of an emerging pluralism in Russia. When he returned to Moscow in 1889, he did so

---

10. *Ibid.,* 94.

"with the presumptuous thought that I will bring Russia together with Europe." [11]

The Moscow to which Maklakov returned was in many respects the most favorable environment in Russia in which to foster societal development and what he called "independent activity" (*samodeiatel'nost'*), which was the basis of Western pluralism. As the second city in a centrally administered empire, Moscow was a natural focal point for resentment against the bureaucratically imposed decrees emanating from Saint Petersburg. As the ancient capital it was the logical center for Slavophile ideas, which, in emphasizing the need for more social autonomy—focusing on society instead of the state—ironically fostered an aspect of Europe's liberal heritage that had not yet developed in Russia.[12]

In the 1890s Moscow experienced a particularly strong surge of social activity aimed at confronting local issues in a way that would involve participation of numerous groups and individuals who were part of the public instead of the state bureaucracy. Educated leaders of Moscow society, such as Paul Vinogradov, became public figures who symbolized the gradual emergence of a pluralistic society in Russia.[13] Commenting on this trend the historian Bernard

---

11. *Ibid.*, 107.

12. Bernard Pares once wrote that "Old Moscow in contradistinction to the new bureaucratic barracks of St. Petersburg, was always the home of the idea of local self-government." "The Public Man," *Slavonic Review*, 4(1926), 546. More recently Martin Malia has written that Moscow in the nineteenth century was "the capital of the gentry and the focus of whatever sentiment of independence that class possessed." *Alexander Herzen and the birth of Russian Socialism* (Cambridge, Mass., 1961), 58.

13. Throughout his writings Maklakov used the abstract noun *obshchestvennost'* to label the emerging nongovernmental public groups composed of civic leaders, journalists, professional men, etc., whose presence constituted an acknowledged social reality by 1900. The word has been variously translated as "society," "community leaders," or "the public." Leontovitsch renders it in German as *Offentlichkeit*, a word that connotes public elements. See his *Geschichte des Liberalismus in Russland*, 32–33n21. The term *public man* (*obschestvennyi deiatel'*) was used in the literature of the period to designate the educated and articulate leaders of the public as distinct from the bureaucracy on the one hand and the people on the other.

Pares, present in Moscow during much of this period, later wrote:

> In the old *regime,* which was an abortive collectivism, there had never yet been that which Vinogradov and his fellow workers tried to create—a school of practical public service, based on direct responsibility to the public, and on the free cooperation of a mass of independent individual wills.[14]

Such organizations as the Moscow zemstvo, the Moscow city duma, the Moscow Society of Jurisprudence, the Moscow Circle of Public Defenders, the Illiteracy Committee and Literary Fund, the Imperial Moscow Society of Agriculture, as well as student associations in Moscow University, became thriving examples of the growing vitality of Russian society and provided a focus through which educated Muscovites could involve themselves in public affairs.[15]

Maklakov was very much a part of the current in Moscow in the 1890s, first as a student and later as a lawyer. He was a member of several student associations, social circles, and lawyer societies that were active in public affairs during the period. Thus, his aspirations for Russian society, though drawn from his observations in Paris, found an outlet in the possibilities for societal development that existed in his native Moscow. These possibilities appeared to him to provide the best hope for dissolving the barriers that separated the isolated intelligentsia from responsible public tasks. They could also contribute to that healthy reciprocal relation between state and society which, to Maklakov, was the essence of Europe.

The emergence of this trend of social Westernization in Russia, along with some parallel trends in law, economic development, and, eventually, national politics, suggested to Maklakov that Russia was merging more completely with those European institutions he admired. His Westernizer outlook still contained a distinctive awareness of the limitations of Westernization in his own time and, more than others of his general persuasion, he acknowledged that the European elements in Russia were overshadowed by

14. Pares, "The Public Man," 545–46.
15. For reports on these activities, see *Sbornik ocherkov po gorodu Moskvy: Obshchiia svedeniia po gorodu i obzor deiatel'-nosti Moskovskago Gorodskago Obshchestvennago Upravleniia* (Moscow, 1897).

the persistence of social, economic, and political realities
that were part of Russia's non-European heritage. He sensed
that these realities crucially limited the pace of Westernization
and could not be ignored.

Here again Maklakov contrasted with the majority of his
colleagues who were Westernizers of the more usual kind.
Though they were not unaware of Russia's non-European
heritage, they tended to disparage its possible influence on
contemporary developments. Paul Miliukov, for example,
acknowledged Russia's past divergencies from Europe, but
regarded them as anachronisms without real relevance for
the future.[16]

Maklakov joined the Constitutional-Democratic party
because he believed it to be the party of Westernization in
Russia. His view of Russia gave him a somewhat different
conception of its role: for him, the Kadet party was a kind
of vanguard, not of revolution, but of Europe.

> Among a backward and therefore generally conservative
> population as were the Russian people, the Kadets were
> the advanced intellectual group, the few advocates of a
> *European ideal* not familiar to Russia.[17]

Maklakov thus made a definite distinction between an
emerging Westernized society of educated Russians and the
mass of the Russian people who were not yet a full part
of the European culture. He suspected that there was not
necessarily an inviolable connection between the European
idea of parliamentary democracy, espoused by the Kadet
party, and the will of the Russian people.[18]

This circumstance was partially acknowledged soon after
the party's birth in 1905 when its Central Committee decided
to add the subtitle "Party of Popular Freedom" to its name
—an indirect admission that the concepts of constitution
and democracy, words foreign and Western, had no real
meaning for the populace at large.[19] Most Kadets continued

---

16. Paul Miliukov, *Russia and its Crisis*, 14–16, 117–21. See
also his article "Dva neprimirimykh tipa," *God bor'by* (St.
Petersburg, 1907), 342.

17. Maklakov, *Pervaia gosudarstvennaia duma*, 9.

18. Maklakov, "1905–1906 gody," in Paul Miliukov et al.,
*M. M. Vinaver i russkaia obshchestvennost' v nachale XX veka:
sbornik statei* (Paris, 1937), 74–75.

19. "Kadety v 1905–1906 gg. (Materialy Tsk Partii Narodnoi
Svobody)," *Krasnyi arkhiv*, 46(1931), 49. Kadet attempts to

to assume that their aspirations for Russia accurately reflected the will of the people. The membership of the party, however, remained essentially that of educated society. Like other intelligentsia-based parties in Russia, it may have thought of itself as representing the people, as being for the people, but it was certainly not *of* the people. Reports sent to its Central Committee from provincial branches, while expressing aspirations to bring the party closer to the people, admitted that such ties were virtually nonexistent. Furthermore, these reports stressed that, to quote from one of them, "a broad layer of the city and especially village population is politically and socially completely undeveloped." [20]

This was a reality that Maklakov always kept in mind. As one of the most active orators during the election campaign to the First Duma, he mixed with the populace more than most in his party.[21] He had few illusions about the tentative nature of the connection between the Kadet party and the people who voted for it in 1906. There were still too many gaps separating the mass of Russians from Europe. The zemstvo was a school for effective local government, but it was barely a beginning. The Judicial Reform of 1864 was an important measure, but a rule of law was far from being an established reality.[22] The proletariat was more peasant than worker in its mentality; and the peasantry, the great majority of the population, was still a class apart. Economically, peasants were no longer serfs, but they were not yet inde-

---

make "constitution," "parliament," and "constituent assembly" intelligible to the populace resulted in the publication of a vast number of election pamphlets that elaborated these concepts in the simplest possible language. See, for example, *Krest'ianam i rabochim o konstitutsionnoi-demokraticheskoi Partii* (Moscow, 1906).

20. *Doklad Kommissii ob obrazovanii partiinykh organizatsii v uezdakh Saratovskoi Gubernii* (Saratov, 1905). According to Kadet records, by mid-1906 the party had local organizations in fifty provinces throughout Russia, but almost all of these were embryonic and usually consisted of members from the educated elite. Their ties to the populace at large remained inconclusive. See *Alfavitnyi spisok adresov mestnykh grupp Konstitutsionnoi-demokraticheskoi partii* (St. Petersburg, 1906).

21. Maklakov, "Sredi izbiratelei," *Russkie vedomosti,* 83(March 26, 1906), 2–3.

22. Maklakov, "Zakonnost' v russkoi zhizni," *Vestnik Evropy,* 44(May, 1909), 238–75.

pendent farmers. Legally, they were free from the arbitrary
judgments and penalties of the landlord; but they were still
separated from other classes by communal restrictions and
subject to special peasant courts that had no jurisdiction over
the rest of the population.[23] While educated Russians in the
nineteenth century had produced cultural works that were
outstanding and European, this culture was as yet not understood by the majority, who still lived in a condition of cultural
backwardness.

Thus, while Maklakov saw that the European elements
within Russia were hopeful signs from his point of view, he
also recognized that they existed in a largely non-European
environment that only time could change. Like infant
industries, they needed protection, and could not flourish in
the midst of upheaval. For this reason, even though his
identification with Europe was full and complete, he felt that
Russia could merge with Europe only through evolution and
gradual change.[24]

This was the basis of Maklakov's instinctive fear of revolution. He knew that in a largely non-European environment
there was no reason to assume that mass revolutionary
upheaval would really follow European precedents or move
Russia any closer to real Westernization. On the contrary,
one might expect that revolution would wipe out those
elements of European civilization that were beginning to be
so apparent.[25]

Thus, Maklakov was a Westernizer of a particular kind. His
priorities for Russian liberalism suggested the importance of
social and legal Westernization more than political and
economic. He identified with the European present rather
than with the European future. In a Russia that appeared to
be moving rapidly towards Europe, he remained painfully
aware of the heritage of the past and the essential fragility of
Russia's European society. He would have agreed with the
Dutch historian Pieter Geyl, who later wrote: "We are
incessantly freeing ourselves from our past, but at the same
time it maintains a sway over us." [26]

23. Maklakov, "The Agrarian Problem in Russia Before the
Revolution," *Russian Review*, 9(1950), 3–15.

24. Maklakov, *Iz vospominanii*, 104.

25. *Ibid.*, 344–51. See also his *Vlast' i obshchestvennost'*,
406–7.

26. Pieter Geyl, *Debates with Historians* (London, 1955), 236.

RELATIONS BETWEEN THE FINNISH RESISTANCE MOVEMENT AND THE RUSSIAN LIBERALS, 1899–1904

William R. Copeland

One of the most persistent and serious deficiencies of the Russian opposition movement was its inability to forge a united front against autocracy. Until the twentieth century, efforts to form alliances against the government failed because of police repression and the unfavorable political conditions prevailing in Russia. A special problem was the doctrinaire and intolerant attitude of antigovernment groups, which tended to expend far more energy in internecine warfare than in political opposition to the government. Cooperation between Russian factions and the opposition organizations of the Russian national minorities was even more problematic. Where common social and political outlook promised the organizations unity, nationalism pulled them apart. The generation of sufficient affinity between the various Russian and minority groups was slow and rarely produced tangible consequences.[1]

Cooperation was achieved before 1905, however, between the Russian liberals and the most separatist oriented national minority resistance organization, the Finnish opposition.[2] As

---

1. The first serious effort at cooperation between the Russian underground and the Polish resistance organizations occurred during the 1825 Decembrist revolt. Finns also became active participants in 1863 when an attempt was made to involve Sweden in the Polish revolt. See Anatole Mazour, *The First Russian Revolution, 1825: The Decembrist Movement* (Stanford, 1961), and Michael Futrell, *Northern Underground* (London, 1963).

2. With minor exceptions, Finnish separatism until 1899 was a highly conservative concept focusing its attention solely on Finland's autonomous position and having no relationship to what transpired in Russia proper. So long as Finland's separateness was respected in St. Petersburg, Finns constituted a force supporting *status quo* in the Empire. Separatism was so force-

the attempted cooperation between the Finnish opposition and the Russian liberals illustrates, several factors were present that served to advance the development of cooperation, but more importantly, strong factors that inhibited the development of closer ties were also present.

For close to nine decades relations between the Grand Duchy of Finland and the Russian government were profoundly influenced by the policies and traditions established by Alexander I in 1809.[3] Finland existed as a contented, autonomous entity retaining nearly all of the indigenous institutions it had inherited from the Swedish period of its history. The stability of Russo-Finnish coexistence was maintained through adroit and farsighted statesmanship on the part of the Finnish administrators in Saint Petersburg and Helsinki. Finnish state secretaries evolved and cultivated a highly pragmatic "foreign policy" designed to maintain a safe margin between the vital interests of Russia and Finland.[4] As time passed, however, Finland's anomalous position became increasingly apparent and the safe margin became threatened as the end of the nineteenth century approached.

A series of largely unrelated developments in the two societies gradually led to a deterioration of Russo-Finnish relations. Of fundamental importance was the rise of aggressive Russian nationalism which, in the second half of the nineteenth century, became an important political factor and reinforced earlier tendencies toward administrative centralization in the Russian Empire. By the early 1890s the Finns experienced increasing difficulty in warding off attempts to extend centralization to Finland. Both Alexander III and Nicholas II displayed a profound preference for conservative advisors whose anti-Finnish agitation formed a part of the broader Russification policy then associated with the complete centralization of government functions and administration.

---

fully ingrained in Finnish thinking that total "deseparatization" did not occur until the personal tie represented by Nicholas II was destroyed in March, 1917.

3. Russia acquired Finland in 1809 from Sweden at which time, for reasons of political and military expediency, Russia granted far-reaching autonomy to Finland. See Päiviö Tommila, *La Finlande dans la politique européenne en 1809–1815* (Lahti, 1962).

4. Keijo Korhonen, *Suomen asian komitea: Suomen korkeimman hallinnon järjestelyt ja toteuttaminen vuosina 1811–1826* (Turku, 1963), 332–33.

By early 1899 these advisors had generated the necessary momentum to reverse long-established traditions and the advantages for the imperial government of the *status quo* in Finland.[5]

The unfolding of Russification in Finland can be traced in a series of laws, manifestoes, and lesser administrative decrees promulgated between February, 1899, and June, 1904.[6] The keynote in the attack upon Finland's autonomy was the February Manifesto of 1899, which attacked "Finnish separatism" piecemeal and prepared the way for and sanctioned all of the subsequent violations of existing agreements. The February Manifesto subordinated Finnish legislative process to imperial legislation, and relations between Russia and Finland were placed on a substantially new footing.

From the very beginning of the "first oppressive period," as Finnish historians call the years 1899–1905, the Finnish population left no doubt that it intended to resist these "illegal" measures. Russo-Finnish relations during these years are the history of the confrontation between Governor-General

---

5. Pressure against Finland's special privileges began very soon after the conclusion of the Porvoo Agreement in 1809, subsiding and flaring into the open again after 1863. Leading publicists, G. Katkov, K. F. Ordin, M. Borodkin, and F. Yelenev hammered away at Finland, precipitating an intense duel between Finnish historians and publicists and the Russian "Finn-eaters," as the Finns called them. The first serious transgression against Finland's autonomy occurred in 1890 when the autonomous Finnish postal system was incorporated into the Russian postal system. For best accounts in English, see Eino Jutikkala and Kauko Pirinen, *A History of Finland* (New York, 1962), 186–237, and John Wuorinen, *A History of Finland* (New York, 1967).

6. The major Russification manifestoes were: Manifesto of February 15, 1899, which transferred the power to legislate from the Finnish Estates to the Sovereign and opened the way for a radical reorganization of the Finnish army and its subordination to the Russian minister of war; Manifesto of June 20, 1900 (the Language Manifesto), which established a timetable for dates by which various Finnish departments had to adopt Russian as the official language; Manifesto of July 12, 1901 (Conscription Manifesto), which decreed the practical reorganization of the Finnish army. Most Finnish military units were disbanded on the authority of this law, and the prospect that Finnish conscripts would have to serve three years in Russia came into being; March 26, 1903, Nicholas Bobrikov, Governor-General of Finland, was granted extraordinary powers "to restore law and order" in Finland.

Nicholas I. Bobrikov and the Finnish resistance movement.[7] The struggle, which may be said in its fullest sense to date from February, 1899, was initially conducted with considerable self-restraint on both sides. The Finns, accustomed to successful dealings with the Russians for nine decades, had no wish to arouse their mighty neighbor by undue intransigeance. The Russians, concerned chiefly with the success of their centralization program, were willing to tolerate opposition as long as no real danger threatened.

Two basic assumptions determined the initial Finnish response to Russification: that West European opinion could significantly alter Russian domestic decision-making, and that the Sovereign remained unaware of developments in Finland. The first assumption was responsible for the mounting of an orchestrated propaganda campaign in Western Europe designed to pressure the Russian government to withdraw the Manifesto of February 15 or at least to obstruct further implementation of it.[8] The direction of Finnish resistance activity was thus determined by its preoccupation with propaganda as a weapon against the Russian threat.

The initial organization of the opposition (1899–1901) was determined primarily by the needs of the domestic-international propaganda campaign.[9] Requirements of the

7. The best general account of the First Oppressive Period is Päiviö Tommila, ed., *Venäläinen sortokausi Soumessa* (Porvoo, 1960).

8. The international propaganda campaign culminated in the ill-fated International Cultural Appeal of June, 1899, which was signed by 1,050 of Europe's most eminent scientists and cultural notables. Nicholas II refused to receive a delegation led by A. E. Nordesjöld, who journeyed to St. Petersburg in late June, 1899, to present the appeal to the Russian Tsar. The most notable consequence of this attempt was to rally the slighted European liberal intellectuals to the defense of the Finnish cause. A "Great Deputation" of 500 Finnish representatives on March 13, 1899, attempted to present to Nicholas II, their Grand Duke, an address signed by 522,931 Finns that sought to inform their Sovereign what was transpiring in Finland. Nicholas II refused to receive them. Adolf Törngren, *På utländsk botten: Från Finlands författningskamp, Åren 1899–1914* (Helsinki, 1930), 41–73; Bernhard Estlander, *Elva årtionden ur Finlands historia, 1898–1908,* which is vol. 3 of 3 vols. (Helsinki, 1922–1923), 33–45.

9. The Finnish propaganda effort was conducted through various loosely organized committees set up in April, 1899. Their functions and responsibilities were redefined in early 1900 and

moment better explain the method, composition, and organization of the various secret committees than do plans to form
a permanent opposition. A number of rather constant factors
accounted for a gradual radicalization of the resistance
effort, the most important of which was the degree of
provocation, or Russification, generated by the Russian
administration. Other factors that influenced the evolution
of Finnish resistance included the success that greeted
resistance, the degree of unity among the Finns,[10] and the
example of the Russian opposition movement. The Finns had
been conscious of the existence of the Russian antigovernment movement for some time, but it had no influence in
Finland until after 1899.

In early 1899 a number of clandestine opposition
organizations experienced in the art of political opposition
flourished in Russia. It was only when they discovered that
the course of Russian policy in Finland was likely to create
opposition in the Grand Duchy that they prepared to establish
relations with Finnish groups. A profusion of contacts took
place between the Finnish resistance movement and members

again in August, 1901. In so far as these committees had a leader,
it was Leo Mechelin. Passive resistance was defined officially in
1901, and in September–October, 1901, a radical faction of the
opposition movement formed the "Kagaali," an involved underground organization aimed at resisting the implementation of the
new conscription laws.

10. The inability of Finland to formulate a unified response to
Russification had its basis in the language struggle of the 1870s
and the 1880s, when the Finnish party made intense effort to give
the Finnish language equality with the Swedish language in Finland. When Russification overtook Finland, elements of this
party took the position that compromise and conciliation
would best limit Russian aims in Finland and that resistance
would be useless and counterproductive in the face of
Russia's superior power. Bobrikov's administration cooperated
with the Fennoman party, which was able to retain and
even capture new administrative positions while the opposition, composed of the Swecomans (Finnish Swedes) and the
Young Finns, was gradually purged from all levels of government. Relations between the Conciliatories and the Opposition
became extremely bitter, and both sides expended much propaganda in this dispute, the chief benefactor of which was, of
course, Bobrikov. Taimi Torvinen, *J. R. Danielson-Kalmari:
Suomen autonomian puolustajana* (Porvoo, 1965), and Pirkko
Rommi, *Myöntyvyyssuuntauksen hahmottuminen Yrjö-Koski-
sen ja Suomalaisen Puolueen toimintalinjaksi,* Historiallisia Tut-
kimuksia, 68(Lahti, 1964).

of the various Russian opposition groups during the so-called formative period (1899–1903) of Russo-Finnish underground collaboration,[11] none of which led to lasting relationships. The determining factor, in most cases, was not so much the attitude of the Russian groups as it was the low level of interest displayed by the Finns. Although stung by Russification, members of the Finnish resistance had acquired (because of Finland's special position in the Russian Empire) certain psychological inhibitions that impeded their identification with the Russian opposition movement.[12] The tradition of Finnish institutional separateness precluded cooperation with the other oppressed nationalities, even while Bobrikov was destroying the foundations of that separateness. The lack of cohesive organization among the Finnish opposition forces and the specific failure to achieve policy decisions about cooperation also served to impede the development of ties with the Russian antigovernment movement.[13]

The promulgation of the Language Manifesto in 1900 and the Conscription Manifesto in July, 1901 weakened the influence of Finnish political leaders who had been advocating restraint, for it was now obvious that little hope of accommodation remained.[14] The Conscription Manifesto was

11. Finland's geographic and political situation was exploited to some extent well before 1899. The attitude of the Finnish population was hostile to the early incursions of Russian dissidents onto Finnish territory. Kenraalikuvernöörinkanslia, 331:1(1891), Akti 16, 37.

12. These restraining factors were only gradually counterbalanced by Russification. Generally speaking, the Finnish reaction was below the level of intensity of the Russification measures during the 1899–1902 period and above the level of provocation in 1904–1905. This characteristic was more pronounced among younger members of the Swedish Finns than among other groups.

13. The exchange of propaganda with Russian journalists was not considered as cooperation by the Finnish opposition. Collaboration on this superficial level began in the 1880s and continued without interruption until 1917.

14. Finnish opposition was markedly hetereogeneous and diffused from the very beginning. Leadership first rested in the hands of the old propagandists, such as Mechelin, Viktor Magnus von Born, and Lennart Gripenberg, but quickly was challenged in May, 1899, by Konni Zilliacus, a newcomer who returned to Finland in early 1899 after an absence of over a decade. Zilliacus had been traveling in North America, Japan, the Middle East, India, and elsewhere. He was free of the inhibitions that con-

particularly important in pushing the Finns to develop more radical forms of opposition.[15] By the end of 1901—less than six months after its promulgation—the radical wing of the Finnish resistance created the first opposition organization that possessed some of the characteristics of a true anti-government movement. Especially important, a clandestine network of resistance groups in various parts of the country emerged and began to coordinate opposition to Saint Petersburg's policy. The clandestine character and the efficiency of this organization earned it the derisive name *kahal,* which was immediately adopted by the Finns.[16]

The most "underdeveloped" sector of Finnish resistance until early 1902 was its limited contacts with other anti-government groups within the Russian Empire. In this sense, the Finns contributed to the chronic lack of unity that had always plagued the Russian opposition movement. The intensification of Russification, as well as the gradual "educating" of the Finnish opposition by the underground press to view Finland's misfortunes as a part of the mis-

---

tinued to dominate veterans of the earlier period, and he allied himself with leaders of the young generation of opposition activists, such as Henry Biaudet, Eugen Wolff, and Arvid Neovius. This basic split became more acute in 1902 and 1903, and in November, 1904, the radicals officially split with the passive opposition to form the Finnish Party of Active Resistance. Herman Gummerus, *Konni Zilliacus: Soumen itsenäisyyden esiteistelija* (Jyväskylä, 1933), 17–63.

15. The Conscription Manifesto represented a challenge almost ideally suited for resistance by passive, nonviolent means. In one resounding blow, Russification was transformed into an issue of direct concern for a vast majority of the population. Its attempted implementation permitted opposition to be mounted at several points, and in the process responsibility for consequences could be extended to the entire population. Einar W. Juva, "Laiton asevelvollisuuslaki, kutsuntalakko ja virkamiesten erottamiset," in *Venäläinen sortokausi Suomessa* (Porvoo, 1960), 63–74.

16. Kahal was a representative committee of Jewish church elders in Russia, Poland, and Latvia. Sulo Haltsonen, *Theodor Schvindt: Kansatieteilijä ja kotiseuduntutkija* (Helsinki, 1947), 273, and *The Jewish Encyclopedia,* vol. 5 of 12 vols. (London, 1905), 525–26. The Finns adopted this name in 1902. For a history of Kagaali activity, see Arne Cederholm, *Kagalens uppkomst och andra episoder* (Helsinki, 1920), and Julio N. Reuter, *"Kagalen": Ett bidrag till Finlands historia 1899–1905,* 2 vols. (Helsinki, 1928–1930).

fortunes of the larger Russian opposition, produced a fundamental shift in Finnish opposition attitudes after early 1902.
The growing awareness of the antigovernment struggle in
Russia created the possibility not only of adopting some of
the resistance techniques utilized by that opposition, but also
of establishing ties with it.

The advantages of cooperation with the Russian resistance
factions had occurred to a few Finnish publicists earlier, most
notably to Konni Zilliacus, Arvid Neovius, and Henry
Biaudet, but this departure did not strike a sympathetic
chord with the majority of the opposition until 1903.[17] An
expanding circle of Finnish resistance leaders understood that
the objectives of the Finnish opposition and the Russian
antigovernment movement were parallel in at least one
important respect: both movements could realize their
objectives more easily if the autocratic government were
weakened. The Finns, of course, sought the restoration of
Finland's position to *status quo* ante-Bobrikov, while the
Russian factions, to a varying degree, aimed at altering the
prevailing *status quo* within the Empire. Although the Finnish
opposition finally developed ties with almost all Russian
resistance factions, their ties with the liberals were most
intimate.[18]

Strong professional ties between certain Finnish publicists
and progressive Russian journalists predate the February
Manifesto of 1899. Several politically liberal journalists in
Russia were eager to publish highly accurate and informative
articles on the "Finnish question," and Finns were equally
interested in having their interpretation of developments in
Finland available to readers of the Russian liberal press.
Such articles were necessary, they felt, to counter the incite-
ment by Russian nationalists against Finland's special position

---

17. Neovius's contacts with Russian journalists predate the
February Manifesto of 1899. Zilliacus probably concluded ties
with London-based Russian publicists in May, 1899, whereas H.
Biaudet's known ties date from the summer of 1900.

18. The International Cultural Appeal of early 1899 served as
an important magnet for bringing Finns into contact with
representatives of the various Russian resistance groups. Initial
ties with the Russian anarchists and Social Revolutionaries date
from this period. Finnish contact with the Russian Social
Democrats dates from 1898, with the earliest contact being with
Russian progressive journalists.

in the Russian Empire.[19] The Finnish opposition possessed no
organization before 1899, and contacts with Russian
journalists were largely the affair of private Finnish journalists.[20]

The crisis of 1899 intensified and expanded contacts
between journalists of the two countries. Dr. Arvid Neovius,
editor of *Nya Pressen* and an important member of the
secret committee (created in January, 1899) to organize
Finnish propaganda in Russia, was the central figure in
this activity.[21] His chief ally on the Russian side was
Dmitri Protopopov who, after being banished from Saint
Petersburg in 1896, had learned Swedish and had lived in
Terijoki, just on the Finnish side of the border. He made
repeated secret trips to Saint Petersburg and acted as a post-
man between the Finns and Russian liberal journalists in
Saint Petersburg, carrying information both ways. He also
scouted the border region for spots to smuggle literature for
publication in *Rabochee delo*.

Protopopov delivered Neovius's articles about a wide range
of events in Finland: student unrest, famine, financial scandals
in the state administration, and court gossip.[22] Russian readers
could find such evidence of Finnish resistance to Russification
in such publications as *Russkoe bogatstvo* and *Vestnik Evropy*.
It is true that government censors issued warnings to the
editors of these periodicals to publish less provocative
accounts,[23] but in Finland censorship was so tightened in

19. Needless to say, not all attempts by the progressive publicists in Russia to come to Finland's defense were inspired by
impulses from Finland. Though sources on early propaganda ties
are extremely sketchy, evidence exists to trace these ties back
to at least 1887.

20. Dmitri Protopopov to Leo Mechelin, January 21, 1898,
Finnish State Archives (hereinafter cited as FSA), and Vladimir
Hessen to Leo Mechelin, January 10, 1898, Folder 33, Leo
Mechelin Collection.

21. In January, 1899, Mechelin and A. Neovius created a
secret committee designed to recommence publishing Finnish
propaganda in Russia in anticipation of renewed attacks against
Finland's autonomy. Sigurd Nordenstreng and Leo Mechelin,
Hans statsmannagärning och politiska personlighet, vol. 2 of
2 vols. (Helsinki, 1937), 70–71.

22. In addition to D. Protopopov, contact was also maintained with Stasulevich of *Vestnik Evropy* and with Boris
Chicherin and V. Notovich, who was editor of *Novosti*.

23. Karl Bernhard Grönhagen, *Från flydda tider* (Helsinki,
1924), 42–43.

1899 that such information could not be published at all. In response to increased censorship, the Finns created in August 1900 the underground paper *Fria Ord* to print such information.[24]

Relations between individual Finnish and Russian journalists remained of this nature until early 1902, when the internal struggle for dominance in the Russian liberal movement reached a crisis. The constitutionalists abandoned the traditional, cautious policies that hitherto had been so characteristic of them and embraced a new policy of greater political activism.[25] The transformation of the "liberation movement" into a clandestine opposition group favoring, among other things, cooperation with other elements of the antigovernment movement in Russia, marked a step forward in the development of ties with the Finnish opposition movement.

Early in 1902 the Russian liberals published abroad their uncensored newspaper *Osvobozhdenie,* an undertaking that quickly involved the Finns.[26] The liberals needed the Finnish underground for smuggling their new publication into Russia from presses located in Germany. Dmitri Protopopov and Andrei Igelström, head of the Slavic Collection of the Alexander Imperial (Helsinki) University Library and a regular contributor to the liberal Russian newspaper *Russkiia vedomosti,* set out in June, 1902 to investigate the possibility that the Finnish underground might be used to transport their newspaper from Sweden into Russia.[27] Arvid Neovius, Konni Zilliacus's chief ally in Helsinki and a friend of Igelström, offered to study the question.[28] Following consultations with Zilliacus, Neovius undertook a journey to Germany to discuss the matter with Peter Struve, the editor in chief of *Osvobozhdenie.* At a meeting in Stuttgart the two reached an agree-

---

24. Dmitri Protopopov to Arvid Neovius, August 13, 1899, and October 18, 1899, Arvid Neovius Collection, FSA.

25. Paul N. Miliukov, *Vospominaniia (1859–1917),* vol. 1 of 2 vols., 197.

26. *Ibid.* Miliukov resided briefly in Finland in 1902, but no proof exists that he was instrumental in the negotiations for Finnish assistance. Loviisa, where Miliukov stayed, was the location of Vladimir Smirnov's summer place, but it is not known if the two men came into contact.

27. Andrei Igelström to Arvid Neovius, July 2, 1902, and July 28, 1902, Arvid Neovius Collection, FSA.

28. Andrei Igelström to Arvid Neovius, July 28, 1902, Carl Mannerheim to Arvid Neovius, July 23, 1902, *ibid.*

ment.[29] In this manner, the Finnish opposition movement had lost enough of its "separatist" prejudice to permit the regular transportation of liberal underground literature into Russia by way of a Zilliacus/Neovius transport system, which had been in existence for other purposes since late 1900.

Although the move to seek the assistance of the Finnish opposition in this matter might have been expected to become the opening wedge of closer organizational collaboration, apparently Neovius and Struve discussed no such possibility in their Stuttgart meeting. Neither side seems to have contemplated at the time that this limited collaboration might deepen to organizational cooperation. The assistance rendered by the Finns came from individuals who were members of what might be called the *Fria Ord* group, which acted essentially on its own responsibility and without the full knowledge of the various opposition committees in Helsinki.[30]

Although the Finnish opposition's relations with the Russian liberals were restricted primarily to matters relating to transport of illicit publications and to the exchange of propaganda materials, these early contacts were important because they served to remove some of the psychological inhibitions and preconceptions among the Finnish opposition toward the antigovernment movement in Russia. Even limited cooperation tended to make the most active members of the Finnish opposition aware of the true proportions and growing importance of the indigenous opposition within Russia. Zilliacus extended this "educating" process to the rank and file of the opposition by publishing a steady diet of articles and books on the antigovernment struggle in Russia.[31]

---

29. Peter Struve to Arvid Neovius, August 23, 1902, *ibid.* Neovius and Struve met between August 24 and 30 in Stuttgart.

30. According to the arrangement, the staff of *Osvobozhdenie* dispatched small packages of their publications and correspondence to Zilliacus in Stockholm. He included this material (named "rojitzo" in code) in larger shipments, which were dispatched to Finland by various surreptitious routes. In Finland the material was transferred to points close to the Russo-Finnish border, from which point Russian liberal couriers carried the publications to St. Petersburg.

31. Zilliacus could manage this because *Fria Ord,* the underground bimonthly published in Stockholm, belonged to him and to Arvid Neovius. The change in Finnish attitudes was most clearly reflected in a number of pamphlets published by the opposition in 1902 and 1903. For example: Toivo (pen name for K. F. Ignatius), *Muutamia mietteitä nykyisestä asemasta*

Gradually the Finnish reserve broke down and each new Russification measure after 1902 served to solidify Finnish affinity with the internal Russian opposition.

The Finnish-Russian cooperation, having reached a new plateau during the summer of 1902, settled down at the new level until the summer of 1903. An end to the Russification policy in 1902 could have reversed the growing involvement of the Finns with the Russian underground. Since no change was forthcoming from the Bobrikov administration and since, instead, Finland was subjected to greater repression in 1903 than before, the tendency for the Finnish resistance toward closer identification with the Russian antigovernment movement grew stronger.

During the autumn of 1902 Bobrikov renewed his request of the previous year for emergency powers, this time fortifying his appeal with new details concerning the resistance movement in Finland. Among other things, Bobrikov was now in a position to reveal damaging information concerning the ties that existed between the Finns and the antigovernment movement in Russia. On this occasion, Bobrikov returned victorious, and on April 15, 1903, the Finnish Senate published (as number nineteen of its code) a law extending dictatorial power to Bobrikov.[32] The law had been prepared in great secrecy in Saint Petersburg in consultation with V. K. von Plehve, minister of the interior.[33] Governor-General Bobrikov now had emergency powers for a period of three years to deal with the "insolent opposition" in Finland. The new law was soon used to arrest and exile fifty-five Finnish opposition activists to Sweden and Russia.[34]

(Stockholm, 1902), 5; Kansalainen (pen name for K. Toppola), *Se Suuri kysymys kaikille, johonka kaikki eivät viela ole wastanneet* (Stockholm, 1903), 8–9.

32. *Sbornik Postanovlenii Velikago Kniazhestva Finliandskago* (April 15, 1903), item no. 19, 32–36. For exile accounts, see Lennart Gripenberg, "Muutamia muistelmia vuodelta 1903," in *Murrosajoilta: Muistoja ja Kokemuksia*, vol. 1 of 2 vols. (Porvoo, 1918), 53–80; Ernst Estlander, *Friherre Viktor Magnus von Born* (Helsinki, 1931), 361–66.

33. V. K. von Plehve was also the Minister-State Secretary for Finland and Chancellor of the Helsinki Alexander University.

34. Between April 21 and early May, 1903, the first twenty resistance leaders received their banishment notice. The last exiles took place in early 1905 when banishment was to the Viatka region of Russia. Bernhard Estlander, *Elva årtionden ur Finlands historia, 1898–1908*, vol. 3, 195–210.

The majority of the exiles chose to take up residence in Stockholm, already the center of Finnish resistance in Sweden. The opposition effort in Finland was temporarily paralyzed while the opposition leadership, now divided between Finland and Stockholm, assessed the new situation and sought to adjust to it. The situation gradually cleared, and the exiles decided to recommence resistance from Sweden. The resistance committee that eventually emerged among the exiles was decidedly more cohesive and radical, although their views on tactics had not greatly changed. Isolated from the moderating influence of the more cautious opposition leaders, subject to the personal influence of the highly persuasive Zilliacus, who lived in Stockholm, and inclined to recognize that passive means of resistance had failed to halt Russification, the exiled group sought to achieve tighter organizational cohesion. In May, 1903, exiles in Sweden and elsewhere began to discuss the possibility of organizing a general meeting in Stockholm of the entire Finnish resistance.[35] The time seemed ripe for bringing together all factions of the resistance for a general examination of the road ahead. Impetus for such a conclave grew in late June when the Finnish opposition received an invitation from the Russian liberals to hold discussions concerning collaboration.[36] This was an issue never before subject to open debate among the Finns, and it necessitated wide concensus.

The fortuitous timing of these two developments—the formation of the Russian constitutionalists into an underground organization and the exile of the most active leaders of the Finnish opposition movement—was important for the future evolution of Finnish-Russian liberal association. It is possible to speculate that events in Finland had some bearing on the quickening of the Russian liberals' interest in the nationalities question generally and in the Finnish question specifically. During the spring of 1903 the liberals took up the question of ties with the Finns and the Poles. Before the middle of 1903 the Russian liberals possessed neither organization nor a formulated program, so that immediate discussion with the Finns was not practicable. During April and

---

35. E. G. V. Becker-Reuterskjöld to Arvid Neovius, May 27, 1903, and Carl Mannerheim to Julio Reuter, June 17, 1903, J. N. Reuter Collection, Åbo Academy, Turku.

36. Konni Zilliacus to Arvid Neovius, June 25, 1903, Arvid Neovius Collection, FSA.

May the Russian liberals created an *ad hoc* committee of three to prepare a preliminary study of the Finnish question. Two prominent liberals in Saint Petersburg, V. von Dehn and I. V. Hessen—both specialists in jurisprudence and government—were appointed to the committee. Prince Peter Dolgorukov, the third member, was responsible for the practical aspects of coordination with the Finns.[37]

Struve sent a letter to Konni Zilliacus on June 24, 1903, inquiring whether the Finnish opposition was prepared to discuss "questions of mutual interest" with an emissary from the Russian liberals.[38] Struve did not identify by name the "royal emissary" who would be contacting the Finns, but he outlined in general terms the questions that the liberals wished to discuss. Struve also failed to clarify the relationship between his initiative and the activities of the *ad hoc* committee. Probably both were concerned with the forthcoming meeting of Russian liberals to be held in Switzerland, and the Russians most likely wanted a preliminary assessment of the attitudes harbored by the Finnish resistance to use in this, their first general planning conference.[39]

At the moment Struve's letter arrived Zilliacus was preoccupied with an attempt to mount an all-opposition propaganda campaign against Von Plehve and a shady, high-level Russian ambassador-at-large, Ivan Manasevich-Manuilov, and he welcomed Struve's initiative as an opportunity to enlist the Russian liberals' support for the anti-Plehve drive.[40] Zilliacus was only mildly interested,

---

37. Törngren's unpublished account (dated May 19, 1904) of his April–May, 1904, journey to Russia, Adolf Törngren Collection, FSA. A number of other liberal leaders, Paul N. Miliukov, Fedor I. Rodichev, F. F. Kokoshkin, and M. I. Petrunkevich, showed considerable interest in the progress of this committee. Only Miliukov's position on the Finnish question remained permanent, and he maintained close ties with the Finns after 1905. Rodichev, of course, became intimately involved with Finnish affairs again in 1917 when he was appointed the Minister–State Secretary for Finland.

38. Konni Zilliacus to Arvid Neovius, June 25, 1903, Arvid Neovius Collection, FSA.

39. George Fischer, *Russian Liberalism: From Gentry to Intelligentsia,* 140.

40. Konni Zilliacus, *Sortovuosilta: Poliittisia Muistelmia* (Porvoo, 1920), 87–92; Zilliacus to A. Neovius, June 25, 1903; K. Zilliacus to A. Neovius, June 1, 1903, Arvid Neovius Collection, FSA.

however, in discussions with Russian liberals. He had already adopted the view that the Russian liberals were nonentities in the struggle to wrest meaningful concessions from the Russian regime.[41]

Zilliacus could not, of course, decide alone on a reply to Struve; the establishing of contact in late June with the Finnish opposition leaders who were scattered throughout Finland, Scandinavia, and Western Europe proved an almost insurmountable task even for Zilliacus. Consultations were finally held with some half-dozen persons who concluded that no substantial opposition would be encountered from the remaining resistance leaders to further investigation of the Struve offer.[42] They directed Zilliacus to send an affirmative reply. To facilitate communication between those members of the Finnish resistance still in Finland and the Russian liberals, the Finnish resistance established, with the aid of Andrei Igelström, a direct line of communication between Helsinki and Saint Petersburg to deal with this question.[43]

Prince Peter Dolgorukov arrived in Helsinki on July 10 for two weeks to represent the Russian liberals and to explore areas of cooperation. He met with Kasten Antell, a Russian-speaking former officer who was part of the more cautious section of the Finnish opposition, and with Igelström, Arvid Neovius, and probably others.[44] Discussions with the Finnish opposition leaders touched upon the whole range of problems that confronted the antigovernment movement in Russia. During this initial encounter, which established close understanding between the Finns and the Russian liberals, Dolgorukov sought to accomplish three objectives: to discover the position the Finnish resistance envisioned for Finland should a constitutional government be established in Russia; to suggest the possibility of official discussions between the Russian liberals and the Finns at some future date; and to study the likelihood of continuing organizational cooperation between the two groups.[45]

41. Zilliacus had maintained very close ties with the Social Revolutionaries since 1899.

42. Konni Zilliacus to Arvid Neovius, July 11, 1903, Arvid Neovius Collection, FSA.

43. Adolf Törngren, *Med Ryska Samhällsbyggare och Stats-män: Åren 1904–1905* (Helsinki, 1929), 8.

44. Arvid Neovius to Ivar Berendsen, July 13, 1903, Ivar Berendsen Collection, Danish State Archives, Copenhagen.

45. Törngren, *Med Ryska Samhällsbyggare,* 8–9; Konni Zilliacus to Arvid Neovius, July 11, 1903, Arvid Neovius Collec-

It did not escape the Finns that Dolgorukov who, the Finns believed, represented one of the more cautious of the Russian opposition groups, spoke quite calmly of the abolition of autocracy and the establishment of a constitutional government in Russia. The Russian liberals seemed prepared to give events a nudge while eliciting the views of the Finnish opposition on this and other plans. To the Russian liberals, the aims of the Finnish opposition must have appeared archaic and timid.

Antell and Neovius found Dolgorukov's proposals captivating and warmly recommended that the Finnish opposition give him serious consideration.[46] They advised Dolgorukov to discuss his proposal with other Finnish opposition leaders in Stockholm and with Leo Mechelin, a central opposition personality and a moderate who was vacationing in Germany. Neovius prepared the way for Dolgorukov by writing Mechelin that the "matter which interests him [Dolgorukov] seemed very important to me and deserves thorough consideration."[47] Antell spoke of Dolgorukov in the warmest terms when he wrote Mechelin in Wildbad that the visitor "is a good friend of Finland, well educated, and an active member of the constitutional party in Russia."[48]

Dolgorukov had good reasons to feel satisfied with the results of his discussions in Finland when he left for Stockholm, supplied with the addresses of three Finnish opposition residents there. The meeting with Eugen Wolff, Jonas Castrén, and Konni Zilliacus in Stockholm during the third week of July confirmed what Dolgorukov had learned in Finland.[49] The Finns, as he was in a position to observe, had no fixed opposition organization at this time but were interested in continuing discussions.

There was no doubt in Dolgorukov's mind that the Finns were sympathetic toward his proposals and toward his faction of the Russian opposition. On July 25, after meeting Viktor

tion, FSA; Karl G. Idman, *Maamme itsenäistymisen vuosilta: Muistelmia* (Porvoo, 1932), 20–21.

46. Arvid Neovius to Leo Mechelin, July 13, 1903, Leo Mechelin Collection, FSA.

47. Arvid Neovius to Leo Mechelin, July 13, 1903, Leo Mechelin Collection, FSA; Törngren, *Med Ryska Samhälls-byggare*, 8.

48. Kasten Antell to Leo Mechelin, July 12, 1903, Leo Mechelin Collection, FSA.

49. Idman, *Maamme itsenäistymisen vuosilta*, 20–21.

von Born, an influential member of the Finnish opposition, in Jonköping, Sweden, he left for Wildbad,[50] Baden-Württtenburg, where Leo Mechelin, the most important Finnish resistance leader, was vacationing. On July 26 Mechelin and Dolgorukov discussed the future of Finnish-Russian liberal ties.[51] Mechelin was not only prepared to meet officially with the liberals, but he also agreed to help draft the constitution for liberated Russia. Without consulting the other leaders, Mechelin undertook the drafting of portions of the liberals' proposed constitution as well as two studies on the resolution of the Finnish question.[52] This immensely important undertaking remained a private matter between Mechelin and the liberals, although it constituted a part of the agenda of the official discussions of the two groups in January, 1904. The same project was responsible for bringing together Struve and Alexis Gripenberg, a moderate Finnish opposition leader.[53]

The meeting between Struve and Gripenberg produced considerable misgivings among the Finns, however. Gripenberg's lengthy letter to Neovius informing the latter of the discussions reveals what were to the Finns some startling facts about the Russian liberals. Struve admitted, Gripenberg wrote, that changes in the Russian government would not necessarily be to Finland's advantage because "the Liberal circles regrettably contain too dominant a nationalistic faction to permit Finland more independence." [54] This statement, so much at variance with the picture painted by Dolgorukov, and coming from the respected editor in chief of the liberal party's organ, *Osvobozhdenie,* dampened the newly generated enthusiasm for cooperation with the liberals. It was clear that the Finns would have to strike a bargain with the Russian moderate group. The achievement of their

50. Telegram from Dolgorukov to Leo Mechelin, July 23, 1903, Folder 23, Leo Mechelin Collection, FSA.
51. Peter Struve to Leo Mechelin, July 30, 1903, Leo Mechelin Collection, FSA; Törngren, *Med Ryska Samhälls-byggare,* 8.
52. Folder 23, Leo Mechelin Collection, FSA; Törngren, *Med Ryska Samhällsbyggare,* 12–13.
53. Peter Struve to Leo Mechelin, July 30, 1903; Alexis Gripenberg to Leo Mechelin, August 15, 1903, Leo Mechelin Collection, FSA.
54. Alexis Gripenberg to Leo Mechelin, August 15, 1903, *ibid.*

objectives would require a much tougher attitude, and their demands would have to be made plain and the bargain secured secretly, if possible, while the Finns still had a reasonably strong bargaining position left.[55] For this reason the Investigative Committee, headed by Mechelin, approached the next discussions with the Russian liberals in January, 1904, with a new and firmer position on the future status of Finland.

In a letter to Leo Mechelin, Gripenberg assured his correspondent that Struve was maintaining close watch on developments in Russia and in Finland as well.[56] The Russian had urged that the Finns use "all possible means" to work toward their objective; otherwise, they would fail to win back their special position after the liberals came to power.[57] Struve had intimated to Gripenberg that the excessively conciliatory Fennoman party in Finland was making defense of Finland's special position difficult for Finland's friends among the Russian liberals. Gripenberg warned, however, that discovery of the liberals' attitude toward the rights of non-Russians within the Empire, if widely disseminated, could have a serious effect upon Finnish enthusiasm for cooperation with the liberals. Gripenberg had other grounds for doubting the wisdom of relying upon the liberals. He had concluded after talking with Struve that the majority of the liberals were too timid to become the likely architects of the postrevolutionary Russian state. Gripenberg's estimation was strikingly close to the views that Konni Zilliacus communicated privately to Arvid Neovius after his meeting with Dolgorukov.[58] Gripenberg's pessimistic conviction was re-enforced by a book he subsequently read on developments in Russia,[59] and the aged Finnish patriot believed that Struve shared his skepticism.

55. Jonas Castrén, one of the opposition leaders who met Dolgorukov in Stockholm, also made this point in a letter to Mechelin on July 20, 1903, *ibid.*

56. This was possible for Struve, since he had received regular reports from Arvid Neovius on developments in Finland since late 1902. Peter Struve to Arvid Neovius, December 5, 1902, Arvid Neovius Collection, FSA; also Peter Struve to Arvid Neovius, March 18, 1903, *ibid.*

57. Alexis Gripenberg to Leo Mechelin, August 15, 1903, Leo Mechelin Collection, FSA.

58. Konni Zilliacus to Arvid Neovius, July 21, 1903, *ibid.*

59. Ernst von Der Brügzen, *Das heutige Russland* (Berlin, 1903).

Contact with the Russian liberals brought a wealth of new light to the Finnish leaders. This insight into Russian domestic developments made even the moderate Finnish opposition view its situation from a new perspective. The sudden realization that they might find themselves detached from Russia by the demise of Nicholas II, the Grand Duke of Finland, underscored the necessity of abandoning the traditional, defensive concept of passive opposition to Russification. The prospect that, with or without their action, the regime of Nicholas II was on the threshold of revolutionary change made a startling difference. Disquieting as it might be to the Finnish opposition, that group now saw the possibility that it might one day have to discuss Finland's future with those Russian groups who were now undermining the stability of the autocracy and who might eventually be its successors.[60]

The deliberations with Dolgorukov and Struve, and particularly the prospect of official negotiations with the Russian liberals, intensified pressure among the Finnish opposition to consider what attitude they should adopt toward the Russian groups who might be responsible for Russia's affairs in the postautocratic Russian government. This realization moved the previous proponents of passive opposition closer to the more radical members, centered around Konni Zilliacus.

The topic of cooperation with the Russian liberals was on the agenda for the September 3–5 general conference of leaders of the Finnish resistance in Stockholm. This first and only general conference abroad was attended by more than fifty Finnish resistance leaders, including about a dozen who made the hazardous journey from Finland.[61] The main problem dominating the conference was the state of the opposition in Finland, and only with great effort did the question of ties with the Russian resistance movement find its way into the deliberations. The issue proved, in fact, too controversial to be debated in a large circle, and the conference decided to establish a special eight-man investigative

60. Jonas Castrén to Leo Mechelin, July 20, 1903, and Alexis Gripenberg to Leo Mechelin, August 17, 1903, Leo Mechelin Collection, FSA.
61. Estlander, *Friherre Viktor Magnus von Born,* 222–23; Eino Parmanen, *Taistelujen Kirja,* vol. 2 of 4 vols. (Porvoo, 1937), 540–50.

committee to study the whole question of ties with outside groups.[62]

Despite its inauspicious beginnings, this committee proved to be a most fruitful agency for promoting cooperation with Russian opposition circles. Through this body the Finnish opposition finally considered the question of closer association with the Russian liberals. The Investigative Committee promptly became active in a number of areas exploring possible cooperative action with various Russian resistance groups. In late October, it established contact with the Polish National League and, a few weeks later, the committee empowered Konni Zilliacus to undertake an extensive fact-finding journey to Western Europe for consultation with the different Russian opposition factions.[63] Zilliacus consciously sought ways to involve the committee and the Finns in activity that would bring these groups into closer contact.[64]

Thus, by autumn of 1903, both the Russian liberals and the Finnish opposition had created organs to deal with each other, and both were searching for specific programs that would be agreeable to the other. The Russian liberals had formed the Union of Liberation at a July meeting in Schaffhausen, Switzerland, and the Stockholm conference in September had officially created the Investigative Committee to coordinate future discussions with the Russian liberals and to consider the possibility of collaboration with other factions within the Russian opposition movement.

By late November or early December the Union of Liberation established January 16–18, 1904, as the date

---

62. Zilliacus, *Sortovuosilta: Poliittisia Muistelmia,* 84–86, and Minutes of the "Stockholm Parliament," Folder 23, Leo Mechelin Collection, FSA.

63. Estlander, *Friherre Viktor Magnus von Born,* 223–25. Estlander's account must be used with caution, because he confuses Zilliacus's initial journey with the later journeys undertaken in April and June, 1904. Zilliacus, *Sortovuosilta: Poliittisia Muistelmia,* 101–8. Zilliacus was also unable to distinguish his various journeys to Western Europe. He fails, for instance, to say anything about his December, 1903, undertaking.

64. Zilliacus exceeded the powers granted him during his fact-finding journeys. He habitually committed the Finnish opposition to more radical forms of cooperation than intended by the Investigative Committee. This strained relations and almost led to a formal split on several occasions.

for its first congress to meet in Saint Petersburg. Preparations for the congress raised once again the nationalities question and the possibility of further negotiations with the Finns. The Union of Liberation decided that the discussions with the Finns would best be held in conjunction with the first congress. Such an arrangement would facilitate closer coordination of the proceedings and would avoid the necessity of convening a special Union of Liberation conference to ratify any results the discussions might produce.[65] The Union of Liberation appointed I. V. Hessen to direct the work of its Finnish Committee, and Dolgorukov again undertook to communicate the Union of Liberation's decision concerning the meeting to the Finnish opposition center in Helsinki.[66] The union's invitation arrived December 15, the very day that Zilliacus was preparing to depart on his initial fact-finding journey to Western Europe.[67]

The Finns began preparations for the negotiations with a certain amount of indecision and confusion. The problem stemmed from the facts that the leadership was divided geographically between Helsinki and Stockholm and, more importantly, that the Finnish opposition had still not arrived at a definite policy on the issue of cooperation. Although the Investigative Committee had labored with the problem for over four months, that body had achieved no specific program nor received any guidelines to regulate its power in negotiating with the Russians. In fact, preparations for the meeting were the prime responsibility of the Helsinki group, and that group coordinated its plans and activities only in part with the Investigative Committee in Stockholm.[68]

In the end, the more moderate opposition leaders in Helsinki decided to conduct the discussions with the Russians independently of the committee. They explained their decision on the basis of security, but were probably more motivated by the fear that the more radical elements in Stockholm would commit the Finnish opposition too deeply.[69]

65. Peter Dolgorukov to Leo Mechelin, December 14 and 19, 1903, and Leo Mechelin to I. V. Hessen, December 3, 1903, Leo Mechelin Collection, FSA.
66. Peter Dolgorukov to Leo Mechelin, December 14, 1903, *ibid.*
67. *Ibid.*
68. Törngren, *Med Ryska Samhällsbyggare*, 10–13.
69. There was some basis in fact for this suspicion of the Stockholm group, because it clearly contained the majority of

The alleged need for security did not deceive the committee; rather, it aggravated the growing split between the Finnish opposition in Stockholm and Helsinki and greatly obstructed progress toward a common program for discussions with the Russians.[70]

Disagreement about the objective of the discussions was so great between the Finnish groups that they experienced considerable difficulty in finding suitable and willing delegates for the talks. Dr. Adolf Törngren, a member of the opposition leadership in Helsinki, and Dr. Julio Reuter, who was temporarily in Finland from London, were finally appointed to represent the Finns. Because of the fear that the Finnish opposition would be committed too deeply, the two Finnish emissaries were given no official accreditation and were empowered to effect no agreements with the Russian liberals. Törngren, annoyed by the procrastination and the whole attitude of the Helsinki group, insisted that another delegate should accompany him so this person "could verify the accuracy of his reporting upon his return home." [71]

Despite such difficulties, the meeting began in Saint Petersburg as scheduled on January 15, 1904, and with elaborate security arrangements.[72] The Finnish resistance organization was anxious to keep the knowledge of this sensitive relationship secret, not only from the Russian authorities, but also from their domestic political rivals, the Fennoman party.[73] To throw off possible police surveillance, the two Finnish emissaries entered Russia through

those opposition leaders who favored more radical measures of opposition. Draft of letter from Arvid Neovius to Konni Zilliacus, February 24, 1903, Arvid Neovius Collection, FSA.

70. Törngren, *Med Ryska Samhällsbyggare*, 24–29.

71. Törngren's unpublished account of the January, 1904, negotiations with the Union of Liberation, Adolf Törngren Collection, FSA.

72. There was ample reason for these measures. Elis Hultin, a member of the Finnish opposition, had been arrested in St. Petersburg in December, 1903, because of his ties with the Russian liberals, an indication that the Okhrana was aware of the ties between the Finns and the Russian liberals. Undated letter from Nina Struve to Arvid Neovius, Arvid Neovius Collection, FSA.

73. The Conciliatory Fennoman party remained on extremely hostile terms with the opposition, although a group of Fennomans closest to the opposition point of view were gradually gravitating toward the opposition at about this time.

central Europe. In Saint Petersburg, Törngren and Reuter received additional instructions concerning the meeting arrangements from a contact at the Free Economic Society. The two delegations met in the private residence of a Saint Petersburg engineer who had placed it at the disposal of the Union of Liberation. The union was represented by its Finnish committeemen Hessen, Von Dehn, and Dolgorukov. With experience in the art of deceiving the Russian authorities, the Russians suggested that the group agree on some plausible alibi for the unusual gathering in case the apartment should be raided.[74]

Although Mechelin had prepared a memorandum on the Finnish question, he had failed to deliver it to the Union of Liberation's Finnish Committee in time for the first meeting.[75] This fact necessitated a change in the agenda. Both sides decided to discuss the question informally and to postpone its official consideration and the question of organizational ties until a later meeting.[76] In the absence of a more formal agenda, the two groups discussed the means each organization was willing to employ to reach its objective. The cautious tone of the discussions, of course, suited the Finnish delegates very well, since they had been instructed to avoid advancing too rapidly and, above all, to avoid commitments binding upon their organization. The delegates were able to exchange views on a number of issues in this setting.[77]

Törngren made abundantly clear the Finnish opposition's commitment to a restoration of Finland's position ante-Bobrikov. This minimum position of the Finnish opposition struck a responsive chord with the Union of Liberation delegates. They stated that they contemplated adopting as a

---

74. Törngren, *Med Ryska Samhällsbyggare,* 12.

75. Undertaken in late July, 1903, as the result of discussions with Peter Dolgorukov and Peter Struve.

76. The Finns certainly did not intend to introduce this question, but expected the Russians to do so because of Dolgorukov's July briefing. The fact that they did not reflects either the inaccuracy of Dolgorukov's information or a shift in the position of the Union of Liberation toward the initial talks. Mechelin's memorandum is in his collection, FSA.

77. The principal sources for the January meeting are Törngren's report of the meeting complemented by the brief account published in his study. Törngren, *Med Ryska Samhällsbyggare,* 13–24.

general principle the *status quo ante* in respect to
all Russian minority peoples subjected to recent Russification.
Dolgorukov, however, showed little enthusiasm for Törngren's
proposal to expand Finland's autonomy under a future
constitutional arrangement. Dolgorukov emphasized that
nationalistic elements in the liberal movement opposed any
arrangement that would extend the powers of the Finnish
Estates beyond those in force previous to the promulgation
of the February Manifesto of 1899. Dolgorukov added that,
"If Finland has managed to get along up to now with a Grand
Duke who was, at the same time, the autocrat of Russia, it
should be able to get along still better with a ruler who, in his
relations with Russia, is restricted by a constitution." [78]

The Union of Liberation delegates repeated the point,
communicated to the Finnish opposition on a number of
occasions since 1902, that the Finns should make additional
efforts to bring about national reconciliation between
themselves and the passive Fennoman party. The Russian
delegates had felt all along that only a common front against
Bobrikov and Plehve would enable the Union of Liberation
to render effective support to a policy of restoring the
status quo ante-Bobrikov in Finland. They believed the
Russian government cleverly exploited the apparent
passiveness of a large portion of the Finnish population
toward the destruction of self-government in their country.
As a consequence, a substantial portion of Russian public
opinion was willing to write off the Finnish opposition
movement as "Swedish separatism." Acquiescence of the
Fennoman party was harmful to the entire Finnish cause.[79]

The preoccupation of the Union of Liberation with a
federalist solution to the Russian nationalities problem was
quite evident to the Finns. Dolgorukov asked if the Finns
would agree to an arrangement in which Finland would retain
her autonomous position but in which the Grand Duchy

---

78. Törngren's report, Adolf Törngren Collection, FSA.
79. The Finnish opposition had become conscious of this fact
as early as 1900 and returned to it repeatedly in their propaganda. See Lauri Hyvämäki, "Perustuslaillinen ideologia," in
Päiviö Tommila, ed., *Venäläinen sortokausi Suomessa* (Porvoo,
1960), 80; Idman, *Maamme itsenäistymisen vuosilta: Muistelmia,*
21; Jonas Castrén to Paavo Ruotsalainen, May 2, 1902, published in T. Hultin, *Taistelun mies. Piirteitä Jonas Castrenin
elämästä ja toiminnasta* (Helsinki, 1927), 69; *Vapaita Lehtisiä*
(December 31, 1903), 2.

would also send delegates to a national Russian Duma. This proposal was an effort to find a suitable arrangement for special cases, such as Finland, that would at the same time mollify the more nationalistic elements within the Union of Liberation. The Finnish delegates had very little room in which to maneuver on this point, however; they had been directed specifically to exclude Finland from any experiments in federal-constitutional solutions. Finland already possessed the framework of an acceptable relationship with Russia, and the Finns' paramount concern was restoration of this relationship. Törngren rejected the proposed departure "because it would tie Finland more closely to Russia." The Russians accepted the Finnish position and did not pursue the matter.[80]

At the request of the Finnish delegates, the Russians provided a general sketch of the fortunes of the antigovernment movement in Russia. Generally speaking, their estimate was reasonably objective, although their evaluation of the importance of the Socialist Revolutionaries was far more modest than the estimate offered by Konni Zilliacus.[81] (This discrepancy prompted several Finnish resistance leaders to make a survey of their own to ascertain the actual situation in Russia.) [82] The Russians admitted that the diversity of views within their movement prevented more resolute action, but they reported a trend toward greater unity. Indeed, they predicted that within a period of one to three years the zemstvo movement would be powerful enough to turn to the Sovereign with a request to convene a constitutional assembly. Cooperation among the various Russian opposition groups was desirable but extremely difficult to achieve, Dolgorukov

---

80. The Finnish position complicated the formulation of the Union of Liberation's position on the nationalities question, or at least necessitated an exception in the case of Finland if an acceptable general solution could be found for the other national minority groups. This explains, for example, the specific reference to Finland in the Union of Liberation program. Törngren, *Med Ryska Samhällsbyggare*, 24.

81. Konni Zilliacus to Arvid Neovius, January 6, 1904, Arvid Neovius Collection, FSA.

82. Undertaken by Adolf Törngren in April, 1904. Törngren returned from Russia in late May. His report represents one of the most interesting and valuable first-hand narratives of the political situation in Russia immediately following the outbreak of the Russo-Japanese War, A. Törngren Collection, FSA.

said. Only the Socialist Revolutionaries had shown an interest in a recent Union of Liberation offer for cooperation.[83]

Near the conclusion of the talks, Dolgorukov explained that a Union of Liberation congress would consider the results of the present meeting in the very near future and that the views of the congress would be communicated to the Finnish opposition as soon as possible.[84] In response to Törngren's question concerning the prevailing view among the members of the Union of Liberation on the Finnish question, Dolgorukov said he was sure that a large part of them fully supported Finland's aspirations to recapture her rights.[85] With these assurances, the Finnish delegation left Saint Petersburg on January 18 to make its report to the Finnish opposition center in Helsinki.

The Union of Liberation's Finnish Committee presented its report to the first congress, and the report, composed of a joint summary of the talks with the Finns, enabled the union to adopt a position on the Finnish question. This position was included in the first general statement of principles published by the union in *Listok osvobozhdeniia* in November, 1904. In an unprecedented move, the Union of Liberation supported the right of self-determination of the different nationalities. As for Finland, the statement specifically called for the restoration "of the [autonomous] status which existed in that country until its illegal abrogation." [86] This paralleled very closely the position of the moderate Finnish opposition leaders in Helsinki. The specific mention of the return to the 1899 position meant that the union interpreted

83. Dolgorukov made this point to Törngren again when the two met in southern Russia some four months later. Törngren's report of his April–May, 1904, fact-finding journey to Russia, A. Törngren Collection, FSA. See Törngren, *Med Ryska Samhällsbyggare,* 18, for the Finnish-Russian protocol.
84. The Finnish Union of Liberation discussions were January 15–16, and the first Union of Liberation congress took place January 16–18, 1904. Törngren, *Med Ryska Samhällsbyggare,* 13.
85. Törngren, *Med Ryska Samhällsbyggare,* 22–23. Specifically, Törngren asked Dolgorukov if the delegates could report back to Finland whether the "party (Union of Liberation) contains a great number of liberal party members who are looking out for the interests of Finland?" Dolgorukov replied that: "We are certain that you can immediately assume that."
86. *Listok osvobozhdeniia,* 17(November 19, 1904), 2. The official adopted program is in *Osvobozhdenie* (May 7/20, 1905).

the contents of the January, 1904 talks to mean that the
Finns, unlike certain other national minorities, did not seek a
total break with Russia. The general declaration of self-
determination, while not specifying the groups to which it
applied, may have reflected the results of discussions the
Russians had with other national minorities, or at least with
the Polish National League which, in late October, 1903, and
early in January, 1904, revealed to the Finns that it had
demanded total independence from Russia.[87]

In Finland the results of the talks met with a mixed
reception. The Investigative Committee in Stockholm felt
that the delegates had been too cautious.[88] This impression
was made all the stronger by the fact that the Finns learned
of the more extreme demands of the Poles during talks in
Copenhagen early in January, 1904,[89] and by the fact that
Konni Zilliacus's journey to various *emigre* centers in Western
Europe had convinced him that a common opposition front
against the Russian government was finally a possibility.
The Stockholm group was also critical because the discussions
had been handled in such a way that that group's authority
on the question of connections with the Russian opposition
groups was being usurped. Its Investigative Committee, of
course, had been created for specifically that purpose, and the
Stockholm Finns wished to find an opportunity to reassert

---

87. During discussions with representatives of the Polish
National League in early January, Zilliacus, at any rate, reported
that the league sought total separation from Russia. The timing
and the program of this meeting strongly suggest that league
representatives were about to meet with some Russian group to
discuss cooperation. Konni Zilliacus to Arvid Neovius, January 6,
1904, Arvid Neovius Collection, FSA.

88. Törngren, *Med Ryska Samhällsbyggare,* 26.

89. Konni Zilliacus to Arvid Neovius, January 6, 1904, Arvid
Neovius Collection, FSA. The Investigative Committee established contact with the moderate Polish opposition, the Polish
National League, in October, 1903, in order to establish what
claims the Poles harbored against the Russian government. The
Finns also needed information on how the resistance in
Poland was organized. Finns hoped for immediate contact and
cooperation with the Poles but, for reasons that are not clear,
the Poles postponed discussions with the Finns until early 1904.
The Finnish delegates to these discussions represented only the
exiles in Stockholm, and the extreme claims of the Poles undoubtedly influenced the Finns to sharpen their demands with
respect to the Union of Liberation.

their authority and influence in these matters. Surprisingly enough, they were led by Leo Mechelin who was actually closer to the moderates in Helsinki in his attitudes than to those of the Stockholm group. In exile, Mechelin saw matters in a more radical light, but he also had other basis for complaint. His active participation in drafting a constitution for Russia had placed him in the very center of relations with the Russian liberals, yet he and his opinions had been almost completely disregarded in the initial deliberations with the Russians. The fact that his memorandum on the Finnish question had not arrived before the talks seems to have been unimportant in shaping his feelings in the case.

Although the Finns met with the Union of Liberation again early in March, 1904, to continue discussions and to finalize the general agreements of the January discussions, the two groups made no significant changes in their previous statement or in the structure of their connections. Developments in Russia and in Finland no longer promoted cooperation. The outbreak of the Russo-Japanese War temporarily strengthened nationalist feelings among the Russians and caused them to abstain from further organizational discussions with the Finnish opposition. Among the Finns the war initially stimulated greater interest and involvement in the anti-government struggle, but this energy was mainly channeled into an attempt by Konni Zilliacus to effect an all-opposition conference to coordinate activity against the autocracy.

During mid-1904 events in Finland reversed the trend that had been developing since 1899 for closer cooperation between Finnish and Russian opposition groups. Assassinations in June and July removed Governor-General Bobrikov and the Minister-State Secretary for Finland, V. K. von Plehve, and these and other events in the Russian Empire resulted in a gradual change in Saint Petersburg's policy toward Finland. In August Saint Petersburg announced that the Finnish Estates would convene late in 1904. In this manner the external stimulants toward interaction between the Finnish opposition and the Union of Liberation no longer played their former role, and the traditional restraining factors reasserted themselves.

The factors motivating both groups in this cautious, closely calculated relationship were quite similar: both groups sought limited objectives through a minimum of commitment. The force of circumstances influenced both to effect alliances with suitable partners against the autocratic government. Despite the intensification of Russification and discussions with the Russian liberals, the Finns were unable to break through the psychological barrier of their separatist-autonomous thinking. Finnish opinion split, and the movement as a whole was left straddling two worlds—one working for the destruction of autocracy and the other agitating for an acceptable *modus vivendi* with the Russian government. The majority of the Russian liberals, according to Dolgorukov, would accept a "withdrawal" of Russian authority from Finland only to *status quo* ante-Bobrikov. This position made impossible a deeper feeling of unity with the Finnish opposition.

The importance of the January discussions was that both groups finally understood the other's position on the crucial question of the future status of the national minorities in the Russian Empire. The majority of the Union of Liberation supported the aspirations of the Finns for a return to the *status quo,* but no more. On this basis, ties with the Russian liberals became regularized, and Dr. Adolf Törngren represented Finnish interests at most of the zemstvo congresses of 1904 and 1905. To the Union of Liberation the deliberations with the Finnish opposition undoubtedly provided a useful point of reference for the mood and aspirations of an important minority group.

The sum of developments during the first half of 1904 led the Finnish opposition to pursue a two-dimensional policy toward Russia. The minority, centered around Zilliacus and Biaudet, was dissatisfied with the results of the discussions with the Union of Liberation and sought closer collaboration with Russian revolutionary groups. In November, 1904, this group formally split away from the Passive Resistance and organized itself into the Finnish Party of Active Resistance. The majority of the Finnish opposition maintained discreet ties with the union, seeking an acceptable resolution of the Russification problem in Finland under the more favorable post-Bobrikov political conditions. The most important immediate consequences of the Finnish-Union of Liberation relationship was a decision reached during the spring of 1904 that the Finns and the union would coordinate their positions regarding the all-opposition conference that was being organized by Konni Zilliacus.

THE KADETS AND THE DUMA, 1905–1907

Judith E. Zimmerman

The formation of the Constitutional-Democratic party in October of 1905 marked the crystallization of a definite trend in Russian political thought, one which had been developing for at least a decade. Despite disagreements within the party, it is probably safe to say that "Kadetism" meant a demand for constitutional government, with a responsible ministry, and based on universal suffrage. Both constitutional and democratic, these Russian liberals were also committed to wide-ranging measures of social legislation, of which by far the most important was the demand for land reform.[1]

Between 1895 and 1905, when liberal demands were formulated, they could not have been fulfilled except by a fundamental change in the Russian state system; in other words, they were revolutionary. The October Manifesto raised the question of whether the satisfaction of the Kadet program still necessitated revolutionary change. In general, the Kadets appear to have believed at first that the revolution they needed had indeed taken place and now had only to be consolidated. As they gradually came to realize that their

---

1. There was, of course, disagreement within the party on this issue; Muromtsev, Rodichev, and Maklakov were only the most prominent opponents of land reform based on expropriation, and Miliukov himself appears to have been a lukewarm supporter at best. See: V. A. Maklakov, *Vtoraia gosudarstvennaia duma* (*vospominaniia sovremennika*) (Paris, n.d.), 134; S. E. Kryzhanovskii, *Vospominaniia iz bumag S. E. Kryzhanovskago, poslednago gosudarstvennago sekretaria Rossiiskoi Imperii* (Berlin, n.d.), 89; Vtoroi Vserossiiskii S"ezd delegatov Konstitutsionno-Demokraticheskoi Partii, *Biulleten' No. 4* (January 9, 1906), 4; P. N. Miliukov, "Rokovye Gody," *Russkiia zapiski*, 8–9(August–September, 1938), 120; 17(May, 1939), 115. Thomas Riha, in *A Russian European: Paul Miliukov in Russian Politics*, 76, states that Miliukov "fully agreed with the general outlines" of what would become the Kadet program, but generally this book attests to his lack of interest in the subject.

initial impression was mistaken, the party developed a strategy that remained revolutionary in that it attempted to force further structural change, with the Duma the key weapon in their arsenal. Kadet policy in the First Duma, then, was aimed not at using the Duma in the manner for which it had been designed, but as a means of extorting major concessions from the government—a strategy that today we would call "confrontation politics." It was only after the dissolution of the First Duma that the party shifted to a reformist position, aimed at working for change within the existing system. At no time, however, did the Kadets show a willingness to dispense with their agrarian program, and it was this, I feel, that torpedoed the relatively democratic system of 1905–1907.

The Kadets' attitude toward the Duma changed with their changing perception of Russia's constitutional structure. At a moment of revolutionary turmoil, the October Manifesto could easily be interpreted to mean that their demands had been satisfied. The manifesto's promise that, to the extent possible in the short time remaining before elections, "those classes of the population which at present are altogether deprived of electoral rights," should be given a vote, reserving "the further development of the principle of universal suffrage to the newly established Legislative Order," could mean governmental recognition of the principle of universal suffrage in the West European sense of the term. Point three of the manifesto, establishing "as an unchangeable principle, that no law can obtain force without the consent of the State Duma," certainly appeared to promise a genuinely constitutional system.[2]

On the other hand, the manifesto, while promising to expand the electorate, said nothing about changing the curial basis of elections, with its unequal representation of different classes. Furthermore, the Duma's constitutional position was not defined by the manifesto, which said nothing about other institutions that would share power with it. The party's immediate reaction to the October Manifesto was, consequently, a statement that it was not satisfactory:

The State Duma cannot be recognized as a proper popular representative body; therefore, the task of the Constitu-

2. Translation of the manifesto cited from Bernard Pares, *The Fall of the Russian Monarchy: A Study of the Evidence* (New York, 1939), 503.

tional Democratic Party remains the achievement . . . of
a constituent assembly on the basis of universal and equal
suffrage with direct and secret voting; and the State Duma
reformed by the Manifesto of October 17 can serve the
party only as one of the means for the realization of this
goal, while it preserves a constant and close connection
with the general course of the liberation movement outside
of the Duma.[3]

Most Kadets, however, felt that the manifesto implied
nothing about the future state structure except that autocracy
had come to an end, and therefore a constitution was needed
to define the new system. Further, they appear to have
believed that the tsarist regime, by its recognition of defeat
in October, had disqualified itself as a source of the constitution;[4] the government henceforth was qualified to act only
in a caretaker capacity with the obligation to call a constituent
assembly and to provide a framework of civil liberty within
which elections could take place. Even the moderate V. D.
Nabokov wrote in October, 1905: "The basic elements of
this reform must be universal suffrage, freedom, and a
constitution drawn up by a constituent assembly. The calling
of the latter is thus the direct and immediate task of the party's
activity."[5]

At the last of the zemstvo congresses, meeting a few
weeks later, the constituent assembly was identified with the
Duma; the term "constituent assembly" was replaced by

3. This position is associated with Miliukov. Maklakov reported Miliukov's lack of enthusiasm about the manifesto, which
Miliukov did not deny. Maklakov, *Vlast' i obshchestvennost'
na zakate staroi Rossii* (*vospominaniia*) (n.p., n.d.), 431;
Miliukov, *Vospominaniia* (*1859–1917*), vol. 1 of 2 vols., ed.
M. M. Karpovich and B. I. Elkin (New York, 1955), 311. The
party resolution issued on October 18 is printed in V. V. Vodovozov, *Sbornik programm politicheskikh partii v Rossii* (St.
Petersburg, 1905–1906), 54–55.

4. Miliukov reported in his memoirs that he suggested to
Witte in a meeting at the end of October that the prime minister
avoid the problem of a constituent assembly by granting a
constitution on the Belgian or Bulgarian model. Miliukov, *Vospominaniia,* 1:325–28; *Tri popytki* (*K istorii russkago lzhe-
konstitutsionalizma* (Paris, 1921), 22–25. It is apparent from
these accounts that in so doing he was acting counter to the
general party position.

5. V. D. Nabokov, "Sovremennoe polozhenie i takticheskiia
zadachi konstitutsionno-demokraticheskoi partii," *Pravo,* 41
(October 25, 1905), 3404–7.

"Duma with constituent functions." The latter was defined as a popular representative body elected by universal, equal, secret, and direct suffrage, which would formally be given constituent powers. Presumably the constitution would have to be ratified by the Emperor.[6] This position was straightforward, provided the assumptions that the government of Russia had to be totally reconstituted and that the Duma would be elected on the basis of universal, equal, secret, and direct suffrage were correct. The electoral law of December 12, 1905 showed that they were not, and the Kadets had to redefine their attitude to a State Duma elected by an unsatisfactory franchise, and therefore not qualified to undertake constituent functions.

At the same time that government initiative in the electoral law showed the Kadets that the October victory was not as complete as they had dreamed, they found their choice of means for further struggle restricted. In October they had boldly stated that the party would "preserve a constant and close connection with the general course of the liberation movement outside of the Duma." In fact, however, they had never been wholehearted supporters of revolutionary violence.[7] In December, Struve and Miliukov warned against the Moscow uprising;[8] after its failure, the Kadet attitude toward mass revolution hardened. It seemed quite clear that whether or not they approved of revolution, any dependence on it was at best impractical.

---

6. "S"ezd zemskikh i gorodskikh deiatelei," *Pravo*, 44 (November 13, 1905), 3616–20, 3623–25, 3699–3702; *Pravo*, 45–46 (November 20, 1905), 3720–27. Pavel Tolstoi, a left-wing critic of the Kadets, assumed that their definition of the constituent assembly implied monarchical ratification, and quoted Miliukov to the effect that the party did not mean a fully sovereign body by the term. Pavel Tolstoi, "O sovremennykh politicheskikh gruppirovkakh," *Bez zaglaviia*, 1(January 24, 1906), 11–12.

7. One of the major differences separating the Kadets from the former left wing of the Union of Liberation was the Kadet hostility toward the revolutionary parties and distrust of revolutionary mass action. See *ibid.*, 13; E. D. Kuskova, "Otvet na vopros—kto my?" *Bez zaglaviia*, 3(February 5, 1906), 85–87.

8. P. Struve, "Revoliutsiia," *Poliarnaia zvezda*, 1 (December 15, 1905), 11–12; Miliukov articles reprinted in P. N. Miliukov, *God bor'by: publitsisticheskaia khronika 1905–1906* (St. Petersburg, 1907), 170–78.

The Second Kadet Congress in January established the party's position vis-à-vis a Duma elected by the franchise of December 12. The Central Committee leadership took the rigid stand that this Duma could no longer serve as a constituent assembly. Instead, it was to take over the caretaker role originally assigned to the tsarist government. It should institute universal suffrage and establish a framework of civil and national rights. However, in view of the crisis situation, the First Duma was also to begin major legislative work on agrarian reform and local autonomy. Presumably the constitution would be enacted by the next Duma, elected by universal suffrage.[9] After the acceptance of resolutions to this effect, however, the Second Congress broadened the scope of Duma activity by indicating that no definite limits could be set to it.[10]

Before the Duma convened, the whole notion of a constituent Duma was nullified by the promulgation first of the Duma Statute and then of the Fundamental Laws. The Statutes of February 20, 1906 set up a bicameral system with a permanently conservative second chamber enjoying legislative rights equal to those of the Duma. The Kadets in the spring of 1906 were in a belligerent frame of mind after their success in the elections (which they considerably exaggerated at this point) and were in no mood to accommodate themselves to the State Council. The strategy formulated by Miliukov and adopted by the Third Kadet Party Congress directly prior to the opening of the Duma was one of cautious confrontation. The Duma was not to attempt to abolish the State Council, but simply to ignore it. The resolution indicated that the party still felt that the fundamental task of the Duma was to provide a framework for constitutional government, and that it would not be hindered in this aim by the existence of the State Council. Programmatic goals remained civil liberties, universal suffrage, land reform, and the "satisfaction of just national

---

9. Supplement to *Pravo*, 7(February 19, 1906), 25–29.
10. Vtoroi S"ezd, *Biulleten' No. 4* (January 9, 1906), 1–2. Although the resolution was proposed by members of the leadership group—Rodichev and Struve on the right and Koliubakin on the left—it expressed the views of the provincial membership, which was less concerned with theoretical niceties and eager to set about reforming Russia.

demands." In passing this legislation, the Duma was to act as though the State Council did not exist. Points II and III of the congress resolution on tactics stated:

> II. The Party will strive for the achievement of these goals, without hesitating even before the possibility of a break with the government, but it is obliged to take measures in order that all the burden of guilt and responsibility for a clash, if there is one, falls on the government.
> III. The Congress considers that the best plan of action in the Duma is an attack for the realization of the legislative measures enumerated above by means of the introduction of the corresponding bills and discussion of them in the Duma.[11]

Before the Third Congress had ended, the constitutional structure was further rigidified by the publication of the Fundamental Laws, which could be amended only by imperial initiative. The lower house could still draft an electoral law, but it had no power over the State Council, which was defined by the Fundamental Laws. In regard to the immediate Kadet program, amnesty was defined as a monarchical prerogative and no longer within the Duma's competence. The Kadet reaction was to limit their projected legislative activity to those areas still within Duma competence, while requesting imperial action in regard to amnesty and the second chamber; otherwise, their strategy remained unchanged. They would legislate, and the State Council and Emperor would either accede to the Duma's wishes, or else the ensuing stalemate would force a dissolution.

Why did the Kadets feel that their policy of continuing to push for a revised constitutional structure would bear fruit? There can be no definite answer to this question, but analysis of Kadet writings indicates that there were, broadly speaking, two reasons for their belief. The first was the sense of legitimacy created by the opposition victory in the elections. Opinion was divided about the meaning of the Kadet predominance in the Duma; the Central Committee took the position that the victory was not based on real support for Kadet principles, but on the fact that the left-wing boycott of the elections left the party with a monopoly on constitu-

---

11. The Congress resolutions are printed in Miliukov, *God bor'by*, 334–35.

tionalism.[12] The "right Kadets" around Peter Struve, on the other hand, argued that Kadet success meant that the party had succeeded in uniting the Russian masses into a conscious opposition to all the bureaucracy stood for.[13] All the Kadet commentators did believe, and with reason, that the vote signified a thorough repudiation of the old regime.[14] This led to an exaggerated sense of power, which Maklakov described with some bitterness years later:

> The party felt it had been victorious all along the line. It forgot what it had experienced after October 17. All failures were covered by the fact that the "people" were with the Kadets in the election. What could the doomed government, left without support in the country, do against them? Idealism, which believed that right immediately triumphs over might, that the government apparatus was powerless before the people's will, did not sink to the prosaic question of how the people's will could overcome the government's material superiority.[15]

Believing their program represented the minimum demands of the entire nation, the Kadets felt the government would give way. If it did not, there was an unspoken, perhaps

---

12. See, for example, the Central Committee statement, *Vestnik partii narodnoi svobody,* 12(May 25, 1906), 6; for other statements of roughly the same position, see Maklakov, *Vlast' i obshchestvennost',* 514–15; Maklakov, *Iz vospominanii* (New York, 1954), 353–57; N. Ezerskii, *Gosudarstvennaia Duma pervago sozyva* (Penza, 1907), 9–12; N. Kareev, "Vybory v Peterburge v pervuiu Gosudarstvennuiu Dumu," *K 10-letiiu 1-oi Gosudarstvennoi Dumy, 27 aprelia 1906—27 aprelia 1916: Sbornik statei pervodumtsev* (Petrograd, 1916), 3.

13. See, for example, Peter B. Struve, "Narodnaia Partiia Svobody," *Svoboda i Kul'tura,* 1(April 1, 1906), 58–61; S. L. Frank, "Molodaia Demokratiia," *Svoboda i Kul'tura,* 2(April 10, 1906), 68; E. Grimm, "Povorot," *Rech'* (April 2, 1906), 1–2; I. Grevs, "Posle pobed," *Rech'* (April 8, 1906), 2–3.

14. See, for example, Maklakov, "Sredi izbiratelei," *Russkiia vedomosti* (March 26, 1906), 2; Ezerskii, *Duma,* 9–10; Miliukov editorial, *Rech'* (March 21, 1906), 1, reprinted in *God bor'by,* 227.

15. *Vlast' i obshchestvennost',* 546–47. Harder heads in the party, among them Miliukov's, recognized the problem, but probably the rank and file were carried away by the euphoria expressed by Rodichev at the Third Congress. *Biulleteni III Obshcheimperskago delegatskago s"ezda partii Narodnoi Svobody,* 1(April 22, 1906), 4.

unconscious, assumption that revolution would follow.[16]

Once in the Duma, the Kadets' use of their legislative program as a means to force further constitutional change becomes clearer. The party had two major problems in the First Duma: the first was to control the opposition majority. During most of the Duma's short life, this was accomplished. The Kadets, with approximately 175 out of some 500 seats, were the largest single party; next were the approximate 135 members of the Trudoviki, or Labor Group, a parliamentary group formed only in the Duma and made up almost exclusively of peasants, that was led by intellectuals of peasant background. Programmatically the Trudoviki tended toward moderate populism, although a variety of positions was represented in the group. The Trudoviki almost always voted with the Kadets, as did the Polish group, and often the miniscule moderate group as well. There was no organized right wing in the Duma; rightist votes came from a group of about 100 "nonparty" peasants. Consistent opposition to the Kadets came only in June, when a group of Social Democrats elected in Georgia, after the lifting of the Social Democratic boycott, arrived in the Duma. The First Duma was almost unanimous in its positive program, and the drama of maintaining control consisted almost entirely of restraining the Trudoviki from undertaking steps which, because of their illegality, would provide a convenient pretext for dissolution.

The other, more important, and ultimately unsuccessful aspect of their tactics was to use what limited power the Duma did possess to institute a parliamentary system. A change of emphasis took place in the early days of the session; where formerly there had been a general assumption that a parliamentary constitution would be written by some representative assembly, the effort now became one of achieving legislative predominance and a responsible ministry within

16. Interestingly enough, Maklakov did formulate this belief. He wrote that if the Duma were to fail to respond to the people's demands, "the voter will condemn it too; he will lose that faith that made him peaceful and allowed him to wait patiently. . . . He will lose the faith, but his bitterness will not be reconciled, and then the last hope for a peaceful issue will fall, and there will be no barrier to the preaching of violence. That is why not simply personal conviction, but also observation of provincial life convinces me that only the program of the Party of Popular Freedom can—if it is still possible—transform Russia by peaceful means." "Sredi izbiratelei," 3.

the existing framework. The Fundamental Laws made it
unlikely that a new constitution would be written, and so an
effort had to be made to use the existing structure. Furthermore, the Kadets were pushed in the direction of concentrating
on achieving a Duma ministry by the attitude of the Goremykin ministry, which was no more eager than they were to
accept the newly created *status quo*.

The Duma, which had grown out of plans for the Bulygin
Duma of August, 1905, was designed as a consultative, not a
legislative body; it and the State Council were supposed to
discuss, amend, approve, or reject proposals brought to them
by the ministry. Legislation could be initiated by the Duma,
but the process was cumbersome, since it was intended that
this right would be exercised only in the unusual circumstances
when the ministry did not respond to the Duma's expressed
desires. According to the Duma Statute, legislative projects
could be introduced only by a group of at least thirty members.
If the Duma felt the project was desirable, the responsible
minister was to be informed, and he then had a month to
prepare the necessary legislation. If he failed to prepare the
bill requested, the Duma would write and pass its own law,
which was then subject to the approval of the upper house and
the Emperor.

The system could function only if both the ministry and the
Duma wished it to. In the First Duma neither side accepted
it, and the result was continuous conflict. The Goremykin
ministry proceeded to ignore the Duma and, when the Duma
convened in April possessed by an urgent need to set about the
task of reforming Russia, the ministry had no bills prepared.
The first measures presented to it, in mid-May, were appropriation requests for a new laundry and greenhouse at Dorpat
University, and these were introduced immediately after
government spokesmen had formally rejected most of the
Duma's plans for major structural reform.[17]

---

17. On May 13 Goremykin responded to the Duma's "Reply
to the Speech from the Throne," in which it had stated its own
legislative program and requested amendment of the Fundamental Laws, amnesty, and repeal of the extraordinary laws.
Goremykin ignored the Duma's distinction between its intentions
and its desires and attacked it for infringing upon the monarchical prerogative. He further stated that agrarian reform on
the basis of expropriation of private lands was "inadmissible,"
rejected the requests for amnesty and repeal of the extraordinary laws, and stressed the government's intention of struggling

The Duma was at least as intransigeant. Ministry bills were not simply rejected; with only one exception, they were not even placed on the agenda.[18] Under Kadet leadership, the Duma attempted to shift the locus of legislative initiative from the ministry to itself. A Kadet bill introduced a rather half-hearted modification of the Duma Statute, shortening the period between the original Duma statement of its desire for a bill from a month to one week. The Kadet project went to committee, a proposal was drawn up, but it was never reported out.[19] More importantly, the Duma evaded the possible month delay by utilizing an article of the statute that enabled it to elect a committee to draw up the "basic principles" of a law once its desirability had been established. Through this article the discussion of whether or not the Duma would request a bill from the ministry was transformed into a full-scale substantive debate, and the committee would report in a month not on basic principles, but on a completed project ready for Duma action.[20] This was the procedure used in the only bill that went through the entire Duma legislative process—a measure abolishing capital punishment.[21]

True to their program, the Kadets opposed government inaction with a broad series of legislative projects first expounded in the Duma's "Reply to the Speech from the

against revolutionary unrest and restoring order. *Pervaia Gosudarstvennaia Duma, Stenograficheskie otchety* (St. Petersburg, 1906), 294–95.

18. Before the Duma opened, I. V. Hessen had indicated that the Duma would not be seduced from its real function of basic reform by action on government bills. *Vestnik partii narodnoi svobody,* 6(April 11, 1906), 359–60.

Ministry bills were submitted on the reorganization of local courts, the criminal responsibility of officials, and the agrarian question, the latter similar to the legislation Stolypin would enact during the summer and fall. *Pervaia Duma, Stenograficheskie otchety,* 1213; *Rech'* (June 1, 1906), 3; S. M. Dubrovskii, *Stolypinskaia zemel'naia reforma* (Moscow, 1963), 97–102. The measure acted upon was an appropriation for supplemental famine relief. *Pervaia Duma, Stenograficheskie otchety,* 1449–52, 1646–65.

19. *Ibid.,* 592–603; M. M. Vinaver, "Konflikty v pervoi dume," *Pervaia gosudarstvennaia duma: sbornik statei,* vol. 1 of 3 vols. (St. Petersburg, 1907), 225–26.

20. The moderates questioned the legality of this procedure, but Muromtsev, the Kadet president of the Duma, defended it. *Pervaia Duma, Stenograficheskie otchety,* 302–4, 307–8.

21. *Ibid.,* 422–44, 640–42, 900–916, 1469–1504.

Throne," which was largely drawn up by the Kadets. It expressed the chamber's intention to undertake measures implementing universal suffrage, inviolability of person, freedom of speech, press, association, assembly, and strike, equality before the law, agrarian reform, labor legislation, local government reform, free education, and satisfaction of the demands of the national minorities. It also expressed the Duma's desire for constitutional reform leading to legislative predominance in a parliamentary system.[22] The party had either submitted or was working up bills in most of these areas at the time of dissolution.[23]

In addition to countering ministerial passivity with their own positive reform program, the Kadets led the Duma in its attack on the Goremykin government. The negative ministerial response to the Duma's "Reply" was greeted by angry speeches and a resolution expressing no confidence in the government and calling for its resignation.[24] All future confrontations resulted in more angry speeches and condemnatory resolutions.

The interpellation was another weapon used with great frequency by the First Duma; nearly 400 were introduced in the course of the short session, each illuminating a specific grievance against the system. Their subject matter included governmental involvement with pogroms, attacks on the competence and prerogatives of the Duma, failure to provide adequate famine relief, instances of Cossack brutality, and, by far the majority, instances of illegal imprisonment and exile. The Duma's interpellation power was limited, the ministers often refused to reply (usually only the ministries of the interior and justice attempted to justify their actions), and

22. *Ibid.*, 73–235, 239–43.
23. The following bills were sent to committee: civil equality, inviolability of person, freedom of speech, freedom of assembly, agrarian reform, abolition of capital punishment, amendment of the Duma Statute, and immunity of Duma members. The following were submitted to the Duma but not acted upon: freedom of conscience, judicial reform, freedom of association, freedom of the press, and the right to strike. Bills on universal suffrage and local government reform were still in the planning stage at dissolution. P. N. Novgorodtsev, "Zakonodatel'naia deiatel'nost' Gosudarstvennoi Dumy," *Pervaia gosudarstvennaia duma*, 2:11–12; F. F. Kokoshkin, "Proekt reformy zemskago samoupravleniia, vyrabotannyi v parlamentskoi fraktsii partii narodnoi svobody," *ibid.*, 2:26.
24. Pervaia Duma, *Stenograficheskie otchety*, 324–54.

the Duma usually found the answers unsatisfactory; but they did provide an outlet for the deputies' anger and maintained a high level of tension in the chamber.

By June it was clear that the stalemate had to be broken by either the resignation of the ministry or the dissolution of the Duma. Kadet confrontation politics were successful enough that negotiations toward a more responsive ministry began in mid-June, although it is impossible to tell how seriously the Emperor took them.[25] The decision to dissolve the Duma, instead of appointing a Duma ministry, may be partly attributable to the fact that unanimity in the Duma broke down with the arrival of the Social Democrats and loss of Trudovik support on the Kadet bill on freedom of assembly.[26] As I shall attempt to show later, the Duma's uncompromising stand on the question of land reform was probably of great importance in convincing the government to go ahead with dissolution.

The events of the summer of 1906 brought home to the Kadets the bitter truth that there was no hope of further change in a liberalizing direction. A majority Duma was not omnipotent, the Duma could not count on passive support from the population, and Stolypin amply proved that the government had the resources and the ruthlessness to crush the revolutionary movement. The government had demonstrated its ability to dissolve the Duma, and there was danger

---

25. Negotiations with the Kadets are summarized in Robert L. Tuck, "Paul Miljukov and Negotiations for a Duma Ministry, 1906," *The American Slavic and East European Review,* 10(April, 1951), 117–30; and in greater detail in Frederick J. Piotrow, "Paul Milyukov and the Constitutional-Democratic Party" (Ph.D. diss., Oxford University, 1962), 163–89. Miliukov's recollections can be found in: "Moe svidanie s generalom Trepovym," *Rech'* (February 17, 1909); "Sergei Andreevich Muromtsev: Biograficheskii ocherk," *Sergei Andreevich Muromtsev,* ed. D. I. Shakhovskoi (Moscow, 1911), 47–48; *Tri popytki: vospominaniia,* 377–85. Other memoir material includes: I. V. Hessen, *V dvukh vekakh: Zhiznennyi otchet* (Berlin, 1937), 229, which is vol. 22 of the 22-volume series *Arkhiv russkoi revoliutsii; Out of My Past: The Memoirs of Count Kokovtsev,* ed. H. H. Fisher, trans. Laura Matveev, The Hoover War Library Publications, 6(Stanford, 1935), 147–48; A. Izvolskii, *Recollections of a Foreign Minister,* trans. Charles Louis Seeger (New York, 1921), 183–218.

26. Discussion in Pervaia Duma, *Stenograficheskie otchety,* 1400–1423, 1424–40, 1452–66, 1523–49.

that the next dissolution would lead to an amended electoral law.[27]

After the failure of the Vyborg Manifesto, then, the Kadets shifted to an essentially defensive strategy, expressed by the slogan, "Preserve the Duma." Their eight-point platform represented a generalized, if slight, moderation of demands.[28] Tactics changed more fundamentally. No longer could the Kadets count on outside support for the Duma—it was isolated and vulnerable—and this meant the party had to concentrate on using the powers it did possess, and on lasting long enough to make an impact on the national mentality.[29]

Once the session had begun, in February, 1907, the Kadets scarcely wavered from their new, cautious line.[30] That they were able to do this with decreased representation in a polarized Duma is a tribute to their political skill.[31] In every

---

27. A changed electoral law had been recommended by the first congress of representatives of noble societies, which was held the first week in May and attended by members of the government. Appeals for the abolition of the Duma had been printed in government publications. Dubrovskii, *Stolypinskaia zemel'naia reforma*, 112. Changing the electoral law was under discussion at this time. Fisher, ed., *Out of My Past*, 154, 165–66.

28. *Russkiia vedomosti* (October 31, 1906), 4; platform reprinted in *Novaia duma: platforma partii narodnoi svobody*, (n.p., n.d.), 15–16; and *Partiia narodnoi svobody*, volume consists of *Programma pervoi dumy; Otvet dumy na tronnuiu rech';* and *Platforma k vyboram vo Vtoruiu Dumu*, (n.p., n.d.), 15–16.

29. See, for example, *Novaia duma*, 5; V. D. Nabokov, "Takticheskiia zadachi partii k-d," *Vestnik partii narodnoi svobody*, 38(November 23, 1906), 2010–11; *Rech'* (January 1, 1907), 1; S. Kotliarevskii, "Budet li raspushchena vtoraia duma?" *Russkiia vedomosti* (January 24, 1907), 2; G. N. Shtil'man, "Duma i obshchestvo," *Russkiia vedomosti* (February 16, 1907), 2; editorial, *Rech'* (February 4, 1907), 1.

30. The most notable exception to this is the repeal of the field courts-martial, a resounding piece of propaganda of no practical utility, accomplished with some violation of legality. For discussions, see Vtoraia Gosudarstvennaia Duma, *Stenograficheskie otchety: Sessiia vtoraia* (St. Petersburg, 1907), 1:359–438, 445–534, 2282. For criticism of the measure, see Maklakov, *Vtoraia duma*, 115.

31. The Kadets' representation was reduced to about 130, and with the Cossack and Moslem groups they commanded about one-third of the votes. The end of the socialist boycott brought in sixty-five Social Democrats and about half as many Socialist Revolutionaries, and they were joined by the Popular

aspect of Duma work, from the most routine details to major
policy questions, the Kadets consistently tried to evade
controversial issues and to defuse potential conflicts.

Thus, where in the First Duma the proceedings on opening
day had been interrupted by a plea for amnesty by Ivan
Petrunkevich, in the Second the Kadets were worried about
the same kind of intervention from the right.[32] Where the
First Duma had opened with the "Reply"—a dramatic
statement of principle—in the Second nothing at all was done
before the body had legally constituted itself by verifying the
credentials and seating one-half of the delegates.[33] In contrast
to the ringing declaration of nonconfidence that had greeted
Goremykin, the Kadets hoped for a silent reception of
Stolypin's programmatic statement on March 6; while they
were unable to convince the Social Democrats to go along,
they did succeed in ending the discussion with an unmotivated
formula of passage.[34] The Kadet attempt to avoid discussion
of a resolution on terrorism constituted a saga in itself.[35] The
party also tried to limit the time and attention devoted to
interpellations.

The Kadets actually attempted to downgrade the general
sessions altogether, replacing them with committee work, and
the Duma met fewer hours per week than it had before.[36]
Standing committees were elected almost immediately, and
the Kadet decision that ministerial bills would no longer
simply be ignored was reflected in the rulings that all minor
government money bills, and measures dealing with local
courts, inviolability of person, religious policy, freedom of

Socialist party. On the other wing, there were about twenty
reactionaries and forty moderates.

32. *Ibid.*, 65.

33. Vtoraia Duma, *Stenograficheskie otchety*, 1:65–120. The
First Duma had begun verification only on May 12. Pervaia
Duma, *Stenograficheskie otchety*, 285–94.

34. *Russkiia vedomosti* (February 27, 1907), 3; *Rech'*
(March 1, 1907), 1, and (March 2, 1907), 3. Discussion of the
Stolypin statement is in Vtoraia Duma, *Stenograficheskie otchety*,
1:120–74.

35. Alfred Levin, *The Second Duma: A Study of the Social-
Democratic Party and the Russian Constitutional Experiment*,
2nd ed. (Hamden, Conn., 1966), 261–78; Judith Zimmerman,
"Between Revolution and Reaction: The Russian Constitutional Democratic Party, October, 1905 to June, 1907" (Ph.D.
diss., Columbia University, 1967), 355–67.

36. Almost at once the Duma accepted the four day a week

conscience, local government, and the regulation of working hours would be sent to committee without debate.[37] At the same time, the revised Duma rules, largely formulated by Maklakov, did away with the precedent established in the First Duma of using preliminary debate for substantive discussion of a bill; on measures initiated by the Duma the chamber would submit proposals to the ministry and then wait one month before taking any action at all; the only exception to this involved procedure for dealing with proposals of doubtful constitutionality.[38]

The decision to send government-sponsored bills to committee was not a Platonic gesture. A number of minor bills were acted upon, most of which were either ministerial requests for extension of measures instituted by means of the decree power (Article 87 of the Fundamental Laws) or minor money bills.[39] Debate on the first major ministry bill, a measure reforming the local court system, was underway at the time of dissolution.

The crucial test of Kadet ability to control the unwieldy Second Duma was passage of the budget and the annual military levy. Passage of these measures was a major test of the Duma's good faith, while failure to do so would result only in the continuation of the laws in force for the preceding year. Despite the limitations on the Duma's budgetary powers the Kadets argued against rejecting Minister of Finance Kokovtsev's project, and at the same time promised a bill broadening these powers. With support from the Trudoviki the budget was sent to committee.[40] More difficulty was

schedule that eventually evolved for the First Duma. The sessions began three hours later, leaving the mornings free for committee work, and rarely ran over the 6:00 P.M. closing. Toward the end, however, the Duma added two night meetings a week for dealing with minor money bills. *Vtoraia Duma, Stenograficheskie otchety*, 1:341–59, 1403–8.

37. *Ibid.*, 1:876–90, 1278; 2:577–84.
38. *Ibid.*, 2:303–11.
39. *Ibid.*, 809–25, 829–80, 882–948, 980–1019, 1025–70, 1249–92, 1437–80.
40. *Ibid.*, 1:793–876, 896–934, 937–80, 987–1052, 1160–1268. The bill broadening the Duma's powers was approved by the Kadets' parliamentary faction on March 29 and was submitted soon after. *Rech'* (March 31, 1907), 2; *Rech'* supplement (March 30, 1907), 3. The budget committee did not have time to report out the amended project. The problem of ministerial noncooperation with the budget committee added a new strain

created by the recruits bill, when suddenly the Trudoviki and
Popular Socialists decided to oppose passage of the measure.
At the last minute the Polish group reversed its decision to
abstain and provided the margin needed to pass the measure,
but Nicholas was little happier about having his army bill
saved by Poles than he was at the thought of its being rejected
altogether.[41] The real crisis arose from the intemperate
remarks of the Social Democrat A. G. Zurabov in the course
of debate. The Duma's fate hung in the balance for several
days, and it was probably spared only by the intervention of
Stolypin.[42]

In the First Duma the Kadets gambled on a strategy of
confrontation; although they played their hand well, the
gamble did not pay off. In the Second they successfully
readjusted their strategy to the far more difficult task of
conducting a moderate policy in an extremely radical Duma.
Nonetheless, the Second Duma followed the First to dissolution, and to the *coup d'état* of June 3, 1907. It was not Kadet
tactics that were to blame, but their program; had they
assumed governmental power in the spring of 1906, they
would have attempted to introduce their agrarian program
based on the compulsory expropriation of private land. Had
the Second Duma not been dispersed, the Stolypin program
would have come before it for repeal or amendment. It is
my belief that this accounts for the failure of the constitutional
experiment of 1905.

The official pretext for dissolving the First Duma was its
resolution on the agrarian question. On June 20 the government had issued a communiqué stating that the agrarian
problem would be resolved without expropriation of private
land. On July 6, the Duma passed its controversial refutation
of the government position. It was never very clear what
purpose the Duma's statement was supposed to serve—the
Kadets insisted it was an attempt to pacify the anger of the
peasants, and asked them to wait patiently for the Duma to
provide them with land—but others felt that it was a

to Duma activity. See Vtoraia Duma, *Stenograficheskie otchety*,
1:1747–50; Levin, *The Second Duma*, 134–37, 225–26.

41. *Russkiia vedomosti* (April 15, 1907); Levin, *The Second
Duma*, 294–97.

42. For the Zurabov affair, see: "Zapiski F. A. Golovina,"
Krasnyi arkhiv, 19(1926), 142–45; Levin, *The Second Duma*,
294–304; Maklakov, *Vtoraia duma*, 181–82.

revolutionary proclamation.[43] In any case, even so severe a
critic of the Kadets' parliamentary tactics as Maklakov
argued that it was not, in fact, illegal.[44] The government,
however, had already stated that all programs involving the
expropriation of privately owned land were inadmissible.

In his memoirs Sergei Witte stated that at a conference
held to discuss the draft of the Fundamental Laws Goremykin
had indicated the need to dissolve the Duma if it broached the
question of land reform. Having put himself on record, Witte
felt Goremykin had no choice but to keep to his word.[45] The
Soviet historian S. M. Dubrovskii has found a memorandum
to this effect which indicates that the decision to dissolve was
made on June 8. Miliukov, in 1917, also stated that the
agrarian question lay behind dissolution.[46]

Ostensibly, the dissolution of the Second Duma had
nothing whatsoever to do with agrarian problems. Stolypin
called a closed session on June 1, where he announced that
he had definite evidence of illegal activities carried out by
the Social Democratic group and asked that all members of
the parliamentary party be expelled from the Duma so that
legal action could be taken against them. The Duma failed
to satisfy his twenty-four-hour ultimatum and was dissolved.
The case against the Social Democrats was quite obviously
a pretext. Despite evidence obtained from a police agent, the
attempt to link the Duma delegation with an illegal Social

43. For the history of the Duma project, see *Pervaia Duma,
Stenograficheskie otchety,* 1751–52, 1950–75; Gosudarstvennaia
Duma Pervago Sozyva, *Materialy k stenograficheskim otchetam
1906 g.: Korrekturnye ottiski po zasedaniiam 39 i 40 (6 i 7 Iiulia)*
(St. Petersburg, 1907), 2019–82; Vinaver, "Konflikty," 263–
73; Viktor Obninskii, *Novyi stroi,* Part I (Moscow, 1909), 181–
86; Miliukov, *Vospominaniia,* 1:397–98. The measure as finally
passed by the Kadets alone, all other parties abstaining, was
considerably watered down from the first draft. However, the
decision to dissolve the Duma had probably been taken on July
5, between the introduction of the radical draft and the voting
of the moderate Kadet statement. *Ibid.,* 399; D. N. Shipov,
Vospominaniia i dumy o perezhitom (Moscow, 1918), 460.
44. V. A. Maklakov, *Pervaia gosudarstvennaia duma (vospominaniia sovremennika)* (Paris, 1939), 213–14.
45. Sergei Witte, *The Memoirs of Count Witte,* trans. and ed.
Abraham Yarmolinsky (New York, 1967), 354–55, 372.
46. Dubrovskii, *Stolypinskaia reforma,* 102; Miliukov testimony in P. P. Shchegolev, ed., *Padenie tsarskago rezhima,* vol.
6 of 7 vols. (Moscow-Leningrad, 1924–1927), 295–300.

Democratic group in the army failed, and Stolypin's indictment of the deputies was, essentially, for being Social Democrats in contact with an illegal organization—the Social Democratic party—and attempting to realize their own clearly stated revolutionary goals. Further, the ultimatum, enforced before the Duma had decided whether or not to accede to the request, appears to be more a punitive than a political gesture.[47]

In mid-April, at the time of the Zurabov incident, Stolypin had been largely responsible for prolonging the life of the Duma. Two weeks later, at the beginning of May, he initiated the chain of events that culminated in dissolution. One element in his changed attitude may have been the completion of the new electoral law,[48] but there is also evidence that links his reversal of position with the success of the agrarian reform that bears his name.

Maklakov was one of four members of the Kadet parliamentary party in occasional informal contact with Stolypin during much of the Duma session, and his memoirs provide some information on the prime minister's attitudes. In late April or early May Stolypin told Mikhail V. Chelnokov, the Kadet Duma secretary, that he would dissolve the Duma rather than allow the repeal of the agrarian legislation.[49] Almost simultaneously the agrarian committee of the Kadet parliamentary group decided that all of Stolypin's legislation —aside from the institution of legal equality for the peasantry —should be repealed at once, as it was "unconditionally harmful to the interests of the population." [50] A few days later, on May 6, the ministry of the interior ordered the first of two raids on the headquarters of the Social Democratic parliamentary group, but the raid failed to produce evidence of criminal conspiracy.[51]

The Kadets in touch with Stolypin—Chelnokov, Struve, and Bulgakov, in addition to Maklakov—were eager for a compromise at almost any price, and may have been influential in the Kadets' failure to take any immediate action on their

---

47. See Levin, *The Second Duma*, 307–39.
48. *Ibid.*, 310.
49. Maklakov, *Vtoraia duma*, 233.
50. *Rech'* supplement (May 3, 1907), 4; *Russkiia vedomosti* (May 4, 1907), 2.
51. Vtoraia Duma, *Stenograficheskie otchety*, 2:207–52; Levin, *The Second Duma*, 314–17.

decision about the Stolypin reforms. They further hoped to avoid a definite commitment by the Duma to the principle of compulsory expropriation. They wanted the Duma to consider the Stolypin measures in detail, rather than rejecting them en bloc, so that they would remain in effect if the Duma limited itself to amendment, no matter how drastic, until the entire legislative process was completed; there would then be room for maneuver as the Duma attempted to formulate a bill that would pass the State Council and receive imperial confirmation. (Repeal could be effected by a simple majority vote.) When this plan was reported to Stolypin, he indicated that he found it satisfactory.[52]

On May 10 Stolypin addressed the chamber on the agrarian question, and while he did not unconditionally condemn all expropriation, he did reject all the schemes that had been introduced.[53] Maklakov was undoubtedly a major influence in convincing the Kadets that the Duma should make no formal response to the speech, and this was carried in the Duma.[54]

At the end of May the Kadets decided on their alternative to the Stolypin legislation on withdrawal from the commune and announced their decision on May 30.[55] The same day, Stolypin told the Emperor he would demand the lifting of parliamentary immunity of the Social Democratic deputies. On May 31 he sent Nicholas the dissolution order for signature and the following day made the demand in the Duma, which meant

52. For Kadet hesitation, see *Rech'* (May 15, 1907), 3; for the tactics of the four Kadets, see Maklakov, *Vtoraia duma*, 233–34. *Rossiia,* the paper expressing the government's position, indicated acceptance of this plan early in the Duma session; its implications of preserving the bulk of the Stolypin program were not lost on the Kadet journalist Izgoev, who also noted that the prime minister's tolerance of the radical Duma hinged on the agrarian program. A. S. Izgoev, "Obshchestvennoe dvizhenie v Rossii (Zametki publitsista)," *Russkaia mysl',* 28:3(March, 1907), part 2, 177–78.

53. Vtoraia Duma, *Stenograficheskie otchety,* 2:433–45.

54. *Ibid.,* 527–32; *Rech'* (May 26, 1907), 2; Maklakov, *Vtoraia duma,* 238–40.

55. *Rech'* (May 30, 1907), 2. This was confirmation of a unanimous decision of the party's committee on peasant equality arrived at on May 14. *Rech'* supplement (May 16, 1907), 4. The Kadet plan was far more careful of the rights of the commune as a whole than was the Stolypin program; any member of the commune could demand to withdraw his land, but withdrawal would normally take place only at repartition. At any other time agreement between the individual and the commune

dissolution.[56] On the night of June 1 the four Kadet deputies went to see the prime minister in an attempt to stave off the inevitable. Stolypin insisted the Duma should give up the Social Democrats, but, when pressed by Struve for the reason for his changed attitude to the legislature, indicated it was concern over the agrarian question.[57]

Relations between the First Duma and the government consisted of a rather straightforward struggle for power—the Goremykin ministry had no desire to compromise with any legislative body, much less one that intended to expropriate landowners' land. Stolypin did wish to work with the Second Duma, but only on his own terms.

The Kadets might have been able to persuade the assembly to give up the Social Democratic deputies and renounce compulsory expropriation—thereby saving the Duma—but this would have meant denying all they believed about parliamentary government and repudiating an integral part of their program. In a slightly different context, *Rech'* had editorialized on May 21:

> Indeed, our task is not the formation of a Duma majority at whatever cost. The majority we are working for must be able to realize—or approximate—our programmatic goals. If we had to sacrifice something vital from our own goals or assume obligations incompatible with our own intentions, then we would be turning *a means* into an end, and an end into a means.[58]

---

was necessary. If there were no general repartition, and the commune would not agree to withdrawal, the individual had no choice but to sell his land to the commune at the price determined by mutual agreement or court settlement.

56. Levin, *The Second Duma*, 322.
57. Maklakov, *Vtoraia duma*, 246–47.
58. *Rech'* (May 21, 1907), 1.

KADETS AND THE POLITICS OF AMBIVALENCE, 1905–1917

William G. Rosenberg

Preoccupied with biography and the ideological facets of "right" and "left" liberal outlooks, historians have generally glossed over the basic dynamics of Kadet party politics. This is surprising since, with the formation of the Kadet party in 1905, politics superseded ideology, in my judgment, in structuring the development of Russian liberalism. It is true, of course, that party members continually analyzed the appropriateness of their views to Russian society, while re-examining as well the philosophical validity of their political theories. Both the *Vekhi* controversy and the later publications of *Iz glubiny* and *Smena vekh* show this quite dramatically. Yet the fate of Russian liberals is only fully understandable in terms of Kadet party behavior; and the Kadets themselves must be studied in light of the obvious but neglected fact that from 1906 onward their behavior was constantly circumscribed by a need to preserve organizational cohesion, a dependence on voter support, and the necessity of acting as a party so as to prompt the government to alter its own political institutions.

My purpose here is not, however, to fill any gaps in our study of Kadet politics, or otherwise chart new waters. These must be the fruits of a full-scale investigation. Nor is it to enter into the discussion—which seems to me by now to have been virtually exhausted—about alternatives to revolution. Rather, my effort will be to suggest certain important aspects of the Kadets' behavior as a party between 1905 and 1917, and to raise several questions about the character of Kadet politics generally. This might set the political development of Russian liberalism in a somewhat clearer light, while also offering a further basis for thinking about the outcome of the revolution when, in fact, it did occur.

Our starting point must be the general task Kadets set for their party, which was nothing less than apocalyptic. (In this, incidentally, they much more resembled Marxists than they did Russian equivalents to the followers of Gladstone.) As national, *nadklassnye* (literally, "above class," or not oriented to class interests) liberals, Kadets saw their party lifting Russian society *as a whole* from its general condition of backwardness, championing the "good of the entire nation" rather than any specific social group or interest. Even the differences in outlook and temperament of men like Ivan Petrunkevich, Peter Struve, Paul Miliukov, and Vasilii Maklakov, failed to obscure the party's vision of itself as the true heir to the nineteenth-century intelligentsia tradition, which held selflessness as a supreme virtue. Throughout the party's entire existence, its pamphlet literature insisted that Kadets looked beyond the bounds of a political organization in the narrow, partisan sense, and struggled to meet the broad needs and desires of *all* social sectors.[1]

In practical terms, this national orientation meant that the divisions that rent Liberationists and Zemstvoists over whether to ally with the worker-peasant mass or the regime, the two principal forces of prerevolutionary Russia, could never be effectively resolved. In 1905, of course, the question caused a fracturing of the liberal movement. Early liberationist slogans like "No Enemies on the Left" drove right-liberals like A. I. Guchkov and D. N. Shipov to form their own political groups, while left-liberals like S. N. Prokopovich and V. Ia. Bogucharskii broke from the Kadets in part because of a difference of opinion over the question of how strongly the party would press the demands of the masses.[2] Nonetheless, the Kadets' task of demonstrating to both a self-serving autocracy and to self-interested workers and peasants that Russian progress could only be measured in national terms caused those who stayed with the party to continue to believe they should maintain working associations with all sides.

1. See P. Struve, "Ideinyia osnovy partii narodnoi svobody," *Vestnik partii narodnoi svobody* (hereinafter cited as *VPNS*), 36(November 10, 1906), 1863–78; A. Kizevetter, ed., *Napadki na partiiu narodnoi svobody i vozrazheniia na nikh* (Moscow, 1906), 7 ff.; K-D Partiia, *S"ezd 12–18 oktiabria 1905 g.* (Moscow, 1905), 5; Tsentral'nyi komitet partii narodnoi svobody, "K rabochim," *VPNS*, 2(March 5, 1906), 65–71; N. Losskii, *Chego khochet partiia narodnoi sovobody (konstitutsionno-demokraticheskaia)?* (Petrograd, 1917), 6; A. Izgoev, *Nashi politicheskiia partii* (Petrograd, 1917), 38–39; A. Kornilov, *Partiia narodnoi svobody* (Petrograd, 1917).
2. See the discussion in Donald Treadgold, *Lenin and his Rivals* (London, 1955), chaps. 6 and 8.

Kadets had to make *all* social classes and groups believe that Russian development required a rule of law, and that parliamentary government, civil liberties, social improvement, economic welfare, and domestic peace all related to each other in an integral way.[3]

As party leaders themselves recognized, the question of association was always one of degree. Kadets had to convince the regime of their loyalty to Russian national interests, but had to do so without alienating the masses whose support they wanted not only to win elections, but also to weaken the appeal of violence. The Kadets consequently had to champion popular demands without incurring the hostility of those who exercised real power, upon whom they depended for the development of parliamentary institutions.

The real danger of this position, of course, was that Kadets could be pressed by both sides, as indeed they were. But while Miliukov and others saw this dilemma clearly, they believed right up until the emigration of 1920–1921—when the party finally split on precisely the question of whether or not to become a class party and support wholeheartedly the demands of the peasants—that these were the risks of maintaining a national orientation, rather than a class-based or partisan one.

With few Western traditions, Russia was simply unready for the adversary politics of Britain or France, where parties pressed particularistic interests. Kadets subsequently felt they had to accept their party's difficult position as a result, simply, of Russia's backwardness. Somewhat curiously, considering they were a political party, Kadets referred to this posture with some pride as *nadpartiinost'* (standing "above partisan politics") or at least aside from narrow partisan concerns.[4]

---

3. This was the formulation of N. Astrov in an untitled short manuscript in the Panina Collection, Archive of Russian and East European History and Culture, Columbia University (hereinafter cited as Columbia Russian Archive), Box 1, Packet 1, Folder 3. I wish here to thank Philip Mosely for permission to use the Columbia Russian Archive, and especially its able curator, Lev Magerovsky, who graciously assisted me in using its materials.

4. The Kadets were not the only prerevolutionary group to adopt the pose of *nadpartiinost'*. A large number of deputies running simply under the *nadpartiinyi* label were elected to both the First and Second Dumas. They lacked the Kadets' organized political base, though, and it is fair to assert that the Kadets were Russia's only significant party with this outlook.

These were the general underpinnings of Kadet party
behavior that must be borne in mind while characterizing
their politics in each of the major periods of their prerevolutionary career. In the first of these, from roughly the summer
of 1905 until the Second Duma elections, the party formed
around a revolutionary program, as Professor Zimmerman
points out elsewhere in this volume. These were, of course, the
months in which party leaders became fully cognizant of the
power of mass movements to provoke change and issued a
number of radical appeals. Thus, Miliukov in the summer of
1905 believed that "all methods" were legitimate against the
autocracy; Petrunkevich regarded "the people" as "our sole
hope"; the First Kadet Congress declared "complete solidarity"
with the strike movement; and Kadets insisted even after the
October Manifesto that they would fight on for a true political
democracy.[5] The result was the beginning of what Professor
Zimmerman regards as a period of "confrontation politics,"
and what Leonard Schapiro considers the "tragedy" of liberal
delusion. "It was Miliukov's tragedy," Schapiro writes in his
discussion of the *Vekhi* essays, "that he believed he was a
liberal when he was in reality a radical."[6]

These were also months in which both right and left Kadets
increasingly worried about revolutionary destructiveness,
and the "fragility" of Russian social existence.[7] As Professor
Zimmerman points out, the party came out against the Moscow
insurrection and decided at its Second Congress to participate
in the Duma, despite the restrictive electoral law of December 11 which, many felt, destroyed its function as a constituent
assembly.[8] If we paraphrase Vladimir Hessen, Kadets

5. P. Miliukov, *Vospominaniia (1859–1917)*, vol. 1, 290–
91; E. D. Chermenskii, *Burzhuaziia i tsarizm v revoliutsii, 1905–
1907 gg.* (Moscow-Leningrad, 1939), 109–10; K-D Partiia,
S"ezd 12–18 oktiabria, 21; Resolution of the Kadet Central Committee, December 10, 1905, in the Miliukov Collection,
Columbia Russian Archive, Box 8131, Section 13, Folder 1.
6. L. Schapiro, "The *Vekhi* Group and the Mystique of Revolution," *Slavonic and East European Review*, 34(1955–
1956), 67.
7. See especially the discussion in V. Maklakov, *Vlast' i
obshchestvennost' na zakate staroi Rossii* (Paris, 1936), 369 ff.;
and I. Petrunkevich, *Iz zapisok obshchestvennago deiatelia:
vospominaniia*, 402 ff., which is vol. 21 of *Arkhiv russkoi
revoliutsii*.
8. K-D Partiia, *Postanovleniia II-go S"ezda 5–11 ianvaria
1906 g. i programma* (St. Petersburg, 1906). The statutes of

committed themselves firmly at this time to the realization of legality in Russian life. What this means in practical terms is that the party determined to press for its program only *within* the institutional bounds set by the regime.[9]

Radical in program, cautious in tactics, the Kadets assumed a deliberately ambiguous position in the winter of 1906, and they did so for strategic reasons. Believing that the mass of Russian voters was also leery of revolution "from below" and that the voters would support party candidates who were *of* the left but not *in* the left, the Kadets sought to build their political power through an election victory and thereby harness popular wrath to legal methods.[10] The problem was that a successful implementation of their program did not depend on the number of votes Kadets received, but on the voluntary acquiescence of the government. Nicholas and his advisors had to accept Kadet electoral success as evidence of the nation's will and feel compelled on that basis to grant the party power.[11]

Kadets did, of course, win something of an election victory, though the boycott of left-wing parties made determining the true nature of their support difficult. Even *before* the balloting, however, Nicholas and his ministers had already decided what type of parliamentary system Russia would have. On February 20, 1906, the government had published the Duma Statute, which drastically limited that body's power as an independent parliament. Shortly afterwards, the

December 11, providing for unequal and indirect suffrage, and only limited worker representation, were bitterly resented on the left and were a major reason for boycotting the elections. The Kadets were also highly dissatisfied. See P. Miliukov, "Izbiratel'nyi zakon 11 dekabria," *God bor'by* (St. Petersburg, 1907), 78–81; and N. Kareev, "K voprosu ob uchreditel'nykh funktsiiakh gosudarstvennoi dumy," *VPNS*, 3(March 12, 1906), 142–50.

9. V. Hessen, "Taktika partii v pervoi gosudarstvennoi dume," in A. Mukhanov and V. Nabokov, eds., *Pervaia gosudarstvennaia duma* (St. Petersburg, 1907), vol. 1 of 2 vols., 119–53; Kadet Central Committee discussions on this question appear in B. Grave, ed., "Kadety v 1905–1906 gg." *Krasnyi arkhiv*, 46(1931), 38–68, and 47–48(1931), 111–19.

10. P. Dmitrenko, "Vospominaniia," unpublished manuscript in the Columbia Russian Archive (n.p., n.d.), 100–115. Dmitrenko was a Kadet party organizer in Petersburg.

11. Kadet leaders fully expected this to happen. See *Rech'* (February 23, 1906); V. Nabokov, "K voprosu o boikote dumy," *VPNS*, 2(March 5, 1906), 71–79.

Tsar appointed a "tottering relic," Goremykin, as prime minister, and in April the Tsar issued an unamendable constitution: the Fundamental Laws. The importance of these familiar developments from the standpoint of Kadet politics is that they undermined the party's strategic position and rendered its relations with its constituents extremely tenuous. By ignoring what Kadets regarded as the popular will, the regime was indicating that Kadet party politics would not lead to a genuine constitutional democracy.

But what course now for the Kadets? It becomes obvious from Professor Zimmerman's details that the party faced a dilemma. On the one hand, Kadet cooperation with the government would drive many supporters into the hands of left-wing parties, particularly if the latter lifted their boycott in future elections. If, on the other hand, the Kadets called for workers and peasants to "use all necessary means," as some party members had done the previous summer, the Kadets would pour oil on the smoldering embers of uncontrollable mass unrest. A third alternative was to confront Goremykin directly through their own Duma boycott, but this action might further deprive them of the government's regard. Kadets still cherished the thought that they themselves would eventually be appointed to ministerial positions. Besides, they very much valued even a rump Duma as a public forum, for it was the primary vehicle through which Russia as a whole might be politically educated.[12]

The party's resolution emerged in the ambivalent declarations of the Third Congress: Kadets would "struggle" for their goals within a system clearly designed to thwart achievement of those goals—a curious brand of confrontation politics, indeed. And it is in these terms that one must understand the nature of Kadet "radicalism" in the First Duma. If one reads the speeches of Kadet Duma delegates —later published in huge editions as if to prove the party's radicalism to potential supporters— one finds extremely forceful language. Also, Kadets did indeed treat ministers harshly and replied to the "Address from the Throne" with a clarion call for change,[13] but none of the constitutional demands in the "Reply" ever found their way into draft

---

12. See the discussion in V. Nabokov, "Pered dumoi," *VPNS*, 6(April 11, 1906), 353–58.

13. For example, the "Statement of the 42" on the agrarian question was published in a run of 50,000 copies for public

legislation. In all their proposals, Kadets showed their loyalty to the system by staying within the permissible limits of the Fundamental Laws.[14] On the amnesty issue, the party not only discarded its own program, but convinced the Trudoviki to do the same, since the Fundamental Laws made amnesty an exclusive prerogative of the Crown. They also beat back a proposal that the Duma abolish capital punishment—a reform they supposedly very much wanted—on the grounds that constitutional *procedures* had not been used in presenting the question.[15]

The underlying reason for Kadet acquiescence is obvious with even a cursory reading of memoirs and party reports and has been pointed out in many places: Kadets feared the violence of a new revolutionary wave. The seedling Duma needed time, and Russia had to grow accustomed to this first institutional product of political adolescence. Kadets still had to maintain their electoral following and cater to popular militance, since only their party embraced the interests of the entire nation, and Russian progress thus depended on their popularity.

Rather than a strategy to force change from Nicholas and Goremykin—who thought of the Duma, of course, as simply another tool with which to lance the abcess of revolution—Kadet radicalism was a verbal mood or attitude in the First Duma, designed to appease radical supporters and dampen revolutionary fires, to say to the masses, as a young Central Committee member declared in the Duma: "Wait a little longer, we are struggling for you, believe us, stay peaceful and calm." [16] Lenin recognized this, and so

distribution, while the party issued 500,000 copies of their radical "Reply" to Nicholas' "Speech from the Throne." See *Otchet tsentral'nago komiteta konstitutsionno-demokraticheskoi partii* (St. Petersburg, 1907), 80–81.

14. The Kadet "Reply" is in Pervaia Gosudarstvennaia Duma, *Stenograficheskie otchety* (St. Petersburg, 1906), 1:239–43. It can be compared with the Kadet draft legislation in Mukhanov and Nabokov, or N. Astrov et al., eds., *Zakonodatel'nye proekty i predpolozheniia partii narodnoi svobody 1905–1907 gg.* (St. Petersburg, 1907). See also *Otchet tsentral'nago komiteta*, 56; M. Vinaver, *Konflikty v pervoi dume* (St. Petersburg, 1907), 15–59.

15. Pervaia Duma, *Stenograficheskie otchety*, 1:642, 660–61, 1469–82; Vinaver, *Konflikty*, 143–46.

16. Pervaia Duma, *Stenograficheskie otchety*, 1:1984–85.

did some Kadets themselves, who worried that verbal confrontation was devoid of any real coercive content.[17]

On this basis, moreover, one might reconsider the Vyborg affair. With Evgenii de Roberti, who insisted to his Central Committee colleagues that the "poorly cultured Russian people" needed some symbol of popular representation to keep their brutal instincts in check, Kadet leaders feared the Duma's dissolution might spark wild disorders. The Duma therefore had to act, as much to stave off riots by showing it still existed as to indicate to the regime that the peoples' representatives could not be treated with impunity. Thus Kadets led fellow delegates across the Finnish border.[18]

Once across, party leaders worked assiduously to prevent their socialist colleagues from calling a general strike or otherwise taking advantage of the expected revolutionary wave to advance their own partisan causes. Despite the fact that the Vyborg Manifesto itself urged peasants to resist the draft and not pay taxes until the Duma reconvened, Kadets were certain it was preventing widespread disorder, rather than promoting it, by channeling potentially violent energies

---

17. See V. I. Lenin, *Polnoe sobranie sochineniia*, 5th ed., (Moscow, 1968), vol. 12 of 55 vols., 91–94, 103–5, 115–16; Dmitrenko, "Vospominaniia," 113–15.

18. See Grave, "Kadety," 64–65, for discussion of Central Committee on June 4, 1906. Kadet fears concerning popular response to the dissolution of the Duma are discussed by M. Vinaver, *Istoriia Vyborgskago vozzvaniia*, 7–9; and in *Delo o Vyborgskom vozzvanii: Otchet o zasedanii osobago prisutstviia S-Peterburgskoi sudebnoi palaty* (St. Petersburg, 1908), 14–15, which contains the testimony of I. I. Petrunkevich. See also *Rech'* (July 16 and 18, 1906). The government also feared that dissolution might spark popular disorders. Taking Kadet rhetoric more seriously than the radicals, Goremykin thought the Duma was strong enough to rally the country in a direct confrontation with the regime and make good Kizevetter's rhetorical boast to the Third Kadet Congress that, "If they dissolve the Duma, it will be the government's last act, since they will cease to exist." It may have been this fear that underlay both Trepov's and Stolypin's tenuous efforts to negotiate a Kadet ministry. And it was precisely this fear that caused Goremykin to ring the Taurida Palace with machine guns when the Duma was, in fact, dissolved. See A. Izvolskii, *Recollections of a Foreign Minister*, trans. Charles Louis Seeger (New York, 1921), 184 ff.; V. Maklakov, *The First State Duma*, trans. M. Belkin (Bloomington, Ind., 1964), chap. 13; and R. Tuck, "Paul Miliukov and Negotiations for a Duma Ministry," *American Slavic and East European Review*, 2(1951), 117–29.

toward the paths of passive resistance.[19] Not surprisingly,
once it was clear that peasants and workers would not respond
in any active way to the Duma's dissolution, Kadets made
virtually no effort to gain support for the Vyborg demands; at
the Fourth Congress in September they disavowed them
altogether.[20]

The aftermath of Vyborg divides what might be called the
Kadet's nonrevolutionary radicalism from a new period in
their politics, which might be described as one of antigovernment conservatism. Politically the Kadets were in considerable
disarray; not only was their First Duma strategy discredited,
but a host of prominent party figures also were barred from
further Duma activity. Kadets, moreover, seeing a growing
reaction in the fall of 1906, became more anxious than ever to
control the government's temper; hence their strategy of
"protecting" the Duma.[21]

If one must question the nature of Kadet radicalism in the
First Duma period, there is also cause to re-examine the
thoroughness of the party's new commitment to cooperation, a
posture ostensibly maintained through the Second and most of
the Third Dumas. One must first note, however, that the
party's *parliamentary* behavior in both the Second and Third
Dumas was eminently suited to a cooperative policy. Again
Professor Zimmerman provides essential details: Kadets used
interpellations cautiously, refrained from direct attacks on
ministers, concerned themselves primarily with government
bills, and forced other parties, as much as possible, to act
strictly "within the Duma's legal competence as a legislative
body."[22] While failing to keep the Second Duma alive, they at

19. *Delo o Vyborge,* 16–17, contains the Kokoshkin testimony;
Vinaver, *Isotoriia Vyborgskago vozzvaniia,* esp. 21–22. The
Vyborg debates appear in A. Sergeev, ed., "Pervaia gosudarstven-
naia duma v Vyborge," *Krasnyi arkhiv,* 57(1933), 85–99.

20. For discussion of the Kadet Central Committee on the
provincial response to the Vyborg Manifesto, see the Miliukov
Collection, Columbia Russian Archive, Box 8122, Group 2,
Section 5, Folder 15; the Fourth Kadet Congress discussions
appear in *Russkiia vedomosti* (September 26–30, 1906). See also
the editorial in *Rech'* (September 29, 1906).

21. P. Miliukov, "Novaia takticheskaia postanovka pro-
grammnykh voprosov," *VPNS,* 35(November 5, 1906), 1781–93,
and his *Vospominaniia,* 1:409–24.

22. P. Miliukov, "Taktika K-D v dume," in *Russkiia vedomosti*
(February 20, 1907). See also Miliukov, "Novaia," 1791–93;
V. Nabokov, "Takticheskiia zadachi partii K-D," *VPNS,*

least felt some measure of success in the Third, where as opponents *to* His Majesty, rather than His Majesty's Opposition (as Miliukov remarked in an ungarded moment),[23] various party leaders established their expertise on different government problems and earned the respect of radicals and bureaucrats alike. At least in the Third Duma's first three sessions, lasting almost until the end of 1910, Kadets felt they were making progress. The government responded to Duma interpellations and accepted the Duma's use of its budgetary rights to raise questions of policy. Generally, Kadets thought they were preparing for the time when the "natural liberalization" of government attitudes, as *Rech'* once described Russia's "inevitable" political modernization,[24] would offer their own projects more chance of success.[25]

That which restrained this effort at accommodation and made the party's cooperative posture ambivalent at best was the electoral mechanism of the Duma campaigns and the necessity to win votes. Throughout the entire period when Kadets in the Duma were trying to tame government reactionaries, local party committees all over Russia were conducting election campaigns on the premise that voters were radical and that radical socialists, entering the competition for the first time, would sap Kadet strength. This was the case in the Second Duma election campaign, and to some extent, at least, it was the case as well in the Third Duma campaign of 1907 and the Third Duma bielections of 1909.

The election activities of the Petersburg group serve as a good example. This was perhaps the Kadets' most illustrious local committee, including in its membership such eminent figures as Miliukov, Maxim Vinaver, Fedor Rodichev, and Ivan Petrunkevich. On November 4, 1906, when it formally opened its Second Duma campaign, the Petersburg group was evenly split as to whether or not it should block its slate of delegates with left-wing parties. At first, by a margin of a

---

38(November 23, 1906), 1999–2014; and especially A. Kaminka and V. Nabokov, eds., *Vtoraia gosudarstvennaia duma* (St. Petersburg, 1907).

23. T. Riha, *A Russian European: Paul Miliukov in Russian Politics,* 178.

24. *Rech'* (June 2, 1907).

25. K-D Partiia, *Tret'ia gosudarstvennaia duma: Materialy dlia otsenki eia deiatel'nosti* (St. Petersburg, 1912), esp. vi–vii.

single vote, the group decided on an independent slate,[26] but
the split was so dramatic the question remained open. On
November 25, the group declared it was "necessary to try to
follow [the party's] own line, but to remain ready at the
same time, in case it seems necessary, to enter into an
agreement with the [Social Democrats]."[27]

The debate continued through December, with one faction
arguing in favor of an open alliance with the socialists and
another opposed. What distinguished these discussions from
earlier debates on tactics in the Union of Liberation and the
zemstvo movement is that Kadets were now consciously
trying to set their posture as a party, determining which was
the best way to maintain their electoral support. Some wanted
a complete bloc; some wanted three slots on the Kadet slate
given to Social Democrats; some wanted two, and some one
slot to a genuine worker, and several slots to socialist
moderates. Finally, on January 1, 1907, well after the party's
national leadership determined to follow a policy of
"cooperation" in the Duma, the Petersburg city committee
finally voted to give one place on its slate to a militant
worker, and one place to a "genuine" leftist. It was Miliukov
himself who insisted this step be taken "to calm our electors
who want us to bloc with the left very much."[28]

That the socialists in Petersburg failed to respond to the
Kadets' rather offhanded tender is less important than the fact
that district committees here and elsewhere campaigned as
if they had. The government consequently had good reason to
continue regarding the party's "cooperative" posture with
suspicion. Moreover, Kadet concern for leftist sympathies
continued past the electoral reform of June 3, 1907. Though
drastically restrictive, the June 3 reform still left Petersburg
Kadets (along with their party comrades in other major cities)
to contend with voter sentiment in the so-called second
curia, where the franchise was still sufficiently broad to allow
the election of a number of left-wing deputies.[29] And while

26. D. Protopopov, ed., *Ocherk deiatel'nosti S.-Peterburgskoi gorodskoi gruppy partii narodnoi svobody* (St. Petersburg, 1908), 8–9.

27. *Ibid.,* 10.

28. *Ibid.,* 14.

29. A. Levin, "June 3, 1907: Action and Reaction," in A. Ferguson and A. Levin, eds., *Essays in Russian History* (Hamden, Conn., 1964), 233–73.

apathy, depression, and the absence of arguments about political blocs characterized the Petersburg Kadet group's Third Duma campaign, party spokesmen continued their efforts to identify constitutional democracy with the programs, values, and spirit of the left.[30] A similar pattern also appears —rather dramatically, in fact—in the supplementary elections of September, 1909, in Petersburg for the seat of the expelled Kadet deputy Koliubakin. Here N. N. Kutler ran hard against the Bolshevik Sokolov, his closest competitor, by advancing the Duma as the best weapon to struggle for the realization of popular objectives. "The Kadets," party spokesmen argued, "have done more for the *real* interests of the working masses than have all of the Social Democrats." [31]

The conflicting demands of local and national politics thus led Kadets into a position where the disparity between "cooperation" with the government and a practical defense of the "real interests of the working masses" was increasingly less tenable. Party leaders were still reaching inconsistently in several directions, unsure of their tactics. Moreover, since the Kadets' conception of the "real" interests of workers was inextricably bound to their conception of Russia's national development as a whole, in which the interests of *all* social classes would be protected, they refused to stand as "special" champions for particular class interests, as did the Social Democrats on one hand, or Trade Industrialists and other explicitly bourgeois groups on the other. Hence they invited electoral indifference—workers regarding them as bourgeois, tradesmen and manufacturers regarding them as left. At the same time, however, the fact that Kadet leaders continued to insist on their own basic militance only increased the

---

30. For example, on September 30, 1907, two weeks after the campaign for the Third Duma had gotten underway, *Rech'* editorialized that "a number of special 'democratic parties' have not, in fact, taken upon themselves the defense of the interests of all democratic strata of society, but this had been done rather by political parties organized entirely on non-class principles. . . . The Party of People's Freedom not only does not stand in opposition to a democratic program, but on the contrary, gives the possibility of its practical realization." See also *Rech'* editorial (September 20, 1907), where Octobrists are described as "fish out of water," and other campaign materials on September 27 and 28, and October 2, 1907.

31. *Rech'* (September 14, 1909). The results of the election are in *Rech'* (September 23, 1909).

hostility of the government. The implementation of the liberals' own program "from above" thus seemed increasingly less likely. By the spring of 1910, in fact, the disparity between the party's posture in practical local politics and its cooperative attitude at the level of state administration was so obviously contributing to the party's over-all weakness that Central Committee members themselves began discussing ways to resolve it before the Fourth Duma elections, still two years away.[32] The general feeling seems to have been that Duma posture should be brought in line with election strategy, rather than vice versa. If the party turned leftward and mobilized new popular support, Kadet delegates hopefully might replace Octobrists as the "pivotal force" in the Duma.[33]

There was, of course, no unity of view within the party. Kadets remained the same diversified group of liberal professionals and intellectuals they were at the time of the party's formation. Fedor Kokoshkin, Andrei Shingarev, Ariadna Tyrkova, and even Miliukov himself were impressed, for example, by the way in which the State Council seemed to be cooperating with the Duma, and with the readiness of many Octobrists to work with the left in defense of Finnish autonomy and the rights of non-Russian nationalities. Some saw this as an indication that the regime would come around, that Russia was well on her way to a new political order.[34]

Others recognized, however, that cooperation of this sort bore precisely the difficulties Liberationists and Zemstvo-Constitutionalists had faced a decade earlier. The regime was still opposed to any changes that would weaken its power. Rather than a step toward the eventual implementation of a liberal program, Kadets like Mandel'shtam, Nicholas Shchepkin, and Nicholas Kishkin worried that improved relations between the ministers and the party might simply vitiate the latter as an effective force for reform, the same fear radicals in 1905 and earlier had had about liberals in general.

The ministers, moreover, were relying on arbitrary

---

32. A. Avrekh, *Stolypin i tret'ia duma* (Moscow, 1968), 433, quoting Central State Archive of the October Revolution, hereinafter cited as TsGAOR, SSSR, *fond* 523, *opis'* 1, *delo* 10, 36, 39–41.

33. Correspondence from F. Kokoshkin to I. Petrunkevich, October 20, 1911, in the Panina Collection, Columbia Russian Archive, Box 1, Folder 6.

34. S. Ol'denburg, *Tsarstvovanie imperatora Nikolaia II* (Munich, 1949), vol. 2 of 2 vols., 35, 65–76.

bureaucrats, who acted with scant regard for a rule of law, and Article 87 of the Fundamental Laws, which in practice allowed officials to bypass the Duma completely. Both right and left Kadets worried, therefore, that if the party became more closely involved in official policy, it might only be postponing new popular disorders, rather than dealing with their causes.[35] As conservative a Kadet as Vasilii Maklakov was so convinced administrative arbitrariness would provoke new upheavals that on one occasion, in February, 1910, he suggested his Duma colleagues could only prevent a revolution by making one themselves.[36]

Equally important was the fact that many Kadets saw little real progress being made toward the realization of their goals. The Third Duma was surviving, but with only limited powers, and with no real control over government policy or behavior. Some success had been gained in developing local government, particularly in land reform, but many Kadets bitterly resented the procedures by which Stolypin had introduced his legislation of November, 1906, and they were soon convinced as well that eventually the government's plan would prove disastrous for landless or poor peasants who would have little opportunity to develop consolidated homesteads. At the same time all discussions of national defense issues, which were of vital interest to the nationalistic Kadets, were closed to the party as an officially proscribed group; and there seemed little progress concerning questions on health, sanitation, living conditions, and other critical social areas. Most of all, Kadets resented the government's failure to submit to the Duma any significant civil rights legislation and saw this as a device to screen administrative malfeasance. Even as the Third Duma came to a close, delegates themselves were still prohibited from receiving subscriptions to foreign periodicals whose contents were critical of the regime. Yet it was precisely because of such questions that liberal professionals had begun organizing their movement more than fifteen years before.

---

35. P. Miliukov, "Politicheskiia partii v gosudarstvennoi dume za piat let," *Ezhegodnik gazety Rech' na 1912 god* (St. Petersburg, 1912), 77–96, esp. 95; M. Ganfman, "Zakonodatel'stvo," *ibid.*, 49–76; V. Nabokov, "Printsip zakonnosti v administratsii sude i gosudarstvennoi dume," *ibid.*, 35–48, esp. 36.

36. Gosudarstvennaia Duma, Tretii sozyv, *Stenograficheskie otchety,* sess. 3, 1774–91.

A new radical spirit thus began to develop in Kadet ranks in 1910, increasingly disdainful of both intransigent ministers and the so-called *verkhovniki* within the party (like A. S. Izgoev, Ariadna Tyrkova, and Peter Struve) who continued to advocate what was in effect a policy of ambivalent conciliation.[37] The hope of this resurgent leftism, represented in part by Nicholas Nekrasov, Nicholas Kishkin, and Ivan Petrunkevich, was to dissociate Kadets from the Octobrist center in the Duma and take advantage both of growing unrest in the countryside and a marked rise in strike activity to create what Nekrasov described in Central Committee meetings as a new Union of Liberation. In Nekrasov's design the new union, like the old one, would be broader than the Kadet party itself, but sharply demarcated on the basis of its political and civil libertarian objectives from those who supported the established order. According to Kishkin, Kadets were to take the lead in creating the new alliance by emphasizing their differences with Octobrists in the election campaign and by making them, rather than the socialists, the party's chief opponents.[38]

The arguments for a change in Kadet orientation rapidly gained support—a development that may have been related to the growth of Russian masonry around this time—though some who supported it in the Central Committee were not masons, or otherwise part of Nekrasov's clique.[39] Petrunkevich, for example, was convinced that Russia was entering a new revolutionary period, similar to the years between 1903 and 1906, and felt Kadets should respond accordingly. The majority of his committee colleagues apparently agreed.[40]

At a series of party meetings in the fall of 1911, Kadet

---

37. Kokoshkin to I. I. Petrunkevich, September 23, 1910, Panina Collection, Columbia Russian Archive, Box 1, Folder 6. Testimony given to B. Nicolaevsky in 1927, in the Nicolaevsky personal archives, Stanford, Calif., graciously provided to me by A. M. Bourgina. See also the discussion in Avrekh, *Stolypin i tret'ia duma*, 461–64.

38. Avrekh, *Stolypin i tret'ia duma*, 430, quoting TsGAOR, *fond* 523, *opis'* 1, *delo* 5, 54. See also the editorial discussion in *Rech'* (January 21, 1911).

39. G. Aronson, *Rossiia nakanune revoliutsii* (New York, 1962), 138–41. Nekrasov was a prominent mason himself.

40. Correspondence from I. I. Petrunkevich to his son, September 13, 1911, in the A. I. Petrunkevich Collection, Yale University.

leaders finally defined their new "union" to include the left wing of the right as well as the right wing of the left (to borrow Leninist phrasing).[41] The Kadet strategy that finally emerged for the Fourth Duma elections was "to unite all progressive elements in the country." [42] While the formula was ambiguous—as so often in the past—the Central Committee was implicitly excluding Octobrists from the ranks of "progressives" and including Social Democrats, though local committees were free to define specific alliances as they pleased.

It is known today that Kadet election tactics failed to alter the Duma's composition in any significant way. As Thomas Riha suggests, this was partly due to government interference, as the deputies themselves complained,[43] and in part simply the result of popular apathy and disdain for the Duma. Moreover, when the new delegates took their seats in November, 1912, Prime Minister Kokovtsev showed the regime's antipathy for new Kadet "radicalism" by failing to include in his program any bills which either the Constitutional Democrats or the left considered worthwhile.[44]

All these events pushed Kadets to the left. Disgusted by what Kokoshkin now called a "moral rot" in Russian politics, some even insisted the party discard as useless the tactics of "organic opposition," as the party's politics in the Third Duma were described, and become a "declarative" opposition instead.[45] As Professor Leopold Haimson has pointed out, these sympathies were shared by other moderate parties of the time, notably the Progressists.[46] When the Fourth Duma

41. Avrekh, *Stolypin i tret'ia duma*, 433, 446–48, 450.
42. *Rech'* (March 28, 1912). See also the discussions in March 8 and 18.
43. Riha, *Miliukov*, 199.
44. *Ibid.*, 205. See Kokovtsev's speech in Gosudarstvennaia Duma, Chetvertyi sozyv, *Stenograficheskie otchety*, sess. 1, 260–81. For the Kadet response, see *Rech'* (December 6 and 8, 1912).
45. Kokoshkin to Petrunkevich, October 11, 1912, Panina Collection, Columbia Russian Archive, Box 1, Folder 6.
46. Leopold Haimson, "The Problem of Social Stability in Urban Russia, 1905–1917," part 2, *Slavic Review*, 24:1 (March, 1965), 1–22. It was the Progressist faction that introduced a resolution in the Duma calling for recognition of the regime's own October Manifesto. If the Duma could not be a parliament, the new "liberationists" reasoned, it might at least again be a forum for calls for reform. See Ol'denburg, *Tsarstvovanie*, 2:91–93; Riha, *Miliukov*, 200–204.

opened, Kadets began to reintroduce their old First and
Second Duma bills on political freedom, inviolability of
person, freedom of the press, and the like. According to
Miliukov, the party was again going to mobilize popular
dissidence and lead a radical thrust for nonpartisan reform, as
it had in 1905–1906.[47]

The evidence still suggests that Kadet politics were again
constrained, and the credibility of the party as a whole again
left open to challenge, this time by Kadet conservatives
working actively against radical tendencies. An organizational
base for such a division existed in the division of the Kadet
Central Committee into Moscow and Petersburg branches.
Generally, though with important exceptions, the Moscow
branch sided at this time with Pavel Novgorodtsev and
Mikhail Chelnokov, who opposed the new liberationist concept
as both harmful and tactically hopeless. According to recent
research by Soviet historian A. Ia. Avrekh, at precisely the
time Petrunkevich and others were advancing their idea of a
new union of liberation, another group of Kadets also sought a
review of the party's program, but with an eye toward
making it more acceptable to the right. This group wanted to
underscore the monarchist character of liberalism, re-examine
the party's efforts with respect to military reform in a
"patriotic spirit," approve Stolypin's agrarian reforms, and
rework nationality questions to align Kadets with Octobrists.[48]
When the Fourth Duma campaign began, Kadet "conservatives" did not hesitate to stress *their* association with
the right; [49] and when Kadet Duma deputies began toying
with the concept of a declarative opposition, Tyrkova,
Maklakov, Chelnokov and others publicly expressed their
fears that this would harden reactionary tendencies within the
government and stimulate the growth of a *genuine* revolu-

---

47. Miliukov's notes on the Kadet faction in the Fourth Duma
(n.p., n.d.), manuscript in the Miliukov Collection, Columbia
Russian Archive, Box 8122A, Section 8; Miliukov testimony in the
Nicolaevsky personal archives. See also *Rech'* (January 5, 1913)
on Kadet bitterness over Kokovtsev's unwillingness to accept a
plan for police reform, and (January 31, 1913) on a "united opposition sharply and energetically struggling against the government's policies."

48. Avrekh, *Stolypin i tret'ia duma,* 459–60, based on TsGAOR
police files, 1911.

49. See *Russkiia vedomosti* (September 27, 1912, and October
6, 1912).

tionary movement.[50] Tyrkova even began in 1912 to publish a right-wing Kadet journal, *Russkaia molva,* expressly to counter what she and others thought was the "dangerous leftism" of *Rech'*.[51]

A careful investigation of Soviet archives is necessary before one can write confidently about the degree to which right-wing opposition affected the new liberationists in the Fourth Duma election campaign. Also open is the question of an actual splintering of the Kadet party at this time. (According to testimony given in 1927 by Miliukov, the two groups of Kadets engaged in increasingly bitter clashes throughout 1913, making a break-up a real possibility.) [52] Split or not, nonetheless, it is clear that divisions within the party in the 1911–1913 period set a pattern for Kadets that lasted through World War I. This became the pivotal factor structuring the politics of the party as a whole in the last crucial prewar period, the thirty months from July, 1914, until the February Revolution. The ambivalent quality of Kadet politics in these months was not simply a function of the war itself, or the fear of struggling with the government under conditions of national emergency; instead, as police records and memoirs indicate (and Thomas Riha indirectly implies in his recent book on Miliukov), the ambivalence was the result of the Kadet party's ceasing to remain a coherent, organized, political whole.

In analyzing this period, one must first note that the picture given by Miliukov and Riha of Kadet unity at the war's outbreak is misleading.[53] The party's well-known official decision to postpone its opposition to the government, which Miliukov announced so eloquently at the Duma session of July 26, 1914, was taken by the Central Committee only after considerable debate. A number of committee members believed that the Kadet party should make its support of the

50. Miliukov testimony in the Nicolaevsky personal archives. See also M. Novikov, *Ot Moskvy do N'iu-Iorka* (New York, 1952), 163ff.

51. Unpublished memoirs of A. V. Tyrkova, Columbia Russian Archive, chap. 38, 740–42. Tyrkova insisted her action in no way breached party discipline, since *Rech'* was not an official party organ.

52. Miliukov testimony in the Nicolaevsky personal archives.

53. Miliukov, *Vospominaniia,* 2:189–91; see also his "Moe otnoshenie k poslednei voine," *Posledniia novosti* (August 1, 1924); Riha, *Miliukov,* 213–18.

regime conditional on the promulgation of reforms, since Russia simply could not win the war with her antiquated form of government. Others, however, like Tyrkova, led an assault from the other direction. They accused party leaders like Miliukov and Petrunkevich of a lack of patriotism and considered the government's decision to suspend publication of *Rech'* a disgrace not to the regime, but to the party. They berated Miliukov in particular for not convening the Central Committee until the last possible moment, thus depriving Kadets of the chance to organize local demonstrations in support of the war. In Tyrkova's view, the struggle with Germany allowed true Russians to shed politics altogether and become "simple patriots." [54]

From the war's very beginning, then, there were two sides to the question of postponing the antigovernment struggle, though all Kadets stood staunchly behind Russia's military effort. In the summer of 1914 party harmony rested largely on the conviction that the conflict would not last more than nine months. Miliukov could thus persuade his colleagues to make the war an effort of total national involvement, one in which a developed awareness of citizenship and its responsibilities could carry over into the postwar period as a basis for broad liberal reconstruction.[55] This conception of how Russia might develop epitomized the liberals' underlying belief in the necessity of elevating or lifting both the government and the masses toward a progressive constitutional democracy. However, as it became apparent that the war would be long, that Russia's administration *was* unfit for its task, and that Nicholas so feared the Duma's becoming a base of opposition that he intended, as much as possible, to prevent its convocation, Kadets rapidly lost their motivation for unity.

There is some evidence, suggested by the Soviet historian V. S. Diakin, that the new oppositionists regrouped as early as August, 1914. The grounds for resistance seem to have been the ministers' own lack of commitment to the war, as well as the obvious inaccuracies appearing in *Pravitel'stvennyi vestnik,* the government's journal, and the army's extremely

---

54. Tyrkova memoirs, chap. 2, 15–17; unpublished memoirs of V. Obolenskii, 391–93, loaned to me by Professor Nathan Smith.
55. P. Miliukov, *Taktika fraktsii narodnoi svobody vo vremia voiny* (Petrograd, 1916), 11. See also M. Rodzianko, "Iz vospominanii," *Byloe,* 21(1923), 220–21.

158 · Essays on Russian Liberalism

callous treatment of its wounded.[56] No change in party
policy was decided upon this early, however, nor was one
formulated four months later when Kadets planned their
strategy for the upcoming Duma session.[57] In June, 1915, at
the first full-fledged Kadet conference since the war's
outbreak, unconditional support for the regime was replaced
as the party's official position by a program of demands that
shortly afterwards became the basis of the Progressive Bloc.
Riha and Diakin give the details.[58]

What was the significance of the Progressive Bloc from
the standpoint of Kadet politics? I would argue it was not so
much in terms of a "last chance" for Kadets to obtain political
power short of revolution, though the regime's decision to
reject the bloc at this juncture certainly accelerated its eventual
collapse,[59] but rather that the bloc held significance for Kadets
primarily as a strategic recommitment to the principles of
political nonpartisanship—*nadklassnost'* and *nadpartiinost'*—
with their related notions of progress being obtained through
the championship of national rather than particularistic
interests, and without radical change in existing social and
political structures.

The important—though perhaps familiar—point in this
regard is that Kadets supporting the bloc saw it primarily as
the parliamentary equivalent to public organizations like
the War Industries Committee or the Union of Zemstvos and
Cities in whose branches party members were so active. Its
function was to coordinate relations between these
organizations and the bureaucracy and to bridge the gap
between regime and society, creating conditions for the
emergence of a new Russian society.

56. V. S. Diakin, *Russkaia burzhuaziia i tsarizm v gody pervoi
mirovoi voiny (1914–1917)* (Leningrad, 1967), 63–64.

57. B. Grave, ed., *Burzhuaziia nakanune fevral'skoi revoliutsii*
(Moscow-Leningrad, 1927), 1–5. This and Grave's *K istorii
klassovoi bor'by v Rossii* (Moscow-Leningrad, 1926), are largely
collections of police reports published from archival holdings. See
also N. Lapin, ed., "Kadety v dni galitsiiskogo razgroma,"
Krasnyi arkhiv, 59(1933), 113.

58. Riha, *Miliukov*, 221–23; Diakin, *Russkaia burzhuaziia*, 84–
85. See also: Grave, *Burzhuaziia*, 61; Lapin, "Kadety," 121–23;
Miliukov, *Taktika*, 15; Grave, *K istorii*, 269.

59. See T. Riha, "Miliukov and the Progressive Bloc: A Study
in Last-Chance Politics," *Journal of Modern History*, 32:
1(March, 1960), 16–24.

Ministers enjoying the nation's confidence were necessary for obtaining these ends; structural change was not, nor was a political strategy that pitted one social interest against another. Miliukov specifically rejected the idea of having the bloc demand a ministry responsible to the Duma, while he was present at party meetings in the summer of 1915, on the grounds that it would require writing a new constitution.[60] Not one of the proposals offered in the bloc's program demanded basic changes in Russia's political system.[61] At the same time, once the bloc was formed, some of its members were themselves surprised when Miliukov and Shingarev refused to instruct them on how to vote on various Duma issues. They were told instead that decisions of this sort would commit the bloc in a "partisan" way, and should be left to their own party committees.[62]

While some Kadets—particularly Maklakov, Tyrkova, and A. V. Vasil'ev—worried that the bloc was perhaps too much an expression of disloyalty to the regime,[63] its practical import in terms of Kadet politics was that it committed the party to perpetuating what many had come to believe was an anachronistic system of government. It was this that bothered even notables like Kishkin, Dolgorukov, Kizevetter, and Kokoshkin, who were not in the party's left wing. Part of their argument was the nationalist one heard earlier in 1914 —that Russia simply could not win the war with her present governmental system. But part of it centered as well on a fear that the general orientation of the party was no longer appropriate, particularly considering Russia's military crisis.[64]

Kadet strategy, with its underpinnings of *nadklassnost'* and *nadpartiinost'*, was already a major bone of contention at the Central Committee meetings in January, 1915, among those who were moving away from a policy of postponing antigovernment criticism.[65] When the Progressive Bloc emerged, party members muted their quarrels until they could

60. Miliukov, *Taktika,* 15–23.
61. A. Kornilov, *Parlamentskii bloc* (Moscow, 1915), 13–16. See also Grave, *K istorii,* 283–86; *Rech'* (August 25–27, 1915).
62. S. Shidlovskii, *Vospominaniia* (Berlin, 1923), 2:46.
63. A. Tyrkova, *From Liberty to Brest-Litovsk* (London, 1919), 18.
64. Kokoshkin to Petrunkevich, February, 1915, Panina Collection, Columbia Russian Archive, Box I, Folder 1.
65. Grave, *Burzhuaziia,* 2–4.

measure its success; but when the regime responded by dismissing the Duma, those hoping Kadets would take a more active and forceful approach grew rapidly in numbers and influence. Some went so far as to demand a strike of all social organizations as a means of forcing constitutional reforms and a ministry responsible to parliament.[66] At a party conference in October, 1915, Victor Obninskii, Kizevetter, and others attacked Miliukov's politics broadside, accusing him and the Progressive Bloc of compromising liberal goals. More importantly, these Kadets also wanted to cultivate relations with soldiers, workers, and peasants. The party needed new allies for a direct struggle with the government.[67]

Again, many of the details are in Riha and Diakin, and in the police records published by Grave in *Krasnyi arkhiv*. These and other materials suggest that the question for most Kadets was still one of degree; they were more frightened of mass upheavals than they were of perpetuating the regime. It is also known that Mandel'shtam, Nekrasov, and a small group of Kadet provincial representatives finally concluded that if political opposition was necessary to reform, the use of partisan, revolutionary tactics was necessary for effective political opposition. By the end of 1915 yet another Kadet faction existed, one which believed that the party should champion the demands of workers and actively cooperate with Social Democrats in pressing for change "from below." Nekrasov and Mandel'shtam also wanted Kadets to forge militant new unions among Russia's different social groups so that mass protests could be politically coordinated. They had come full circle, back to the Union of Unions idea of 1905.[68]

By 1916, tsarist police could write confidently about the fragmentation in Kadet party ranks. There were indeed, as Riha points out, open divisions between various Kadet leaders. Many party officials did not even know which "official" line to follow.[69] Whether or not an organized, coordinated liberal party would have affected the course of events between 1914 and the February Revolution, divisions among Kadets

---

66. *Ibid.*, 33–35, 39–40, 42–43, 46, 63–64.
67. *Ibid.*, 43, 68–70.
68. *Ibid.*, 94–95; Grave, *K istorii*, 310–15. See also *Rech'* (February 23, 1916).
69. For example, at the Sixth Kadet Congress in February, 1916, the party became hopelessly confused. After hearing

could not help but dissipate whatever influence the party might have brought to bear in any given direction. The result of party fragmentation was political weakness. And it was in this awkward posture that Kadets heard Miliukov fire his famous "stupidity or treason?" salvo and watched the revolution begin.

When seen against this background of consistently ambivalent politics, the Kadets' approach to the kaleideoscopic events of 1917 and the party's subsequent history must gain respect. As a party, Kadets entered the revolution committed to achieving social progress through legal methods, but aware that legitimacy cloaked ineptitude and abuse; nagged by an awareness that popular rebellion could be an effective instrument for change, but fearful of unleashing a politically backward people whose actions could not be controlled; convinced as to the rightness of their cause and ideals, but bitterly divided on how to achieve success; unsure in wartime whether to sacrifice principle for the sake of military victory, or whether the sacrifice itself might contribute to Russia's defeat. The Kadet party thus entered the revolution without having solved basic questions concerning its political role and lacking a tactical firmness. On the basis of its internal development alone, one can hardly be surprised that the Kadet party never gained any substantial strength in 1917.

To some extent, Kadet politics were ambivalent because the party tried to unite several diverse and basically incompatible elements within one organizational framework, as Vasilii Maklakov and others have since pointed out.[70] The cohesion preserved by party leaders was consequently quite misleading. Superficial unity was gained at the cost of political effectiveness, while widespread discontent developed toward the whole party as different sectors went in different directions. Kadets never actually wanted organizational rigidity. As national liberals, committed to *nadklassnost'*

Mandel'shtam, the 87 delegates voted 46 to 27 in favor of *rapproachement* with the left. But hearing Shingarev one day later, the vote was 73 to 14 in favor of continued participation in the Progressive Bloc, now anathema to the radicals. See Riha, *Miliukov*, 245, and *Rech'* (February 23–24, 1916).

70. V. Maklakov, *Vlast' i obshchestvennost'*, 482–89; M. Karpovich, "Two Types of Russian Liberalism: Maklakov and Miliukov," in E. J. Simmons, ed., *Continuity and Change in Russian and Soviet Thought*, 129–43.

and *nadpartiinost'*, virtually all party members felt this type
of structure was inappropriate to Russia at her stage of
development. The Central Committee thus made little effort
to dictate to local groups, or even to force a rigid line in
the party's fraction in the Duma. For much of the time the
committee itself was divided into Moscow and Petersburg
sections, a condition party members accepted as facilitating
the broadest possible contacts.

While Kadets felt their commitments served the task of
lifting Russia out of her backwardness by championing the
real needs of all social classes, they never seemed to recognize
the difficulties of getting either the regime or the masses to
appreciate their position. Party members expected to obtain
power from above. Nicholas, however, thought he was serving
"the good of the nation as a whole"; and the posture of
nadklassnost' was not likely to prompt him to surrender his
own authority. At the same time, not only were workers and
peasants unlikely to think that Kadets served their interests
better than Social Democrats or Socialist Revolutionaries,
but also, throughout its history, the party had tried to
instruct them via hundreds of thousands of special pamphlets,
whose language was more appropriate to a salon on Nevskii
Prospekt than a factory or village. Meanwhile, Kadets
constantly excluded themselves in the government's eyes from
the ranks of those capable of working "cooperatively" for
Russian progress. They were making themselves *of* the left but
not *in* it in 1906 by attempting to channel radical passion
constructively at Vyborg; by appealing to radical voters in
1907 and 1909 while stoically maintaining the face of
compromise in the Duma; and by mounting temporarily a
policy of declarative opposition before the war. By staying
strictly within the confines of the Fundamental Laws in
preparing legislation; renouncing their own Vyborg Manifesto;
laying a slow seige and attempting to legitimize the activities
of radicals; and fragmenting over the question of political
opposition during the war, Kadets constantly alienated
themselves from the very constituencies capable of giving
political force to their arguments.

One might take the position that, given Russia's industrial
underdevelopment and the absence of a substantial liberal
bourgeoisie, the politics of ambivalence was ideally suited to
Russia's prerevolutionary context. Had Kadets been given
the opportunity to exercise governmental power, the party's

radicalism might well have sapped the strength of revolution, while its concern for legitimacy smoothed relations with the established bureaucracy. This would have allowed peaceful transition to a new order, but the problem again was that Kadets could not *obtain* power on their own. Consequently their political task remained either to secure mass support or to obtain acquiescence from the regime, neither of which was served by ambivalent politics. One might also argue that Kadet failure simply reinforces the notion that revolutionary change was inevitable in Russia—that industrial and social underdevelopment left political stresses that moderates like the Kadets could not overcome. But while it seems likely that the various imperatives of industrial modernization did indeed predestine drastic political changes in Russia, this view ignores the fact that Miliukov and his followers did have a range of choices in defining their politics.

The drama of Russian liberals lay in the difficulty of reconciling principles and politics. Ultimately, however, one must agree with the views of many Kadets themselves when they reconsidered their past in emigration: the Russian context demanded either movement to the left, and tactics designed to press mass partisan demands; or consistent conservatism, with a corresponding decision to work for change only after having become part of the established bureaucratic order. However reasonable the derivation of their ambivalence, Kadet politics did not advance the party's goals.

THE PROSPECTS OF LIBERAL DEMOCRACY IN TSARIST RUSSIA

Theodore H. Von Laue

The fact that my remarks come toward the end of the volume does not imply that they are related by design or cause to the preceding chapters. *Post hoc,* so Hume reminded us a long time ago, does not necessarily mean *propter hoc,* in this as in all other cases. In other words, this chapter was written without knowledge of the preceding ones.

Invoking Hume we need no further introduction, for we have already found the heart of our topic. What is the relationship between the nature and the prospects of liberalism in tsarist Russia on the one hand and, on the other, the fact that the Bolshevik Revolution and the Soviet regime have made short shrift of all forms of Russian liberalism? The temptation, obviously, has been to argue that, because of their ultimate and total failure, liberal institutions never had a chance for survival in Russia. Soviet historical scholarship, always suspect of serving transscholarly considerations, has had no difficulty in documenting this conclusion. It is also implicit in our own efforts to establish continuities from the tsars to the Bolsheviks.

These conclusions, however, have not gone unchallenged. Citing Hume, a different set of scholars have denied any causal relationship between the fate of liberalism in Russia and the victory of the Bolsheviks and have buttressed their plea with impressive scholarship. The tsarist regime, according to their version, was in the process of stabilization under the constitution of 1905–1906 on an increasingly liberal course. A profusion of nongovernmental institutions was springing up, demonstrating the creative vitality of the Russian public (including the peasantry). Had the growth continued, they would have grown into the pluralist web of liberal-democratic society, and the tsarist autocracy would have given way, slowly but surely, to effective constitutional government. What stopped the promising process was something unrelated to it

—the First World War. Except for the war there was, in short, every indication that Russia would have followed the mainstream of West European development. The debate between these two points of view is still in full swing, with obvious benefits to historical scholarship. More relevant material is being turned over and sifted, with each side trying to marshal more convincing proof.

There is a catch, however, in the competition: what evidence is considered convincing? Will our final judgment depend on more research into the "silver age" of Russian culture in the decade before the war, on more evidence of the growth of semipublic and nongovernmental public institutions, or on the proof of greater ease of public discussion and political agitation? Will we be convinced by further details on the life and activities of Russian liberals in this or earlier periods of Russian history? Or, contrariwise, will our knowledge of subsequent events persuade us to investigate instead the shortcomings of all these promising beginnings and point out the persistence and proportionate progress of illiberal forces and tendencies? Can we, for that matter, stop in the deliberation of these issues with a consideration of Russian conditions alone or must we take a larger, comparative point of view, setting Russia into the general development of Europe before, during, and after the First World War, or even into the global context—was this not the age of imperialism?

Venturing a summary answer to these questions, I would say that in the long run the more inclusive perspectives (or, perhaps better, the researches based on them) are apt to carry the palm. The conclusions reached by scholars must be able to match the best contemporary understanding of such comprehensive questions as are being considered in this discussion, with due awareness of basic methodological difficulties.

As Americans, using American words and concepts, and relying on American patterns of sociopolitical analysis and civic experience, we are trying to investigate the complexities of a crucial turn of Russian development in the early twentieth century. Any such comparison is understandably surcharged with the high voltage of political tension between the United States and the Soviet Union. In transcultural comparison, scholarship and politics intersect, not necessarily in the deliberate manner frequently assumed, but subtly, almost imperceptibly, and yet ineradicably.[1] Americans generally agree that liberal democracy is the ideal form of government for themselves and universally as well. This loyalty to their own form of government inclines them to support a liberal-democratic movement wherever they see it. If someone asserts that there exist conditions under which liberal democracy cannot work, as say in Russia, the ideal loses its universal significance. Liberal democracy becomes a relative truth; relativism gives rise to dissent.

It is no wonder then that the threatened destruction of one of the key absolutes of American tradition arouses a deep-seated and for the most part unconscious resistance. If we argue, on the grounds of long-range historical evidence, that liberal democracy in Russia had no chance, we are indeed helping to make liberal democracy a relative concept and contributing to a contagious relativism that subverts the bases of the American consensus. (Our reluctance to formulate such subversive conclusions should make us more sympathetic to the traditional Russian and Soviet defense mechanisms against foreign influences.) Even in our privileged American condition, an underlying necessity of collective existence and statehood precludes objectivity and clarity of vision; we too want to safeguard the foundations of our society. Such are the inevitable consequences of the coexistence of separate polities—or value systems—in the global state system.[2]

Another problem in the study of distant cultures and polities is the relationship between our empirical research and the conclusions we are likely to draw from it. At first sight, no difficulty may be evident: our conclusions arise organically out of our scholarly investigations. On closer inspection, however, it is obvious that our research, with its positivist bent for precision, is by necessity concerned with relatively miniscule phenomena, while our conclusions are likely to pertain to substantial questions like that concerning liberal democracy. To be specific: what bearing, for instance,

---

1. A good illustration and analysis of the political implications and overtones in the study of prerevolutionary Russia may be found in the chapter by Arthur Mendel, "On Interpreting the Fate of Imperial Russia" in Theofamis George Stavrou, ed., *Russia Under the Last Tsar* (Minneapolis, 1969).

2. The author has spelled out these conditions in detail in *The Global City* (Philadelphia, 1969).

does a study of the agrarian policy or nationality policy of the
Kadets have on an assessment of the prospects of liberal
democracy in tsarist Russia? Information on what these
policies have been does not necessarily provide an answer, or
even a clue, to the all-comprehensive question.

Our research can provide suitable insights only if it is
conducted with an a priori assessment of how a liberal
democratic society with all its complex and multifarious
ingredients functions in its indigenous setting. We must set
the process of policy formulation in the Kadet party into the
contexts of social action, asking: for what contingencies and
under what circumstances were these policies designed? What
were the chances of their receiving effective support among
the bulk of the population? How, precisely, were they
formulated? What promise did the process of policy formulation give for effective liberal-democratic forms of decision-
making among the bulk of the population? In short, no matter
how narrowly conceived, the inquiry demands a command
of the sophisticated instrumentation of comparative studies.

Stretching limited and inappropriate evidence to cover large
and basic aspects of sociopolitical development all over the
world is a common occurrence of current research in history
and even more in the behavioral sciences. Our conclusions
are constantly in danger of outrunning our research capacities.
The authors of monographs as well as of general works over-
expand the limited expertise emerging from their specialized
competence in order to reach imposing, all-inclusive conclusions. Conclusions of sufficient solidity can emerge only from
research that has covered the totality of the endless number
of factors contributing to a polity's course of development
—obviously an impossible condition. If our pointillist
methods of research [3] are inadequate for solving these crucial
questions, the quest for improved research techniques must
continue.

Two familiar concepts of scholastic philosophy may add
clarity to our condition. The word "nominalist" could be

---

3. The danger of this approach may be seen in a recent study
of the Bolshevik Revolution. Putting the events of the Bolshevik
coup under a powerful magnifying glass and observing each step
separately, one can indeed come to the conclusion that this event
was no more than a complexity of accidents. The political and
ideological implications of this technique are obvious: it plays
down the importance of the Bolshevik Revolution.

applied to our routine research procedures, to the "empirical" gathering of facts and data from sources and to our hard-nosed conclusions about the relationships emerging from them—all strictly within the limits of the surface evidence. This is the most effective way to begin any historical investigation, although such strict adherence to documented evidence should leave a nagging doubt. How much do these facts reveal about basic historical reality? After a lengthy exposure to his sources, the historian develops a sixth sense that transcends his immediate evidence. While the sixth sense does not yet go beyond the range of topics encompassed by his sources, it suggests the existence of another dimension of historical reality that does not necessarily assume concrete and documentable forms, yet exerts a powerful pull upon the course of development of individual careers, institutions, and entire collectivities. Inquiries into that set of historical factors we might call "realist."

Because it assumes the efficacy of abstract and generally invisible forces in history, the realist approach perforce must remain rather theoretical and abstract. It ascribes causal power to a given set of circumstances, to constellations of events, to the spirit of the times, to general concepts like Westernization or industrialization, or to shorthand approximations of vast complexities. It accepts abstractions like "culture," "the nation," and "state," as active agents of history; it assumes the intelligibility of the patterned mosaics of random facts; and it insists on the totality of contexts. An all-wise historian of miraculous longevity and energy might find these realities organically emerging from his ceaseless researches. His lesser brethren will by necessity draw on the conclusions of philosophers and political or social theorists, as well as, more basically, on the collective human experience laid down in abstractions like culture, nation, or state. They may even accept the validity of the term "national character," meaning thereby a common set of human responses conditioned over a long period of time by exposure to a common authority or destiny (and find it much more real than the Marxist concept of "class character"). They take for granted, in other words, that nobody (including historians) can live and judge effectively without accepting the reality of such abstractions. The reliance on them becomes even more extensive as the social interdependence of human existence expands. In large-scale human association such as prevails in our age, men necessarily live by abstractions and generalizations.

Applying these reflections to our discussion we find that nominalist (or pointillist) research will not suffice. As we deal with Russian liberalism we have to rely, in short, on theory, on abstract and summary considerations, to guide our research, proceeding with a theoretical awareness of the nature of liberalism, putting our detailed investigations into the contexts of a patently illiberal and antiliberal tradition and, more generally, keeping our minds open to the adversities constantly encountered by any form of liberalism in Russia. It is also necessary to be alert to the illiberal features in the personalities and careers of Russian liberals, as well as to the total context of Russia in the European and global state system.

At this point it may be objected that, in promoting the realist approach, we may aggravate all the distortions stemming from the very nature of intercultural studies. Nothing could be more self-evident than the dependence of these "realities" on the crosscurrents of ideology and political tension or, at any rate, on the limited peculiar experience of one polity. In reply we should first remember that even nominalist research can never escape from these distortions; it uses American (or West European) terms for things Russian and, devoid of a sense of the Russian connotations, unwittingly substitutes American meanings. As for the larger issue, the objection is well taken. We cannot match the total contexts of a distant culture from our own experience. But does this admission rule out the realist position? It may instead merely bring us face to face with the central problem in all intercultural comprehensive studies, forcing us to take a more honest look at what we do and to treat all our conclusions with greater caution. As we embark upon the search for answers to summary questions like that raised in this volume, we must forever ask what chance there is for American scholars conditioned in the cultural envelope of American (and Western) experience to comprehend the crucial totality of the Russian experience. Our terminology, our methodology, and our working equipment are, in short, derived from our own past needs and conditions. Is there any guarantee that they allow meaningful conclusions about the needs and conditions of people patently raised under very different circumstances?

These are hard and disagreeable questions for Americans brought up in the universalizing tradition of the Enlightenment and accustomed to spreading their concepts and achievements all over the world as common yardsticks.[4]

Yet, these observations are not meant to discredit all foreign-area studies, but only to point out the complexity and obstinacy of the problems confronting scholars engaged in intercultural and comparative research. Comparative studies of this exacting nature lie at the very frontier of our experience in the Age of the Global Confluence.

II

Moving closer now to the historical realities of tsarist Russia, we start from the assertion that the basic drawback to liberal democracy—or of any form of liberalism—in Russia was that it was un-Russian. The best authorities in the field leave no doubt on that point. Victor Leontovitsch wrote that "in Russia liberalism faced different tasks than in the West; it therefore assumed different forms. It was, on the whole, the fruit of the reception of west European liberal ideals." [5] Or again: "Liberalism in Russia had essentially a receptive character." [6] If we may equate liberalism with freedom as Miliukov viewed it, we may also quote that eminent historian speaking in May, 1917: "Our freedom is a young, new-born babe; it is from the Allies that we must learn the ways in which mankind gained freedom for itself." [7] The fact that the genes of that newborn babe were of foreign origin raises the basic problem of the viability of cultural transplants. Let it here be approached from the holistic—or realist—point of view, as a matter of general consideration.

The proper theory of cultural transplantation would start by asserting that liberalism (as a political ideology shaping institutions and the very character of nations) grew out of a

4. A good example of this tendency, just because it tries to escape from it, is the book by G. A. Almond and S. Verba, *The Civic Culture* (Princeton, 1963).

5. V. Leontovitsch, *Geschichte des Liberalismus in Russland* (Frankfurt, 1957), vii.

6. *Ibid.*, 2.

7. Quoted from Thomas Riha, *A Russian European: Paul Miliukov in Russian Politics* (Notre Dame, 1969), 329.

given historical matrix. It is no undue oversimplification to
say that the matrix was England and Great Britain, with
amplification also from both the United States and France.[8]
In the British matrix it grew out of a widening popular
resentment directed against absolute monarchy and privilege,
against sociopolitical regulations not founded on the consensus
of all those affected by them. It was an ideology of liberation,
devised and advanced by activists within the framework of
British life, which in time created its own institutions, values,
habits, and even instincts. As a force for change operating in
the context of British society and government—and of British
security and insularity as well—it was concerned with only a
relatively small part of the sociopolitical factors at work in
the British Isles. It affected only those aspects that needed
to be changed, leaving all others, i.e. the great bulk of human
relations, untouched. The liberal-democratic movement, its
ideology, and all that followed from it comprised only a
segment of the matrix of British state and society, related
to it as the key is related to the lock for which it was designed.

In the instrumentalist view here set forth ideologies or
institutions are merely extrusions from an unstated totality,
designed for accomplishing certain purposes within larger
contexts. In their visible, articulate aspects they touch only a
few skeins of the underlying—and generally invisible—web
of human relations. In other words, their justifications and
explanations remain highly incomplete, revealing only so
much as is necessary for accomplishing their purpose, though
they can be understood (from an outsider's perspective) only
in relation to their full context. How can we understand the
full context when it is never spelled out, when men are not
even aware of its intricacies, of its unspoken or even unformu-
lated assumptions?[9] What we can afford to take for granted
we never bother to investigate or rationalize. No ideology or
politically effective theory of social change, in short, offers a

---

8. Leontovitsch's explanation of the peculiarities of the Russian
matrix, while useful, is perhaps too much oriented toward the
European continent.

9. Since I have been taken to task for pleading the effects of
"invisible" factors in Russian history, I would like to elevate the
point into a maxim of scholarship: there is considerably more
happening in human relations on any level than can be seen at
first glance or summarized in inadequate words. This is especially
true in comparative studies.

full account of the social mechanism, though it usually pretends to do so.

What, then, could be more alien to the Russian setting than the conditions that gave rise to liberal democracy in England? We can here mention but a few highlights of English development merely to indicate the lines of thought involved in our argument and omit the obscure realms of the influence of geography, climate, ethnic traits, and other long-range factors beyond human control. It should be noted that there had existed since the eleventh century a common government closely related to common law, producing common institutions, habits, loyalties, and achieving over the centuries a depth of unity unique even in the Western world. We must also point to the widespread sense of public responsibility cultivated over centuries by men in authority, by monarchs and aristocrats, and filtered down to the grass-roots layer among the population. Together with the sense of public responsibility went a high degree of self-discipline and self-reliance oriented toward conformity and social cooperation as well as toward diligence in the performance of one's work.

In the global experience English society presented an astounding and unparalleled miracle. Under a laissez-faire permissiveness it allowed its citizens to do as they pleased, and their actions, by the end of the nineteenth century, made their country into the most powerful and prosperous empire in all history. The Whig interpretation of English history, much maligned though it is, nevertheless still serves as the best explanation available in the global comparison for that extraordinary feat, with one exception: it does not sufficiently take into account the unique advantages of external security that Britain enjoyed over many centuries. The absence of a real danger of invasion and the resulting relative neglect of the realities and pressures of power politics have deeply permeated British liberal theory. From liberalism they evolved into Marxism and all its derivatives. In the Marxist theory of the primacy of the class struggle the powerful exigencies of international power politics play but a secondary part (despite the fact that in man's experience, particularly in recent times, the exactions of government outbid the pressures of employment and material survival). It is not too farfetched to trace the liberal obtuseness to power politics into the controversy over the prospects of liberalism in tsarist Russia. Only liberals and those brought up in the liberal tradition elsewhere could have ruled out the influence of power politics on Russia's development and viewed the First World War as an extraneous factor.[10]

How different, by contrast, was the matrix of Russian development! To serve as reminders to illustrate the coordinates into which we must set our study of Russian history, let us point to the painful process of gathering the Russian lands and of building up a common government—a government that always acted harshly without even trying to relate itself to the customs or wishes of its subjects, always treated them as minors in the overriding pressure of extemporizing defenses against foreign aggression, and always tried to hold its own against odds more oppressive and burdensome than those faced by any Western country. All students of the subject are aware of the absence of any autonomous civic development capable of holding the government in check, or of the crushing of individual initiative and creativity to the point of raising up serfdom as a guarantee of progress when it was dying out in Western Europe. We also know of the havoc wrought in the self-esteem of individual Russians by the absence of any stability of law and institutions, by the abysmal inequality between lord and serf, tsar and subject. The "plasticity" of the Russian character stressed by Miliukov [11] was poor building material indeed for the self-reliant, rational, sovereign individual of liberal ideology.

We also remember that in the process of nation building the tsars tried to substitute compulsory Russification for the century-long spontaneous growth of consensus that had characterized the British experience, and that they built up, by the same token, a deep-seated resistance that always offset all centripetal tendencies. We cannot afford, furthermore, to disregard the long series of defeats and failures that tripped up the tsars and their government. The final failure came in 1917–1918, when the Germans would have destroyed Russia as a Great Power, except for American help on the French front. Most people do not realize that if Russia had not been a Great Power, she would most likely not have preserved her

---

10. The absence of any consideration of power politics and its effects is strikingly marked in Barrington Moore's recent book, *Social Origins of Dictatorship and Democracy* (Boston, 1966); it is also part of Max Weber's explanation of the Puritan Ethic, and of the work of many sociologists and anthropologists concerned with the sociopolitical evolution of the contemporary world.

11. Miliukov, *Russia and Its Crisis* (Collier, 1962), 25.

sovereignty, like Poland or the Baltic states. The great open
plains of Eastern Europe did not furnish any natural defensive
bastions—the only bastions were the bodies of soldiers,
crudely equipped, poorly led, and put into the field at great
sacrifice to the entire population. The only boon conferred by
the tsars upon their people, one might say, was the fact that
the people were ruled by men speaking their own language
and representing their own cultural tradition—although even
that somewhat imperfectly at times.

Even with survival assured, attempts at invidious comparison with the Western model brought successive failures.
The comparisons were not only of arms, but also of cultural
creativity, of economic productivity and the standard of living,
and of the freedom and happiness of the individual. Tsarist
Russia consistently compared unfavorably to the competition.
The defeats undermined the loyalty of the most valuable
subjects and made the tsars' tasks of nation building even
more difficult. While the English imperially dished out cultural
and political guidelines to the rest of the world, the Russian
government and the Russian intelligentsia begged and
borrowed in all essentials of statehood, forever in the shadow
of a superior model and unable to catch up and to enjoy full
and secure political and cultural sovereignty. The basic
inequality produced another source of profound weakness—
the alienation of a divided loyalty in the innermost recesses
of the mind of educated Russia. Part of it looked to the
Western model with admiration, while part of the educated
despised it. It was a division unknown to the English mind,
which at the very source of volition possessed a singleness of
basic purpose, a solid integrity, and a profound invisible
homogeneity derived from the beneficial uniformity of civic
experience under a long-established and truly sovereign native
government.

There is no room here for improvising a scaffold of Russian
cultural and political evolution. Let us instead probe into a
few lesser aspects illustrating the incompatibility of the liberal
key with the Russian lock, returning for a moment to Leontovitsch's assessment of liberalism in Russia. He argued that,
as a method for realizing the freedom of the individual,
liberalism was not a constructive but a destructive force,[12]

---

12. V. Leontovitsch, *Geschichte des Liberalismus in Russland*,
1.

which tried to remove all trammels on individual initiative. This interpretation obviously overlooks the fact that in the American practice the destruction of restraints merely preceded the formulation of new ones, self-imposed, collective in nature, and usually more demanding. Wherever liberal democracy prevailed, the free individual used his liberties in combination and cooperation with other individuals, in a manner which, through some invisible benevolent hand, generally enhanced the common weal as well. Liberal freedom, in short, was felt to be for English-speaking organization men only. Leontovitsch further argued that liberalism was not suitable for activists,[13] which again hardly applies to the British prototype. The British liberals had created, with spry, collectivist vitality and conviviality, a liberal England and an empire with a liberal life style that permeated all pores of the body politic. When necessary they could put up a good fight. In Russia, one might argue by contrast, liberals were weaklings who would never fight. It is in those colors that Saltykov-Shchedrin has characterized the type. The activists were found in the camp of the socialist revolutionaries (or of the rulers).

We might argue, however, that Leontovitsch was basically right in stressing the destructive character of liberalism in Russia; it counteracted all efforts of the autocracy to cement the unity of the Empire, whether by the doctrine of official nationality, the spirituality of the Orthodox church, or Russification, thereby preventing the rise of the very unity that in the British matrix had been the precondition of its success. Freedom in Russia encouraged self-determination among the subject nationalities, which in turn endangered the security of the Empire still further. It helped to mobilize the population of the Empire for political action, encouraged everyone to speak his divisive mind, and brought to life all the repressed furies. Given the basic atomism of Russian society, its tensions and lack of civic experience, individualism inevitably produced anarchy and political disintegration— and, predictably, political disintegration produced weakness for the entire polity. Yet no Russian liberal wanted to weaken his country still further; on the contrary, he always hoped to make Russia more powerful through liberation. How, then, under Russian conditions, could he guarantee a repetition of

13. *Ibid.*

the British miracle that combined freedom for the individual with power and glory for the country? What political cement did the liberals keep in reserve for achieving the consensus necessary for their ideal government?

Political mobilization in the name of freedom, however, was not only destructive to Russian power in the European (or nascent global) state system or to autocracy, but also to the liberals themselves. They knew from bitter personal experience among peasants and workers that the masses were not yet ready for self-determination. Deep down they dreaded universal suffrage, but they included it in their program on the wishful assumption that the masses would turn for leadership to the liberal critics of autocracy, to the educated, nongovernmental elite. In effect, they were following the trends of West European liberalism. If there was one single conclusive demonstration of the radical incapacity of the Russian liberals, it was their failure to come to grips realistically with the consequences of universal suffrage in the Russian Empire.

The liberals likewise failed to assess realistically the economic conditions and needs of their country. Their democratic bias inclined them to favor the peasant bulk of the population; their own material as well as spiritual ties were to agriculture and to the agrarian way of life—at a time when the worldwide trend was toward industry and cities. Western liberals representing the industrial wealth and skill of their countries could afford to oppose state regulation of economic development or even industry itself. Their Russian counterparts in a country without much industry were in an altogether different position. Could they afford their persistent opposition to forced industrialization or to any kind of economic planning that took into account their country's weaknesses in the emerging world economy? What, furthermore, was their prescription for effective handling of the peculiarities of economic development in the Russian Empire? And how were they to deal with the unrest among the peasants in the factories? Economic activity, like citizenship, requires strong habits of voluntary cooperation—a fact which liberals are apt to take for granted even though it may be lacking in reality.

Another facet of liberal illiberalism in Russia questions the Russian capacity, even among the Europeanized elite itself, for voluntary cooperation, compromise, and mutual accommodation. Long deprived by the autocracy of any experience in autonomous social and civic action, Russian society was more profoundly divided than any other West European society; the skills of the liberal organization man were lacking. About three-quarters of the population lived under law and customs of their own barely touched by—and deeply afraid of—the Europeanized social and political super-structure. Yet even that elite was deeply marred by a self-conscious individualism that bore little resemblance to the highly socialized individualism of liberal doctrine. As Leopold Haimson has recently shown,[14] even during the heyday of liberal stabilization the liberal opposition manifested no durable internal coherence. Its last resource of cement for common action was free masonism, an esoteric institution with insufficient sticking power.

Even in the psychic households of their individual motiva-tion we find, in scratching below the surface, not a solid liberal, but an illiberal autocratic or messianic urge, as in the case of Kerensky, or an illiberally doctrinaire one, as in the case of Miliukov. Analysis of liberal character is admittedly a difficult task; it is, in fact, nearly hopeless in intercultural comparison where there exists no set of common denomi-nators of cultural traits. Any spirited American dealing with individual Russians cannot help but speculate on such differences. The trouble is, however, that in most cases our sources or our methods of inquiry do not allow us the close scrutiny needed for a grasp of character—or else as foreigners we do not know how to recognize the clues.

The foregoing will show, on reflection, how subtle yet complex is the notion of freedom and how problematical its use becomes in intercultural comparisons. It is a highly convoluted cultural molecule composed of promptings of the will and instinct, of personal attitudes and quality of conduct, and of moral imperatives embedded in society—all structured in a unique mold by a common association over long periods of time. The English prototype had built into it a multitude of precautions against anarchy and willfulness, a series of restraints that modify, not deny, the openness of choice. Freedom is a matter of choice between accepting or rejecting self-imposed limitations, and certainly not a choice between restriction on the one hand and unrestraint on the other. It

14. Leopold Haimson, "The Problem of Social Stability in Urban Russia, 1905–1917," *Slavic Review*, 23:4(December, 1964), 619–42, and 24:1(March, 1965), 1–22.

is, in short, a highly deliberate—or civilized—motivation that in the name of freedom makes our decisions for us.

It was the good fortune of the English-speaking peoples that in the matrix of their collective development man's outward discipline in state and society developed in consonance with his inward sense of self-discipline. British life and politics were "free," although from an outsider's perspective they often seem strangely constrictive. In the Russian experience, on the other hand, individual volition and state necessity constantly clashed. As a result men felt alienated, compelled to live under a sociopolitical order at war with their private conception of their "humanity." When the external restraints of tsarist rule were removed, the newly won freedom revealed both an atrophied self-awareness that did not stretch even halfway to the limits of Russian statehood and an undeveloped sense of self-discipline that proved incapable of fulfilling the duties of social cooperation and statehood as they had been defined by English-speaking society and imposed upon a global world through the exigencies of power politics.

Going one step further in our analysis of liberalism in Russia we might argue that in their moment of liberation all the illiberal, anti-Western forces in Russian life could call the Russian liberal's bluff: "You liberals speak of freedom and self-determination," they might jeer, "but all you do is lay the country under tribute to an alien way of life. You want to shape our country after a foreign model. We, however, want to remain what we always have been, Russians, ourselves. We too, you see, can claim the benefits of freedom." These reflections indicate, I think, that the liberals possessed far less freedom to maneuver in the Russian setting than, say, the socialists. Lenin managed to Russify Marxism by stretching the implicit anti-Western ingredients in that philosophy to cover Russian exigencies. Liberalism, a far less ambiguous ideology than Marxism, could hardly be so adapted, although, as Leontovitsch's volume demonstrates, even liberalism was often stretched out of recognition by its Russian followers. (How liberal, for instance, could a "liberal" *chinovnik* be?) In the liberal vision Russia's future was restricted to the Western, liberal (or "capitalist") track. By contrast, Russian socialism, particularly in its Leninist form, being both Western and anti-Western, could strike out in a slightly more original and nativist direction.

It is not generally recognized that the ability of the Western liberal model to provide guidelines of political, social, and cultural development constitutes a major, though invisible, form of power; nor do we recognize that the desire for cultural sovereignty, for freedom from alien and alienating influences, has raised powerful counterforces against that subversive power. A Russian liberal like Miliukov, his critical acumen notwithstanding, believed to his last that freedom would eventually come to Russia too. He was, in today's terminology, a believer in "straight-line modernization." Russia, as well as mankind, was traveling on the same road as the peoples of Western Europe and America who had turned toward "modernity" at an earlier date. Miliukov was thus trapped in incomprehension like most contemporary theorists of modernization, who in the latest and unconscious stage of imperialism have laid down the Western cultural experience as a universal gauge. Like them he underestimated the vitality and nature of the counterforces. Like them he was blind to the fact that Westernization (whose inevitability one may accept for contemporary history) proceeds in a non-Western pattern, creating unstable mixtures of Western and native elements unique to each culture and forever falling short of their goals. What refuted and disproved the Russian liberals in their hour of seeming opportunity in 1917 was not only their numerical weakness, their aloofness from the masses, etc., but also the widespread popular (not to say democratic) rebellion against any form of Western domination. To an extent not usually recognized the Russian revolution of 1917 stood for a major popular assertion of Russian cultural sovereignty as the political sovereignty of the country was endangered. Miliukov's plea for the imitation of British, French, and American liberty fell indeed on profoundly hostile ears.

One could continue in this critical strain, pointing out causes and symptoms of liberal failure—or liberal illiberalism —in prerevolutionary Russia. It is possible to sum up the liberal predicament by stating that the liberation movement in Russia tended to give a powerful lift to every existing attitude and outlook in the Russian Empire. Encouraging self-expression, it boosted not only the infant transplants of Western ideas and practices but also the most illiberal and antiliberal—autochthonous—tendencies in Russian life. On balance, the latter were by far the more numerous and well entrenched. In the free-for-all of liberal democratic politics the former were bound to be routed, as indeed they were.

For the consideration of those who still follow Miliukov's belief in the inevitability of the victory of freedom outside the original matrix, the consequences of political Westernization might be summarized by saying that the liberal-democratic creed comes as a unit, of which the vision of empire is not the least element; it not only promises freedom but also power commensurate with that of England or the United States. It preaches self-determination for the individual as well as for the polity in which he lives. Applied to a country like Russia —or any "underdeveloped" country—the package breaks apart. A self-determination policy is likely to undermine the traditional political unity of a polity. Worse, the imitation of the Western vision of empire and cultural sovereignty contradicts any other such imitation; one cannot go one's own way and yet copy somebody else's achievement. The liberation of the individual from all hated restraints, moreover, opens the floodgate of nativism and traditionalism at a time when tradition spells backwardness and defeat. The resulting confusion further undermines the validity of the liberal-democratic ideal. The most likely result is the emergence of antiliberal and antidemocratic ideologies and institutions that seem to offer better guarantees of preserving the political and cultural sovereignty of the people concerned. Fumbling with the liberal-democratic key, in short, not only destroys the traditional locks but in the end also breaks the key. The best one can hope for under the circumstances is the eventual emergence of native leaders who will produce both new locks and new keys—a feeble hope as long as these efforts fail to match the continued pace.

To conclude: This chapter has advanced the "realist" concept of political Westernization as an aid to historical studies of liberalism in Russia. Such studies, we have argued, should proceed from an awareness of the special obstacles encountered by those who stood for the liberal-democratic creed in Russia; we should always keep in mind the tragic limitations imposed upon these idealists by their environment and by their own Russia-conditioned human nature.[15] In other

---

15. For instance, we should not, perhaps, treat Miliukov as a Russian European as Thomas Riha has done, but as a Europeanizing Russian. Each approach takes in different matter. The question is: which matter tells us more about liberals and liberalism in Russia?

words, studying Russian history from a distance, we should redouble our efforts to overcome the distortion or misunderstanding stemming from our own imperfect America-conditioned research. Self-analysis might reveal that our curiosity about the prospects for liberal democracy in tsarist Russia is secretly prompted by a psychosocial urge to see liberal democracy succeed all over the world; it may have an ideological as well as a heuristic aim; and it may tell us less about the forces at work in the Russian polity than we imagine.

Viewed from this angle, Hume's stricture quoted at the outset of this chapter becomes inapplicable. In the realist perspective the Bolshevik Revolution of 1917, which ended all prospects for liberalism in Russia, was not a major turning point in Russian history. No question of cause and effect is raised, no alternative posed between Russian liberalism and Soviet Communism. The revolution was merely another milestone—an unusually large one, to be sure, and perhaps the last of its kind—on a road charted long in advance by the position of the Russian Empire at the edge of Europe, and by the fact that Russia was the paradigm of backwardness as well as of self-assertion against the Western model in the Age of the Global Confluence. Events before and after 1917 were part of a common framework that could never be unlocked by the liberal-democratic key, whether in statecraft or in scholarship.

BIBLIOGRAPHICAL ESSAY

The literature on Russian liberalism in Western languages is limited, because the attention of Western scholars and their Soviet counterparts has been focused instead upon the revolutionary movement and foreign policy. Within the past decade, however, several Western scholars and two or three Soviet ones have begun systematic studies of various aspects of the Russian liberal movement. Two substantial monographs by Americans and a significant revision of an earlier monograph by a Soviet scholar have resulted from this research. Several monographs are nearing completion in the West, and others are in progress in the USSR.

For the purposes of this bibliographical essay, I have divided the history of Russian liberalism into three chronological periods, and I have grouped the available literature accordingly. The periods are: (I) from the Great Reforms in the 1860s to the organization of the Union of Liberation in 1903; (II) 1904–1907, including the Revolution of 1905 and the first two dumas; (III) 1907 through the Bolshevik Revolution and emigration of Russia's liberals to Western Europe.

I

Because political parties were illegal in Russia before 1905, the Russian liberals worked through the legal institutions created by the Great Reforms until they founded the conspiratorial Union of Liberation in 1904. The institutions best adapted to the liberals' objectives were the zemstvos, city dumas, judicial institutions, and the gentry assemblies. Of these, the zemstvos had the broadest possibility for influence in the country and were primarily the home of Russian liberalism before 1905. Zemstvo members maintained constant and broad contacts with members of liberal professions, and several of them practiced such professions themselves.

The best study of the role of the zemstvos in the liberal movement is vol. 3 of B. B. Veselovskii's *Istoriia zemstva za sorok let* (St. Petersburg, 1909–1911, 4 vols.). Although this work is unrivaled in scope and vastness of materials consulted, Veselovskii's methodology—that of extracting antigovernment statements from the journals of zemstvo assembly sessions throughout European Russia—stresses the antipathy between the zemstvos and the central government. This approach obscures the process by which the zemstvos functioned, the development of factions within zemstvo assemblies, and ultimately hampers full understanding of the nature of the conflict between the zemstvos and the central government. The series of short histories (ca. 100 pages each) of each zemstvo assembly in vol. 4 partially sets events into their provincial context, but a modern history of each provincial zemstvo would be of enormous value. Veselovskii wrote separate histories of the zemstvo institutions of Tver Province (*Istoricheskii ocherk deiatel'nosti zemskikh uchrezhdenii Tverskoi gubernii, 1864–1913 gg.,* published in Tver in 1914) and of St. Petersburg Province (*Istoricheskii obzor deiatel'nosti zemskikh uchrezhdenii S.-Peterburgskoi (nyne Petrogradskoi) gubernii, 1865–1915 gg., published in* Petrograd in 1917), but each could benefit by a more modern approach.

The gentry origins of zemstvo liberalism can be studied in Terence Emmons's *The Russian Landed Gentry and the Peasant Emancipation of 1861* (Cambridge, England, 1968). The drafting of the Zemstvo Statute has been studied by V. V. Garmiza, *Podgotovka zemskoi reformy 1864 goda* (Moscow, 1957). Charles Timberlake's "The Birth of Zemstvo Liberalism in Russia: Ivan Il'ich Petrunkevich in Chernigov" (Ph.D. diss., University of Washington, Seattle, 1968) is an analysis of the formation of a liberal faction in the zemstvo institutions in Chernigov Province.

Various attempts were made by Russians before 1917, and later in emigration, to trace the history of the zemstvo movement to 1905. The most successful was I. P. Belokonskii, *Zemskoe dvizhenie* (Moscow, 1910). While in emigration Fedor Rodichev published "The Liberal Movement in Russia (1855–1905)" in *Slavonic and East European Review,* 2:4(June, 1923), 1–13; 5(December, 1923), 249–62; and "The Veteran of Russian Liberalism: Ivan Petrunkevich" *ibid.,* 7(January, 1929), 316–26. Paul Miliukov's "The Liberal

Idea," which is chap. 3 of his *Russia and Its Crisis* (originally published in Chicago, 1906, republished in paperbound edition by Collier Books, 1962) remains useful. George Kennan's "The Last Appeal of the Russian Liberals," *The Century Magazine,* 35:1(November, 1887), 55–63, is a translation of an important appeal from a group of Moscow liberals to Minister of Interior M. T. Loris-Melikov in 1880.

Memoirs of zemstvo participants are not plentiful, but those in existence are valuable. See the bibliography in Veselovskii's *Istoriia zemstva za sorok let,* 1:595–628, and at the end of vol. 4, and George Fischer's *Russian Liberalism: From Gentry to Intelligentsia,* Russian Research Center Studies, ser. no. 30 (Cambridge, Mass., 1958), for more detailed lists of memoir materials. Especially useful are I. I. Petrunkevich, *Iz zapisok obshchestvennago deiatelia* (Berlin, 1934), which is vol. 21 of the 22-volume series *Arkhiv russkoi revoliutsii;* V. M. Khizhniakov, *Vospominaniia zemskogo deiatelia* (Petrograd, 1916); and D. N. Shipov, *Vospominaniia i dumy o perezhitom* (Moscow, 1918).

Soviet work on the zemstvo movement prior to the 1905 Revolution is also not highly developed. The major Soviet scholars are L. G. Zakharova nee Mamulova: "Zemskaia kontrreforma 1890 g.," *Nauchnye doklady vysshei shkoly: Istoricheskie nauki,* 4(1960), 60–85; "Sotsial'nyi sostav uezdnykh zemskikh sobranii v 1865–1886 godov," *Vestnik Moskovskogo universiteta, Seriia 9: Istoriia,* 6(1962), 32–48; "Zemskii vopros v russkoi periodicheskoi pechati epokhi kontrreformy [1880–1890], *ibid.,* 2(1966), 57–68; "Dvorianskie proekty zemskoi kontrreformy," *Uchenye zapiski Gor'kogo gosudarstvennogo universiteta,* vypusk 78(1966), 583–602; *Zemskaia kontrreforma 1890 g.* (Moscow, 1968); E. D. Chermenskii, *Russkaia burzhuaziia i tsarizm v pervoi russkoi revoliutsii,* 2nd ed. (Moscow, 1970); and N. L. Klein, "Zemsko-liberal'noe dvizhenie v Samarskoi gubernii v 60–80–e gody XIX v.," *Istoriia SSSR,* 6(1970), 68–82.

II

In addition to the memoir materials cited above that are also useful for this period, other types of materials are available. The semimonthly magazine, *Osvobozhdenie* (June, 1902–October, 1905), founded by a group composed of zemstvo men and men from the liberal professions, is an extremely important source for the period. The most detailed work by one of the participants in the founding of the Union of Liberation is D. I. Shakhovskoi's long essay, "Soiuz osvobozhdeniia," *Zarnitsy: Literaturno-politicheskii zhurnal,* no. 2, pt. 2 (St. Petersburg, 1909), 81–171.

Studies on the formation of the Kadet party and events immediately preceding it are more abundant. Fischer's *Russian Liberalism* treats in detail the events of 1904 and early 1905. Also of note are Donald W. Treadgold, "The Constitutional Democrats and the Russian Liberal Tradition," *American Slavic and East European Review,* 10:2(April, 1951), 85–94; George Putnam, "Russian Liberalism Challenged from Within: Bulgakov and Berdyayev in 1904–1905," *Slavonic and East European Review,* 43(June, 1965), 335–53; Nathan Smith, "The Constitutional-Democratic Movement in Russia, 1902–1906" (Ph.D. diss., University of Illinois, Urbana, 1958); V. V. Shelokhaev, "Programma kadetov v pervoi russkoi revoliutsii" (diss. for the degree *kandidat nauk,* Institute of the History of the USSR of the USSR Academy of Sciences, Moscow, 1971), and "Agrarnaia programma kadetov v pervoi russkoi revoliutsii," *Istoricheskie zapiski,* no. 86(1970), 172–230; E. D. Chermenskii, *Russkaia burzhuaziia i tsarizm v pervoi russkoi revoliutsii,* 2nd ed. (Moscow, 1970); Olga Crisp, "The Russian Liberals and the 1906 Anglo-French Loan to Russia," *Slavonic and East European Review,* 39(June, 1961), 497–511; Michael Karpovich, "Two Types of Russian Liberalism: Maklakov and Miliukov" in Ernest J. Simmons, ed., *Continuity and Change in Russian and Soviet Thought* (Cambridge, Mass., 1955), 129–43; and Gregory Freeze, "A National Liberation Movement and the Shift in Russian Liberalism, 1901–1903," *Slavic Review,* 28(March, 1969), 81–91. See pages 12 to 15 of David Shapiro, *A Select Bibliography of Works in English on Russian History, 1801–1917* (Oxford, England, 1962) for further articles on this period.

Two major studies of participants in the Russian liberal movement especially important for the period of 1904 to 1907 are Richard Pipes, *Peter Struve: Liberal on the Left, 1870–1905* (Cambridge, Mass., 1970), and Thomas Riha, *A Russian European: Paul Miliukov in Russian Politics* (South Bend, 1969).

The role of the Russian liberals in the first two dumas can be studied in such major sets of documents as the stenographic

notes of the dumas, the weekly *Vestnik* of the Kadet party
(published from February, 1906 to February, 1908), the
party's unofficial newspaper, *Rech'* (1906–1917), the minutes
of party congresses, and collections of documents
published by the party's central committee, e.g., *Zakonodatel'nye proekty i predpolozheniia partii narodnoi svobody,
1905–1907 gg.* (St. Petersburg, 1907).

These materials are supplemented by memoirs of partici-
pants. Especially useful are several volumes by V. A.
Maklakov: *The First State Duma* (Bloomington, Ind., 1964);
Vtoraia gosudarstvennaia duma: vospominaniia sovremennika
(Paris, n.d.); and *Vlast'i obshchestvennost' na zakate staroi
Rossii* (Paris, 1936), 3 vols. Also useful are Paul Miliukov,
Vospominaniia (1859–1917) (New York, 1955), 2 vols.,
V. M. Hessen, *Na rubezhe, 1901–1905* (St. Petersburg,
1906), and A. Tyrkova-Williams, *Na putiakh k svobode*
(New York, 1952). For the drafting of the Vyborg Manifesto,
see M. M. Vinaver, *Istoriia Vyborgskago vozzvaniia*
(Petrograd, 1917).

III

This period has received the least attention of the three.
Soviet scholars have contributed only a handful of articles:
E. D. Chermenskii, "IV Gosudarstvennaia duma i sverzhenie
samoderzhaviia v Rossii," *Voprosy istorii,* 6(1969), 63–79;
I. M. Klimov, "K voprosu ob otnoshenii kazanskoi burzhuazii
k 'progressivnomu' bloku," *Uchenye zapiski Kazanskogo
universiteta,* vol. 112, book 5(1952), 55–75; Sh. I. Basilaia,
"Zemskii soiuz i Soiuz gorodov Zakavkaz'ia v gody pervoi
mirovoi voiny," *Vestnik Otdeleniia obshchestvennoi nauki
Akademii nauk Gruziia,* 5(1964), 21–40; V. S. Diakin,
Russkaia burzhuaziia i tsarizm v gody pervoi mirovoi voiny
(Leningrad, 1967); and D. V. Petrova "Gosudarstvennaia
duma i Fevral'skaia revoliutsiia 1917 g.," *Sovetskoe gosu-
darstvo i pravo,* 12(1968), 105–8.

Titles in Western languages on the post-1907 period are, in
addition to Thomas Riha's book on Miliukov, which is also
useful for this period: William G. Rosenberg, "Les libéraux
russes et la changement de pouvoir en mars 1917," *Cahiers
du Monde russe et sovietique,* 9:1(janvier-mars, 1968),
46–57, and his "Russian Liberals and the Bolshevik Coup,"
Journal of Modern History, 40:3(September, 1968), 328–47.

Index